ONE HAND ON THE CLARET JUG

Then catch the moments as they fly,
And use them as ye ought, man;
Believe me, happiness is shy,
And comes not aye when sought, man.
— Robert Burns

One Hand on the Claret Jug

How They Nearly Won the Open

NORMAN DABELL
Foreword by Ernie Els

MAINSTREAM
PUBLISHING
EDINBURGH AND LONDON

First published in Great Britain in 2006 by
MAINSTREAM PUBLISHING COMPANY
(EDINBURGH) LTD
7 Albany Street
Edinburgh EH1 3UG

ISBN 1 84018 983 5

Unless stated, all photographs
© The Phil Sheldon Golf Picture Library

A catalogue record for this book is available
from the British Library

Typeset in Apollo and Trade Gothic

Printed and bound in Great Britain by
William Clowes Ltd, Beccles, Suffolk

This is dedicated to my dear nephew Adam,
who enjoyed life's birdies to the full and
laughed at its occasional bogeys

ACKNOWLEDGEMENTS

FIRST OF ALL, a big thank you to Jock MacVicar, my pal from the *Scottish Daily Express*, for planting the grain of an idea. After Jock had delivered his quarterly lecture on Scotland's best single malts, this time in a bar near Heidelberg, the conversation switched from the merits of his favourite, The Macallan, to the Open Championships. We could remember all the winners. But what about the losers?

My gratitude then goes to Bill Campbell, who allowed the grain to grow and ripen.

To be able to write this book from a position of strength, I needed insights from the men who finished up disappointed in the Open. That meant intruding on personal grief. So I am deeply indebted (in chronological order) to Doug Sanders, Tony Jacklin, Jack Newton, Seve Ballesteros, Jack Nicklaus, Simon Owen, Bobby Clampett, Nick Price, Hale Irwin, Tom Watson, Bernhard Langer, Ian Baker-Finch, Wayne Grady, Jesper Parnevik, Michael Campbell, Costantino Rocca, Jean Van de Velde, Thomas Levet and Ernie Els, who also very kindly provided the foreword, for allowing me to rake up what can only have been rather painful memories. I can tell you, even after over a quarter of a century covering golf, I can still get a dose of the collywobbles when I pick up the phone and the voice on the other end says, 'Hello, Norman, this is Tom Watson. You wanted to talk to me.' Thank you, Tom, for gently putting me right on what has been a major issue over the years. Thanks, Bernhard, for interrupting your New Year holidays to call me. *Muchas gracias*, Seve, for buying me breakfast as well!

I'm grateful, too, to Peter Alliss and Renton Laidlaw for their very worthy contributions.

My gratitude also goes to Nelson Silverio, Scott Tolley, Steve Glassman, Tim Meyer, Gloria Saccoia, Andrew Chandler, Lindi Sue Nicholas, Erwin Langer and Ivan Ballesteros for their help in fixing up interviews. Thanks to Kevin Woodward, once again, for his input.

To Mary Flanagan at Stewart McDougall's office, my eternal gratitude for digging out numerous missing Open interviews and to Stewart for allowing Mary so much time at the photocopier. I'm obliged, too, to Eddie Birchenough, my old pal from *Golf Illustrated*, for turning back the clock to 1970. And to Ireland's golfing memory man, Dermot Gilleece.

Thank you to Lauren St John for giving me permission to use extracts from her excellent *Shooting at Clouds*, published by Mainstream, in order to fill in a couple of blanks from the 1989 and 1990 Opens.

Thanks go to Gill Sheldon for providing the photographic gems taken by my old friend and colleague Phil, who is so sorely missed by everyone. He was 'Simply the Best'.

To all the gang at Mainstream, many thanks for all your help in putting this tome together.

Finally, to my wife, Sharon, as always, thank you for your patience.

CONTENTS

FOREWORD BY ERNIE ELS

(On what it is like winning but also missing out on the Open Championship)

WINNING THE 2002 Open Championship was the highlight of my career so far, no question. But what can I say about 2004? Losing was bitterly disappointing. After getting into contention at Lytham twice, in 1996 and 2001, in 2002, at last, I got my name engraved on the Claret Jug. It was a wonderful feeling.

In 1996, it had been the short par-four 16th on Sunday that killed me. Tom Lehman had gone into the final round with a big lead, but I played really well and had a chance. You could get pretty close to the green with a driver on 16, but I played for position with a two-iron and pulled it left into the fairway bunker and took a bogey. That was it.

Then, in 2001, I gave myself a chance again, with a good Saturday round, but on the final day I just couldn't get anywhere near David Duval. It was very frustrating.

It all came right in 2002 at Muirfield. I tell you, the back nine of 32 that I played on Saturday and the front nine of 29 on Friday, they were the key to winning the Championship. They put me where I needed to be on Sunday, which was a perfect day for scoring. Before my final round, I set myself a target of ten-under-par. That was my goal the whole day – I didn't want to go out there and play defensive golf. For a while, it was going great. I was eight-under through thirteen holes, but the tee-shot on 14 into the fairway bunker really threw me. I dropped a shot there and got a little tight after that. Then came the 16th, which was awful. Having missed the green in a tough spot long and left, I made the mistake of trying to make a three. I should have played safe, made certain of getting a four and moved on – you know, make a birdie on 17, par the last and win by one. Instead, I tried to nip a 60° wedge up to the bank but I hit it thin and made double-bogey. Now I had it all to do, just to get into a play-off.

Walking to the next tee, I just tried to remind myself that it was only a game. It was a good thing that my next shot was a drive, because I'd been hitting my driver great all week. And I hit that shot perfect. That settled me down a bit and I hit a great three-iron to 25 ft for an easy birdie-four. Then, on 18, with everything on the line, I hit a great two-iron off the tee and another solid five-iron to make a good par and get into the play-off. After what happened on 16, I was proud of myself for finishing like that.

Then I just had to get myself together. I had to put everything behind me and just think about playing four holes as well as I could. The bunker-shot on the 18th in sudden death was probably one of the best shots of my life. I didn't want to get too cute with the shot. I wanted to hit it almost heavy, so it came out with a lot of run and without any check-spin. It worked out beautifully. Thomas Levet then made a great putt and, all credit to him, he never gave up trying. So I had a three-footer to win the Open! I just told myself to hit it on the line and trust it. I hit it a bit further right than I wanted to, but it took the break nicely and dropped in.

It's hard to describe how it felt when the putt went in. At first, it's a relief. Just a huge, huge relief that you've done it. Then you can start to enjoy the moment, although it takes a while before it sinks in.

Then there was the other side: 2004. Coming this close in a major and not winning is a tough blow to take, but I took a lot of positives from that week. On Sunday, I played the last six holes, one of the toughest closing stretches in golf, in three-under-par. I was proud of the way I holed some of those must-make putts, especially on 16 and 17. On the last green, I gave myself a chance, but with that tricky pin placement it was a difficult putt to make from short of the hole. I just never got the ball running at the hole. So it was into a play-off with Todd Hamilton. For some reason, I didn't play those four holes well, though. And my putter went cold.

To get so close and to come away with nothing is bitterly disappointing. It didn't go my way, but what can you do? I gave it my best shot. Sometimes it's not enough. You just have to accept that and take your hat off to the other guy. Todd played well and kept his nerve when he needed to.

INTRODUCTION

THERE HAVE, OF course, been many, many hard-luck stories at the Open Championship, right from when it began in 1860. Numerous names could have been engraved on the most sought-after stroke-play trophy in golf but weren't.

Who, for instance, could have had his hand more dramatically torn off the Claret Jug than Harry Bradshaw in 1948? And all because of a ball in a broken beer bottle! Going back much further than that, though, what about 1876 when Bob Martin tied with David Strath at St Andrews? In the first Open to finish all-square, Strath could have gone on to place both hands on the jug but refused to take part in a play-off and was pronounced runner-up. It wasn't as if he could have had a plane to catch, either.

In 1888, Jack Burns, Ben Sayers and David Anderson each had one hand on the Claret Jug when they tied for the Championship. Before the chance for a play-off, though, the cards were checked again and somebody's arithmetic was found wanting. It proved to be Burns's night. He was a stroke better off than he thought and was declared winner.

Then, at Muirfield in 1896, it was a close call between the men who dominated the Championship for years, J.H. Taylor and Harry Vardon. Vardon beat Taylor in a play-off. Though J.H. Taylor had his fair share of wins, he was also a perennial hard-luck story, finishing runner-up four years in succession from 1904.

Vardon, the record-holder for Open wins with six, also put the hex on Arnaud Massey at Royal St George's in 1911, pipping the Frenchman in a play-off. In 1921, Roger Wethered so nearly pulled off a rare amateur victory but lost in a play-off at St Andrews against Jock Hutchison, who had become an American but who was born within a couple of par-fives from the Home of Golf. Life was a bit different then. Wethered seemed hardly to care that he had one hand on the trophy at the end of normal play. He had to be persuaded, at some length, apparently, to actually take part in the play-off. He'd agreed to play a cricket match the day after the Open should have ended!

Moving on, Ryder Cup captain Dai Rees was one of the best British players never to quite win an Open. He nearly won in 1954 at Birkdale, where he was joint runner-up, a stroke behind Peter Thomson. Then, in 1961, he was even closer to hugging the jug, finishing a shot away from Arnold Palmer, once again at Birkdale.

In 1957, it wasn't so much a case of hard luck for Peter Thomson – because he finished three strokes behind Bobby Locke at St Andrews – but more of a lucky escape for Locke. He forgot to re-spot his ball after moving it a putter-head's length away from his playing-partner's line. However, because he had already been presented with the trophy, the Royal and Ancient (R & A) showed mercy and didn't disqualify the South African.

A year later, Dave Thomas was runner-up for the first of two times, losing out in a play-off at Royal Lytham and St Annes to Thomson. Two years on, in 1960, Arnold Palmer lost the Centenary Open by just one shot to Kel Nagle, having three-putted the Road Hole 17th on the Old Course three times out of four. That same year, Ireland's wonderful amateur Joe Carr had a hand on the Auld Claret Jug when he raced into the lead in the final round . . . only for a sudden cloudburst to cause play to be abandoned. Carr's score was wiped out, and when they restarted the next day, he could not rekindle the fire and drifted to eighth place.

There have not been many Opens where there was not a

fascinating twist to the tale, but travelling back to the start of the oldest major would have meant producing a tome about as large as the Domesday Book. Also, although getting hold of rugby legend Rob Andrew to talk about his biggest disappointment in sport may seem like an easy task, if it's the Rob Andrew who missed out to Tom Morris in the 1868 Open, a tape-recorded interview with the loser would have been a little more difficult to organise. Besides, Andrew didn't have one hand on the Claret Jug. It was more like half his waist around the Belt, for which the Open was played at that time.

So I've begun the tales of what might have been with the Open of 1970. Most of the hard-luck stories I've written about have come from talking to the players involved years after their disappointments, while others are from interviews I did at the time or from Open press conferences on the day.

Take it away, Doug Sanders. As commentator Henry Longhurst sighed, 'There but for the grace of God . . . '

1970, ST ANDREWS: DOUG SANDERS

(Tied with Jack Nicklaus over 72 holes,
then lost a play-off by just a stroke)

'Do I still keep thinking about missing that putt, after all
these years? Heck, no. Yesterday I went at least five
minutes without it even crossing my mind.'

ARGUABLY, IT TOOK until 1999 for Doug Sanders to shake off his
unwanted association with the most costly moment of an Open
Championship. Until Jean Van de Velde went for a bundle at the
Barry Burn, Sanders's missed three-footer at St Andrews in proper
time in 1970 was the most defining moment in Open calamities.

It is rather ironic, then, that the man to benefit from Van de
Velde's misery at Carnoustie in 1999 was Paul Lawrie. The
Aberdonian might never have got to the stage of being a good-
enough golfer to even play in an Open, let alone win one, if it were
not for Sanders, the man who threw his golden chance away with
one putt. Lawrie attended Sanders's teaching schools when he was a
youngster and has always placed great emphasis on how the affable
and extrovert American helped his game.

If the man born on 24 July 1933 at Cedartown, Georgia, had sunk
that three-footer on the last at the Home of Golf in 1970, he may have
been involved in myriad other projects besides teaching, most of
them highly lucrative. As Sanders observes, 'One putt, only one
putt, and it cost me a fortune.'

Sanders, who had whipped the pros as a young amateur when he won the Canadian Open, won 20 US PGA Tour titles and was one of the most colourful golfers ever to grace the fairways. Gaudy clothes, garish hats and very noticeable shoes were his trademarks. The galleries loved him, and the St Andrews crowd took to him like one of their own.

He had come close to winning the 1966 Open at Muirfield, finishing with Briton Dave Thomas in a tie for second place behind . . . Jack Nicklaus. Sanders knew he had been up there with a chance of lifting the famous Auld Claret Jug. He had matched Nicklaus in the final round, shooting a 70, but the 11th at Muirfield had cost Sanders the Open that year. He double-bogeyed it in the final round from nowhere and finished up a stroke worse than Nicklaus. Sanders had gone home a frustrated man, knowing he'd had the Open in his grasp, determined to go one better next time and beat the Golden Bear, if he got the chance.

As one of the most regular winners on the US PGA Tour, Sanders was one of the shorter-odds contenders for the Open in 1970 and he was in fine fettle. He was also well attuned to Open-week itself, and says he settled in like a local when he got to St Andrews:

'I loved the Open – its history and the nostalgia surrounding it. The Open had a class and style about it. I think coming from the South, as I do, living on a farm, we had more respect for things with tradition and heritage. I always felt so honoured to be there. They said they felt honoured to have me there, but I felt honoured to be there!

'Back in those days, the crowd didn't speak to the players, even though there were no ropes to keep them away. They just got out of the way and you got on with it. The one place that was roped off was the practice range. I ducked under the ropes and spoke to those watching. I told them a couple of jokes and I started to walk away. A guy – nowadays I suppose he'd be security – came running over in a real state, saying, "Is he sick? Is he sick?"

'The crowd said, "No, sir. He's just fine."

'The guy said, "What? He spoke to you and he's not sick?"

'It had been so unusual for a player to talk to the crowd. I'd wanted to start conversations, to be part of them. I didn't want it to be a one-way street. I wanted them to know a little bit about Doug Sanders. If they had a question, I could stop there and answer it.

'I got on really well with them. They liked my loud clothes and my attitude. I think I was the first American to ever rent a house at St Andrews. Tony Lema was my house guest when he won the British Open in 1964 at St Andrews. I used to have parties and put on a tuxedo. We had great fun. When we rented the house that year, we told the owners they had to buy a refrigerator!'

The very thought of drinking warm cocktails! Especially when Sanders and his wife, Scotty, had none other than one of the world's most famous crooners, Buddy Greco, staying with them that week.

Sanders knew his game was on-song coming into the Open and says he knew what was needed at St Andrews:

'In 1970, I knew I was playing well, but that didn't necessarily mean anything at a British Open. A lot of how you go on depends on the weather. I was a good shot-maker, and the more the weather becomes inclement, the more of a chance I had. Being able to manoeuvre the ball around was a great asset. If it had been mandatory in the 1960s and '70s to play the big ball, as happened in the end, I think I could have won three, four, maybe five times. I could move the ball around and hit different shots, more than the average person could. With the little ball, you didn't need to do that so much because you could keep it underneath the wind.'

Sanders had a swing just made for St Andrews. He hoped all of his attributes would work for him at the Old Course.

'Anyway, I felt I was ready to win. I was very confident. I had been second so many times in majors, I was ready to make the move to winner. A bit like Phil Mickelson did in the end. He was, I think, the only person like myself to win 20 tournaments without winning a major. Well, he finally did it and I didn't.'

When recounting his infamous missed putt, Sanders talked about all the amazing things he has done in his life, such as taking the joystick of numerous fighter aircraft, by dint of his friendship with a US Air Force base commander, and even flying the U2 in his own space-suit. Not winning a major, however, has left a huge void in his life. He reached for the sky at St Andrews in 1970, but one putt left him short of gaining the heights.

It all began well. Sanders and Nicklaus started off their week with 68s. Already, Sanders was making sure he kept up with the man he considered the one to beat.

'Nicklaus was such a dominating figure, and while I was determined I was going to make it at last, I know he was just as determined he was going to win at St Andrews. He felt that was the ultimate prize in golf – to win at what is the home of golf.

'I don't remember much about the first round. I just know Jack and I were pretty pleased with our day's work. So much can depend on a good start and I was satisfied with how I'd begun.'

While Sanders doesn't remember this opening round, the same is not true of his great friend and fan Eddie Birchenough, the professional at Royal Lytham and St Annes, who first met him at a Ben Sayers golf-club company get-together in the '60s, when they both played with that manufacturer's clubs.

'Doug didn't get off to the best of starts, and that was another thing you have to remember when you look back on the Open of 1970. He double-bogeyed the very first hole. But he soon got into the swing and I remember him making a few birdies around the middle of the course, the loop. On 13, he made a bit of a mess of the hole. He got the ball to around 20 ft in the end after a bit of a struggle. He turned to his caddie and said, "Come on, George, let's go back and play the loop!" Anyway, he holed it and that steadied him again. He was pretty solid all the way in and for the first three rounds he was pretty solid. The weather got bad in the second round and anything around par was pretty good. Then he came into his own and I was sure he was going to win.'

The battle between Sanders and Nicklaus was already on. They were three strokes behind Neil Coles, whose record opening 65 earned him a two-shot lead. That was over Tony Jacklin, South African Harold Henning, Maurice Bembridge and John Richardson.

If you were looking for a hard-luck story of the first round, it belonged to the defending champion Tony Jacklin. Jacklin had a breathtaking start, savaging the Old Course by going out in just 29 shots, playing magical golf. A St Andrews record looked on the cards, but then a thunderstorm curtailed Jacklin's round with five holes still to go. When he returned to finish off the next day, the magic just wasn't there, and a possible 63 expanded to a 67. Jacklin never got back on a roll and in the end finished fifth. His was a case of a hand on the trophy loosened by an act of God. Jacklin certainly cursed the weather that week. He says:

'It stopped what could have been an exceptionally low round. One never knows what could have happened. It stopped the momentum. I was never the same the next day and the course was completely different. The weather got progressively worse and so did my scores. They went up three shots each day [67, 70, 73, 76] and that was basically due to the weather. I still had a putt on the last green to tie third with Trevino [and Henning], but missed it and finished fifth.'

Coles faded the next day with a 74 and Lee Trevino took over with a second 68, leading by a stroke from Nicklaus. Sanders also went back a little, by shooting a 71 in the second round, and trailed Trevino by three shots.

With conditions even more difficult in the third round, Sanders's short but effective swing reaped dividends. A fine round of 71 left him tied for second place with Nicklaus, two shots behind Trevino. While Trevino was beginning his golden Open age, Sanders still felt Nicklaus was the man to beat. As determined as he was that Nicklaus would not thwart him this time, though, the Golden Bear was equally resolute. He had been told by the legendary Bobby Jones that before anyone could be called a great player they had to win on the Old Course at St Andrews.

In the final round, Sanders went out with Trevino, with Nicklaus playing ahead. Trevino's Open hopes were soon dashed, though, and in the end he was no threat, as he stumbled to a 77. Sanders's feeling that Nicklaus would be the one to beat was well founded. Nicklaus looked set for victory as he went past the turn. However, the Golden

Bear then suddenly ran into putting problems. He three-putted three of the last five greens to shoot a 73, opening the door for Sanders.

While the 18th green still gives Sanders nightmares and is the one everyone remembers, the 14th was unkind to him too. He points out:

'I was going well and I was sure I was going to make a birdie on the par-five, the 14th. I chipped up to about 4 ft, but I missed the putt. A lot of people forget that, when they talk about the finish. That was just as costly. I would have had a two-shot lead going into the last four holes.

'I managed to save par at the Road Hole, the 17th, and it was looking good – one shot ahead with one to play.'

With great modesty, though, Sanders has either forgotten or, more likely, glossed over a telling shot at the Road Hole. Having found the bunker, he could have perished there and then, and there would have been no legend of Doug Sanders's miss on the 18th. Instead, he coolly chipped out of the bunker that had claimed the hopes of many before him, hitting almost stone dead. Eddie Birchenough was watching:

'The bunker-shot Doug played at the 17th, had he won the Open, would have been fêted as the best shot played under pressure to win by anybody at that time. It was a fantastic shot. And it was really windy. That's something else people don't remember. His putt on 17 was about 18 in. and the wind was really howling, whipping his trouser bottoms around and making even a putt of that length very tricky indeed. He had to step back a couple of times before he holed it. That should be taken into consideration when you think about what happened at the 18th.'

Sanders was still in control coming to the last hole, a stroke in front of Nicklaus. He then struck a sound drive. The crowd, whose favourite he had become, bayed their approval. Sanders then carefully hit up about ten yards from the green, just above the Valley of Sin. His third shot, a putt, was nearly the last of the Championship and, as Sanders remembers, would have saved him years of heartache if it had come off:

'Maybe I was a little too cautious with my second shot. I wanted

24

to make sure I got over the Valley of Sin. Then I decided to putt. When I hit the first putt from about 30 ft or so, I believed I had made it. As far as I can remember, it would have been the first birdie there for four days. When I hit that putt, it was heading right for the hole. I said, "Go in, baby," because I knew if it did I'd be the only person to break par all four days. That had been my objective, and I knew if I could do that, I would have a pretty decent chance of winning. It didn't work out that way.'

Had that putt gone in, that would have been more than that. But it wasn't. There was to be an even bigger 'if only'. Arguably the most infamous putt in Open history still had to be made.

It all came down to a three-footer. Sanders was still leading Nicklaus by a stroke. With the crowd hushed and Nicklaus waiting, Sanders prepared himself. He lined up the left-to-right-breaking putt – not a 'gimmee' by any means, on one of the most notoriously fickle greens in the world. Sanders went as if to draw back. But then he stopped, bent down and brushed away a speck of debris. Was the speck imaginary? Were the nerves jangling just that little too much? He went back to his stance. Sanders tapped towards the cup but then arched away almost in one motion. His face bore a look of dejection and resignation, as his ball dived past the cup on the right.

Television commentator Henry Longhurst said it all:

'And so now this is it; this one, with a left-hand borrow; downhill, on the last green at St Andrews, to win the Open . . . Missed it. Yes. That's the side you're bound to miss it. There it is. There but for the grace of God . . .'

Sanders recalls his agony:

'As I looked at the second putt, I was thinking about what I was going to do: hurl my ball to the crowd; throw my putter in the air; bow to everybody. Then I decided I'd try to be a humble winner. And I would have been, believe me. If only that sucker had gone in.

'While I was checking out the putt, I thought I noticed a little brown spot on the line. I bent down to brush it away. But there was nothing there. I then went straight back. And I missed the putt. I was told later that Ben Hogan was watching on television and he'd said, "Walk away, Doug. Walk away from it." I should have. It was the biggest mistake of my career.

'When I thought about it afterwards, I knew the other mistake I made was not letting Trevino putt first, so I could gather my thoughts better. It was all my fault. There's only one person to blame and that's Doug Sanders.'

A closing 73 by Sanders threw the tournament into a play-off. In 1970, that meant Sanders and Nicklaus returning to the course the next day, a Sunday, for an 18-hole shoot-out.

You might expect Sanders's calamitous finish to have taken so much wind out of his sails that he would have been no match for Nicklaus. That was not the case, and the tournament was not decided until that fateful 18th green. Again, Sanders points to pivotal moments before it got that far, though.

'I remember at the 11th hole I left my ball in the bunker. I got up and down to make bogey. That put me three strokes behind. I knew I was better than that. I gathered myself and made two or three birdies coming in.'

With both players now locked together, it looked like sudden death. Nicklaus, though, handed out a body blow to Sanders almost as deadly as Sanders's missed putt the previous day. Nicklaus had only a one-shot lead over Sanders coming to the 18th. The Golden Bear produced a breathtaking drive but, because of being so pumped up, his ball carried over the back of the green. Sanders had a good drive and then played a bump-and-run shot to around 5 ft. Could he again be facing a short putt to win the Open? It never came to that. Nicklaus chipped down to 8 ft. Bobby Jones's words came back: 'The great players are the ones who can say they have won at the Home of Golf.' Time seemed to stand still. Nicklaus finally made his move. He rolled in the curling right-to-left putt which made him one of the 'greats'.

Sanders was stunned, he says. He was convinced Nicklaus's putt would stay out and keep his hopes alive:

'It looked like that putt was going to lip out. And Jack was so fortunate because when he knocked it over the green, that ball could have been buried in that high grass. He might have been lucky to even get it out. But it was laying right on the top of the grass. Jack made a hell of a shot, though, and he made that putt.'

In his jubilation, Nicklaus forgot his cool. He threw his putter in the air. His opponent had to sway out of its way before it hit the deck, to avoid being brained.

'When he threw that putter up into the air, I was trying to cover my head up, because I looked around and I couldn't see the putter. I told him, "Dammit, Jack, it's bad enough to beat me but you didn't have to try and kill me!"'

Finally, Sanders came down to earth too. His dream had gone, broken by a three-foot putt the previous day.

'I told him, "Jack, I gave you the British Open on Saturday. On Sunday, you won it." But, of course, I was heartbroken.

'I was so disappointed. I remember that night going into the field near where we were staying. There were a lot of cows in the field and I took out some sugar for them. First, I lay down near them, just looking up at the sky. Then I took out my lumps of sugar and tried to feed the cows from my hand. They weren't interested. I went back and told my wife, "I'm doing so bad I couldn't even get the cows to eat sugar out of my hand."

'She said, "Honey, they eat salt. They don't eat sugar."

'So I got that wrong too. I'm so unlucky I could buy a pumpkin farm and they'd call off Halloween!'

Sanders reckons that the errant putt cost him millions of dollars per foot.

'Oh, yes, it was costly. It cost me in more ways than people could ever dream. You see, I had been waiting for just that moment. I had done all the other things . . . except to win a major. Do I still keep thinking about missing that putt, after all these years? Heck, no. Yesterday I went at least five minutes without it even crossing my mind.

'If that putt had only gone down, I could probably have signed up right away for millions of dollars. And I would always be known as the guy who beat Jack Nicklaus for the British Open at St Andrews, the Home of Golf.

'I can never be in the PGA Hall of Fame, because I haven't won a major, and, you know, the British Open wasn't that good to me because if I'd parred the 11th at Muirfield in the final round, I'd have won the 1966 Open. I tried to hit a six-iron in, I remember, but the grass caught it and I double-bogeyed. I lost by a stroke. I could have won a Masters, but for one hole. I lost a US Open by a stroke. I lost a US PGA Championship by a stroke. I even finished second in the US Seniors Open.

'It's all been close but no cigar! I don't know what I would give to be able to take that putt again.'

1970 TOP SCORES
J. Nicklaus 68–69–73–73 283
D. Sanders 68–71–71–73 283
(Nicklaus won play-off 72 to Sanders 73)
L. Trevino 68–68–72–77 285
H. Henning 67–72–73–73 285
A. Jacklin 67–70–73–76 286

1972, MUIRFIELD: TONY JACKLIN

(Jacklin shared the lead with eventual winner Lee Trevino
with just two holes to go. Trevino's chip-in at the 17th,
in two days of outrageous fortune,
ended Jacklin's chances)

'It was just the circumstances. I didn't think about three-putting when I was over my fourth shot. I was too aggressive. That was my reaction to the chip-in. It all went away then.'

TONY JACKLIN HAD won the 1969 Open in fine style, but then lady luck seemed to turn her back on him. First, it was heavy rain that thwarted him. Then it was the head of an unfortunate lady spectator that stopped him even being second. Then a string of preposterous twists to an Open tale sank him beyond trace.

Each time, one man stood in his way: Lee Trevino. The wisecracking Mexican-born American seemed to put the hex on Jacklin. Trevino was upset by the galleries in 1971 when he played with Jacklin – not disturbed by the crowd but resentful of their partisan attitude in blatantly urging the British player on. That left Trevino more determined than ever to beat him. He did, two years running. And in the end, Trevino was the player most responsible for ending the major-winning career of England's best golfer of that era.

In 1970, the weather had put paid to Jacklin's chances as he defended his trophy at St Andrews, to leave him in fifth place. Then, in 1971, at Royal Birkdale, he contended strongly but had to settle for third behind Trevino, after a huge stroke of luck for the Formosan Liang Huan Lu, the Chinaman in the pork-pie hat who became 'Mr Lu' with the British public.

Jacklin was hoping for a change in fortune, he says, when he arrived at Muirfield, home of the Honourable Company of Edinburgh Golfers.

'In fairness, I didn't really play that well in 1971. I putted very well. The greens were very difficult. Birkdale had to renovate all their greens a few years ago because, historically, they were not good putting surfaces. The course was always a great links but they seemed to have trouble producing very good greens.

'A lot of putts were missed from short range in 1971 but I managed, somehow, to keep knocking them in. I went close to winning but just came up short. Mr Lu, on the last, hit a woman in the head with his ball, poleaxed her. Instead of possibly losing his ball in the real heavy stuff, it bounced back onto the fairway. He got up and down on 18 to rob me of second place. It's called rub of the green!

'So there had been a few setbacks over the previous two years. But I felt pretty confident going into 1972. I was still playing the American tour full-time, concentrating mainly on playing over there, and it was always a mental lift, gave you inspiration, to come back and play at home in the Open. Together with that, there was obviously added pressure, performing in front of your own home crowd and knowing what they were expecting of you.

'I was happy with the way I was playing coming into the week, but my success was always linked to how I putted on any week. My long game didn't really vary very much. I was just never, consistently, a good putter, as was, for example, Nicklaus. Palmer was, in his heyday, a tremendous putter. My putting sort of went hot and cold.

'Earlier on in that week, I remember trying to work on getting a thought process going, something I could concentrate on and work on. It was down to trying to keep the hands out of the putt and putt with the arms and shoulders more.'

Satisfied enough with his putting, Jacklin fired his first salvoes in the 1972 Open – only 69 salvoes. They were good enough to give him the first-day lead and he was, he says, delighted with a fast start:

'So many of the big championships at that time depended on how you managed to get off the starting blocks. You needed to be in amongst it straight away. On that basis, I was very happy with my start. I was right in there. When you are in the frame early on, it gives you more focus on the tournament. That was especially so for me, because the galleries were out in full strength and I needed to perform in front of them.'

Perform he did. Jacklin led by a stroke from a group that included the inevitable Jack Nicklaus. Trevino was two strokes back. Nicklaus was the big danger, thought Jacklin:

'The talk that week was all about Nicklaus, because he'd won the Masters and the US Open. Was it possible he could do the Grand Slam? The way he was playing, it was definitely on, and we all knew before we were going to win anything at Birkdale we'd have Nicklaus standing in our way. So having Jack close and right up there was something to think about. But I always looked upon the first two rounds as jockeying for position. If you were still in there amongst it after two rounds, that was key.'

Jacklin's key lay in a second-round 72 that left him in a tie on top with Trevino. Nicklaus, meanwhile, was only a stroke off the lead. Jacklin was taking on the two giants of the American game at that time. After the sabre-rattling of the first two rounds, Jacklin says he knew the fight was on in earnest:

'The third round was when the Open started to hot up. Trevino had everything going for him. It wasn't my misfortune, I didn't believe, that was ultimately my downfall; rather, as the commentator Henry Longhurst put it, Trevino's "diabolical luck". He birdied the last five holes, and two of them were chip-ins.'

Trevino had looked as though he was losing ground and in danger of falling out of the running. But he then suddenly took off in spectacular fashion. Birdies came at the 14th and 15th and then came the shot which was to set up his memorable victory. On the 16th, Trevino pitched at pace from the downslope of a bunker. Like a determined bailiff, his ball rapped hard on the flag halfway up the stick – and gained entrance to the hole. It left Jacklin shaking his head.

A transformed Trevino, all gift and gab again, was by no means finished. He picked up a further shot at the 17th and then pointed out to his Scottish caddie Willie Aitchison that he had never made five successive birdies. When he stepped off the 18th, he had. Having hit his ball through the green, Trevino chipped in again.

Though his stomach was churning with dismay, Jacklin says he tried not to show his resentment as Trevino performed his conjuring tricks:

'I was doggedly determined to stay with him, whatever happened. On the 16th, he hit it skinny and it dived straight in the hole on the second bounce, and then on 18 I was on the front of the green and he was off the back. Although it was me to play first, take my putt, as you do sometimes, he said, "I'll come up." So he came up out of this wispy grass and damned if he didn't chip in there as well.

'I was left with a very difficult two-putt. I holed a six-footer for the second putt. That enabled me to at least stay with him, within a shot. Nicklaus was well back by now and it was more or less match play at that stage in the third round and into the start of the fourth round.'

Leader Trevino led Jacklin by a stroke, but any thoughts of it being only a two-man Open were dispelled for the pair of them when the Golden Bear got on a charge. Nicklaus, citing a stiff and painful neck caused by an uncomfortable pillow – he had forgotten to bring his old faithful to Scotland – had looked out of sorts over the first three rounds. With that Grand Slam chance acting like a golden carrot, though, Nicklaus came rampaging after Trevino, whom he trailed by six strokes, and Jacklin.

'We didn't think Jack was going to be able to catch us, but by the time we stood on the 9th tee, Nicklaus was busy birdieing the 11th and going past us both. It was a remarkable performance on his part.

'Trevino turned round to me and said, "Well, he might beat one of us, but he won't beat both of us." Then Trevino and I both eagled. I eagled on top of him on the 9th and we went into the back stretch head-to-head.'

As the pair approached the fateful final two holes, locked together, the news that Nicklaus had bogeyed the 16th, missing an eight-foot par-saving putt, came as relief. Now, surely, one of them must be the winner. And as they played the 17th, it looked for all the world as if it would be Jacklin. Trevino, disturbed twice by cameramen walking in front of him on the fairway, found a fairway bunker, while his chief rival hit down the middle.

'I thought I'd got him. Lee was always a fader of the ball and he hooked into the bunkers. I hit a good drive. Then he came out of the sand sideways and then he hooked it again into the rough. That indicated to me that I'd broken his will. I had every reason to think at that point that I was on top.

'I hit a good second shot down just short of the green by about 20 or 30 yards – the wind was against, so it wasn't reachable – and he hit his pitch out of the rough, his fourth shot, over the back of the green. He turned to me and said something like, "That's me done. Take it. It's yours now."

'I was not naive enough to believe that. You're still out there in a cauldron of pressure. I was too much of a pro to take anything for granted. I knew what could happen in majors.

'My pitch shot didn't quite release the way I thought it would. The green looked brown and hard and I thought the ball would run further. I was left with a 16-, 18-footer. Then he chipped in again. He'd thrown in the towel, more or less, and he'd made five.

'I didn't let that affect my resolve. My feeling was "You son of a gun, you're not going to beat me on that basis."

'I could have two-putted from that distance a hundred times out of a hundred, but my reaction to the chip-in was aggressive: "Right, I'll make this now." Instead of just being patient, rolling it up to the edge of the hole and if it goes in, it goes in, I gave it a rush and it went that awkward distance past: two and a half, three feet.

'I missed the return putt.

'It was just the circumstances. I didn't think about three-putting when I was over my fourth shot. I was too aggressive. That was my reaction to the chip-in. It all went away then.

'He was like a dog with two tails. He then hit a beautiful drive and second shot, and he should have birdied 18. That was it.'

Jacklin was the one who needed to birdie the 18th to have a chance of a play-off with Trevino, but, instead, he bogeyed. That cost him even second place. That honour went to Nicklaus, who, it has to be remembered, also had his hand on the Claret Jug – indeed, one hand and a few fingers on the Grand Slam – until Trevino's magician's stunt at the 17th hole.

A frustrated Jacklin says he had to accept the hand of fate that broke his grip on the famous old trophy:

'You have to take what is given to you. It wasn't to be my week. It turned out to be Lee Trevino's week and not mine. It was a huge disappointment, certainly the biggest disappointment I'd had in golf to that point.'

It was a disappointment that Jacklin freely admits he never got over when it came to trying to win majors again.

'So many chip-ins in 36 holes and witnessing them all. Having that all happen and for it all to unravel at the end the way it did, it affects one's confidence. It shouldn't have been a career-terminator. But it certainly saw me off, as far as major championships were concerned. It changed my outlook in some way. I was always dogged – keep right on to the end. I didn't really believe in fate, just the power of being positive. But up against those sort of odds, it affected my outlook for the future. It shouldn't have done. I've lived long enough to know these things can happen. You soldier on, but you can't pretend that it didn't have some effect. To be a real champion, you can't have any question marks there at all; there's no room for them. When you are at your best, there is never a question mark.

'I'm not saying prior to the 1972 Open I was totally bulletproof, but you have a supreme confidence in your ability. That certainly shook mine.'

1972 TOP SCORES

L. Trevino 71–70–66–71 278
J. Nicklaus 70–72–71–66 279
A. Jacklin 69–72–67–72 280
D. Sanders 71–71–69–70 281

1975, CARNOUSTIE: JACK NEWTON

(Newton lost in an 18-hole play-off with a 72 to Tom Watson's 71)

'The tips I'd been given about Tom Watson were a bit like some of the tips I get at the racetrack. It was bad information. He putted like a demon . . .'

THEY WERE TWO of golf's young bloods, both with the world at their feet, good-looking lads with dashing swings and silky touches to match their looks. In one corner: Tom Watson, America's great hope and a potential challenger to Jack Nicklaus's place at the top of the world order. In the other corner: Australia's blond battler, Jack Newton, the latest to emerge from Down Under and join the pipeline that had produced such wonderful players as Peter Thomson, Kel Nagle, Bruce Devlin, Bruce Crampton, Graham Marsh and David Graham.

Both were only 25 years old when the drama of Carnoustie unfolded in 1975. If anything, Watson held the greater expectations after a good early showing in the US Open a few weeks before coming to Britain. Newton was a bright prospect, had already begun his Open career in 1972 and was, arguably, slightly the more experienced of the two. It was Watson's debut in the oldest major.

Before the curtain came down on a fifth day of breathtaking golf, more like exhilarating swordplay and definitely more akin to matchplay, one man would lift the Auld Claret Jug; the other would face crushing disappointment right in the final throes of a memorable Open.

Newton, New South Wales's finest, had already made a name for himself on the burgeoning PGA European Tour, showing Australia's great production line was in full swing. The ebullient and gregarious Newton's close friend was another man fond of a little of the *bon vivant*, Irishman John O'Leary. Newton recalls how, when Open week began, the pair took on a couple of Open champions:

'John O'Leary and I had won the Sumrie Better-Ball earlier in the year, so we teamed up for practice. Tom Weiskopf [1973 Open champion] had been out in Australia playing and I'd taken a bit of money off him. He was at me about giving him a chance to get it back. So I told him to get himself a partner and we'd play on Tuesday, him and his partner against myself and John O'Leary.

'He turned up to play and brought thousands of people with him. He'd brought Jack Nicklaus along as his partner!

'So we had a bit of a bet and set off for our match. It went pretty well at the start. I birdied two out of the first three holes and John also made a birdie early on. So I said to Weiskopf, "You better send back and get yourself another partner!" Apparently, Nicklaus heard me.

'Anyway, Weiskopf then gets a hole-in-one. He went on to shoot 65. Nicklaus shot 66. I shot 67 and played pretty well, but we got shut out. Of course, Weiskopf wanted me to pay him but I insisted on paying Jack. Jack said, "No, I don't want your money. Just a sandwich and a beer up in the clubhouse will do me." I was more than happy because I'd have lost the best part of 500 quid on the match.

'At that point, I'd never have dreamt I'd be playing with Jack in the third round when I broke the course record. The significance of playing with Jack Nicklaus in that game before the Open was that I watched him and learned a lot from him. I'd also played a practice round with Bobby Locke, just he and I, and I played pretty good but I just wasn't getting the ball in the hole as well as I'd like to. Coming up the 18th, Bobby said, "You know you could win this, Jack, if you can get the 15th club in the bag sorted out," meaning my head.

'So when I watched Weiskopf and Nicklaus, especially Nicklaus, hole these putts from all over the golf course that day, I just noticed something with their putting. I went back out to the practice putting green and worked and worked on it. I putted really well all week.'

It wasn't just his putting fortunes that changed after a little help from his friends and a few leaves taken out of the books of a couple of Open champions, though. Newton's opening round of 69 was a fine overall effort and left him only a stroke off Peter Oosterhuis's lead.

'Going into the tournament, I was in pretty good form, having unlocked a bit of a secret with the putting and feeling pretty comfortable. The weather was pretty good. The course was pretty bouncy, I remember, but it was a course I liked a lot. It was a very strong golf course. It was a good start.'

Newton shared second place after the first round with Nicklaus. It seemed as though fate was drawing the pair together. When Newton shot a second-round 71, they remained inseparable. Nicklaus also shot a 71. That threw the two together in the third round.

Nicklaus and Newton lay two strokes off the four-way tie for the lead. In front was the man making his debut, Watson. Fate was already in the process of matching up him and Newton as well.

Another player who had his hand firmly on the Jug that week, South African Bobby Cole, was to the fore, too. With the then course record 66, Cole shared first place with Watson, Oosterhuis and another South African, Andries Oosthuizen. In a real crush on top of the leaderboard, Newton's fellow-Australian Graham Marsh, Hale Irwin and Bernard Gallacher were only a stroke behind, jammed in between Newton and Nicklaus.

A marvellous record-breaking round by Newton was to follow. And he did it alongside the player he says he probably most admired, the man who had provided his inspiration in a betting match:

'It was just one of those days you don't forget . . . playing at

Carnoustie, playing with Nicklaus, third round of the Open and you shoot 65. I carry a memento around my neck made by Garrards of London which reminds me continually of my round. It's a plate with the two nines of the course on either side, with my scores filled in on each hole. It was the first one they made, so it's a bit special. From then on, they sold them commercially in gold and silver.

'The thing about the third round was that it was quite ironic, having watched Jack hole putt after putt from all over the course when we played the practice round, then to go out with him and score better than him in the tournament. He shot a 68, but he said to me when we finished, "I felt like I shot 80 playing with you." Coming from the great man, that was a pretty good compliment.'

Bobby Cole still had one hand on the old trophy, though, after three rounds. His second successive 66 earned him a one-stroke lead over Newton. Johnny Miller, whose time was to come the following year, was two shots off the lead. Watson lurked a further stroke back. The scene was set for the showdown as the Open drew to what the crowd thought would be its close. Newton knew he was on the brink of glory, and the words of one of his mentors came back as he stepped onto the first tee at Carnoustie.

'Bobby Locke had told me I could win if I could get the 15th club in the bag sorted out, and I felt I'd done that up to now. I just wanted to be able to concentrate fully on the job.

'I played with Bobby Cole in the final round, which was on a Sunday. They hadn't long started to finish the Opens on a Sunday. When I first went to Britain, we used to play in a Variety Club tournament on the Sunday after the Open. I heard there was some old law about not charging admission fee on a Sunday or something, so that's why they originally had Saturday finishes.

'I got off to a pretty good start, and eventually I had the lead.'

The 15th club in the bag was working very well for Newton, but for his playing-partner Cole it all went wrong, as his grip on the Claret Jug wilted and then released altogether. Newton's hold increased. Then it, too, started to slacken, as he allowed what looked like a winning position get away from him. He remembers his cause wasn't helped by a logjam of illustrious names on one of the closing holes:

'I was two shots in front, standing on the 15th tee. But then it went wrong. I bogeyed 15, 16 and 17. At 15, it was a pretty careless bogey. I hit a good drive, but it was quite bouncy. I landed my eight-iron short of the green to bounce it onto the green. But my ball just caught a little bit of a downslope and skipped on just off the back-left edge of the green. I had a fairly easy chip and chipped down about 6 ft, 8 ft – and missed it.'

'Bobby Cole was gone at this stage. He'd struggled all day.

'We walked over the hill to the 16th tee. It was a very difficult hole, anyway – a long par-three. There were three groups waiting on the tee. It was like the 'Who's Who' of golf . . . Watson, Nicklaus, Miller, Floyd: they were all waiting there on the tee. So we had to hang around for 20 minutes or so to play the hole. Not what you want at any stage, but not at that point in an Open when you were where you were.

'It was a hard-enough hole anyway, and I missed the green to the right, which wasn't hard to do. I almost made three but dropped another stroke there.

'Then, on 17, both my caddie and I sort of made a mental error in that we didn't pick up that the wind was coming in a slightly different direction to what it had been all week. It was a two-iron and a five-iron to lay up between the two burns. I hit a good shot and only just got over the first burn. In fact, I had to aim my second shot out over the fence on 18 and hook it back, because I just couldn't get a stance at it. That's how close it went to going in the drink on the 17th!

'Watson was playing a couple of groups in front of me. I heard this roar. What had happened was he'd holed a twenty-five-footer at the last for a three.

'When I bogeyed the 17th, it meant I came to the last needing to make a birdie myself to win. Having just dropped three shots in the last three holes, though, I was more thinking I needed a par to tie. I hit two pretty good shots but left my putt to win just short.'

Newton and Watson had to go to an 18-hole play-off, the second in six years, following Nicklaus's narrow victory on an extra day against Doug Sanders. Nicklaus had needed to chip in on the last to make it a three-way affair but missed. Newton's hunch that something was fatefully drawing him and Nicklaus together was unfounded. The Golden Bear, with the fading Cole and Miller, came up a stroke short of the play-off.

Before Newton could turn his thoughts to how he might beat Watson, there was a small matter of where he was going to spend the night, he recalls:

'We had to go and find out if we could get our hotel room back. We'd checked out that morning. We'd been staying over at St Andrews. They put on a hovercraft that week, across to Dundee from St Andrews, and I'd been getting it each day. They dropped you off right at the practice fairway at Carnoustie. So I'd warm up at St Andrews, then hit a few pitch shots when I got to Carnoustie, then go and play. Before I could think about the play-off, though, I had to go and sort out some new digs.'

Having secured a room, it was time to think about his opponent.

'I didn't know much about him, Watson. He was making his debut, of course. I recall he'd led the US Open earlier in the year, shot 79 and the American press branded him "a choker"! I didn't know what to make of that. And a couple of people told me that he was a bit suspect with the putter.

'So I went out there with the intention of playing a matchplay-type game, where I tried to hole-out first all day and waited for him to miss one. The tips I'd been given about Tom Watson were a bit like some of the tips I get at the racetrack. It was bad information. He putted like a demon – and did so for the next ten years.

'He had a sort of a fast, jerky kind of a "rap" stroke, but at that time he was a very, very good putter. He'd bash them in, and if he missed he'd go up and bash the one coming back in.

'The play-off was a bit of a funny one. He hit a strand of wire on the par-three; his ball was going out of bounds. It dropped down instead and he made three. He holed out with a sand-wedge for an eagle . . . he got a few breaks.'

Watson came flying out of the blocks. He hit a shot into only 3 ft on the 2nd and he was two strokes ahead after three holes. Newton fought back. A pitch into just a few inches on the 5th from just right of the green. Only one behind. A stunning bunker-shot at the 6th to only 3 ft. They were level. Not an inch was given as the two young protagonists produced punch and counter-punch. Then, as the drizzle turned to heavier rain to shroud Carnoustie in a grey shawl, it looked as though Newton was getting the better of his contemporary and Open neophyte.

Then, one moment's magic or luck was to play a major part in deciding whose name went on the Claret Jug that year. On the long 14th, Newton thought he'd done enough to at least stay level with Watson, when he again produced a magnificent chip, this one to 2 ft for his birdie. As with duelling pistoleers, though, Watson produced a crushing riposte, chipping from just off the green into the cup for an eagle. It put him a stroke in front, much to a soaking Newton's chagrin.

'It was raining and it was quite miserable. I hated playing with a jumper or a rain-jacket. A few of my old Scottish friends reckon I lost the Open because I didn't put anything warm on! It was also quite an awkward day: blustery, and it was wet. I thought the golf was pretty good, given the conditions.

'It ebbed and flowed but then I got in front and I stayed in front for a long time, seemed like most of the day. Then he holed out for his eagle on the 14th after I'd put mine close and that was a real body blow.'

Soon it was back to stalemate, though, with a rare mistake in a quality shoot-out. At the 16th, Watson hooked his tee-shot at the par-three to bogey. Newton's ball was on the fringe, a good 40 ft away from the cup. He rolled it up to within a few inches. The pair were level again, as they were after the 17th hole.

It all came down to the final hole of an absorbing play-off, just like it had in 1970 at St Andrews. Carnoustie's formidable finish was to bring dismay for one man and delight for another. For Newton, a brave attempt to be the first Australian to land the Open title since five-times winner Peter Thomson ten years earlier was ended at the 90th hole of the week of the Championship.

'The 18th was playing pretty tough, back into the wind and rain. We both hit good drives. He was more right-middle of the fairway; I was just in the first semi-rough, the low-cut stuff. The pin was back-left. My shot was a bit more difficult but it was no sweat. I was going in with a two-iron and I'd guess he was hitting about the same.

'He hit first. I heard him say, "Get up." He'd obviously hit it a bit heavy and he thought it was in the burn in front of the green. It had just cleared the burn and his ball ran up onto the front third of the green.

'I hit a great shot right at the stick but my ball caught the very top lip of the bunker and came back in it. I played an all-right bunker-shot; just skidded on me a little bit. When sand gets wet, it can skid on you, and that's what happened. Then the ball skidded on again when it went onto the green. It went past the flag. Then I hit a very good putt, but the ball just didn't take the borrow because of the rain and just slid past. It was a left-to-righter, and I hit it just where I wanted to hit it, but when it's wet, greens just don't take the borrow. That was it.'

Watson's 35-ft putt to within a foot for par and a round of 71 and Newton's near-miss from 12 ft for one stroke more finally decided which of the two young guns would lift the Claret Jug in 1975. Newton admits defeat took its toll:

'The breaks certainly went his way in the play-off, but Tom went on to be the best player in the world for ten years. I don't think you can have any sour grapes about getting beaten by a player who was the best in the world for a decade.

'There is definitely some damage when something like that has happened to you, though. I tried to keep playing. In those days, there was not much money around and you played almost every week. It's not like these days, where if they play three weeks in a row they're mentally exhausted!

'Obviously it was playing on your mind. What I should have done was take a few weeks off. Got it out of my system and started again. It took a while before I could get it out of my head.'

While Watson went on to conquer the world of golf and become number one, Newton's playing career was subsequently to be ended in horrific circumstances. He challenged several times in majors over the next few years, running Seve Ballesteros close at Augusta in the 1980 Masters before again having to settle for second best. Newton also won the 1978 Buick Open on the American tour. Then, on 24 July 1983, Newton was rushing to catch a plane at Sydney Airport on a day of poor visibility. As he trotted across the tarmac, he was hit by the propeller of a Cessna. His right arm was severed, a large piece of his trunk ripped off and his right eye torn out. The blade missed his brain by a whisker. Only the battler in Newton brought him through first a coma and then two months in intensive care. No one gave him a chance of survival, but survive he did. After numerous operations, Newton then had to fight off the understandable deep depression at losing a professional golf career, showing the same sort of spirit he had drawn on in 1975.

Nowadays he commentates on golf, always immaculate in blazer and bow tie. He designs courses and encourages youngsters with his junior golf programmes. His life is full. His only regret, he says, is that he didn't quite achieve a dream:

'Growing up, I always wanted to win the Australian Open and the British Open. They were my two chief goals. That's what, I think, most Australian kids who play golf dream about winning. Given what happened after that, I guess it was fate.

'But it was pretty exciting to give it a run in the British Open and also at the Masters. I suppose, on reflection, they were two significant events I did well in, so I can be proud of that.'

1975 TOP SCORES

T. Watson 71–67–69–72 279
J. Newton 69–71–65–74 279
(Watson won play-off 71 to Newton 72)
R. Cole 72–66–66–76 280
J. Nicklaus 69–71–68–72 280

1976, ROYAL BIRKDALE: SEVE BALLESTEROS

(Ballesteros, at 19 years of age, led after three rounds before winner Johnny Miller took over)

'He gave me a look, Johnny. I could tell he was thinking, "Well, I may have more hard work to do today than I expect to beat this young boy." Then, all of a sudden, things happened pretty quickly.'

THE 1976 OPEN will go down as momentous. Not just for its winner, Johnny Miller, the best golfer in the world at that time, but as the launch pad to the most flamboyant career in golf. It was the year Seve Ballesteros first hit the headlines and caught the public's imagination.

It wasn't Seve's first attempt at trying to make off with the Auld Claret Jug. The previous year, he had missed the cut at Carnoustie, limping away after two painful rounds with a foot injury. A year later, though, Ballesteros was back, and at the tender age of 19 nearly became a teenage winner of golf's oldest and most prestigious major championship.

Ballesteros, from Pedreña, near Santander in northern Spain, had been a professional for over two years when he came to play the Lancashire links. His fairly unique swing, fashioned around sublime hands, had been honed from the age of seven on his father's farmland and on the beach near Pedreña. He used an obsolete three-iron head with shafts made from saplings, improvising shots with the roundest stones he could find in lieu of golf balls, which were impossible to come by. When Seve was old enough, he caddied at Pedreña, improving his golfing equipment and technique.

Seve idolised his father, Baldomero, and he was the apple of Dad's eye. When a decision had to be made on Seve's future, his father insisted he should not have a mundane job. Seve was good enough to be a golf professional, like his uncle, Ramon Sota, who had also inspired Seve's brothers, Baldomero Junior, Vicente and Manuel, to try a career in golf.

Soon, his family felt he might be fit for earnest competition. They had been told enough times by Seve that he was ready! Just over three months before turning seventeen, without any experience playing in amateur events, Ballesteros followed his brothers by turning professional too.

Accompanying Manuel, who was playing on the European Tour, Ballesteros played four times in 1974, not really auspiciously, in fact beginning his touring career with a calamitous 89 at Estoril when trying to qualify in Portugal. The following year, though, at 18 years of age, Seve finished 26th on the order of merit.

One year later, Ballesteros became number one in Europe, on the way winning the Dutch Open, the first of 50 victories on the European Tour and 87 worldwide in 30 years. He was to become European number one a further five times and, for a period, rule the world. However, it was at Royal Birkdale, July 1976, that Seve Ballesteros, the most charismatic figure golf has known, first stepped into the spotlight.

Ballesteros had qualified for his second Open Championship by way of a Continental order of merit. Although he already had the machismo and self-belief that would eventually take him to the top of golf's world order, even Seve admits he was not dreaming of an Open win at the start of the week:

'I didn't have any feelings about winning the tournament when I went to Birkdale. I went there because my brother took me to play in the competition and just because it was the Open. As a youngster, you know it's the best tournament in the world and just to be there was very special. The atmosphere was fantastic. My only expectation at that time was just to be there and compete. I had been disappointed at missing the cut in 1975 but I was injured going to Carnoustie. I had a problem with my foot and I could hardly walk, so I was not in good shape.

'But 1975 was very exciting for me, my first time in the Open. I saw Jack Nicklaus, Arnold Palmer, Tom Weiskopf, Johnny Miller . . . So going back to the Open and seeing them all again, like anyone of my age, I thought it was very special.

'I remember in 1976 it was very hot weather. It was very hard to keep cool. We stayed in a bed and breakfast house and it was very hot there. We had all the windows open but it was still very hot.'

In 1975, Ballesteros had met Roberto de Vicenzo, the winner of the 1967 Open Championship. The Argentine player was to play a big part in Seve's Open career. He had one piece of advice in particular before the start of the 1976 Open. Ballesteros remembers:

'I practised with Roberto de Vicenzo, Vicente Fernandez and another Argentine player whose name I only remember as Cabrera. Not the Cabrera we all know today, of course. This was a short guy like Ian Woosnam, a good player. We four enjoyed practising together.

'Roberto told me to watch out for the bunkers. I presumed he had had some bad experiences in the past with the bunkers at Birkdale. From what he told me, I felt he was very scared of the bunkers. He told me, "Once you are in the bunker, don't take any chances. Just try and get out, and if you have to lose one shot then do it. Don't take any risks, because if you do you may pay a very heavy penalty." I was very happy to hear this advice and I remembered it.

'I have some good memories of that week, away from the course. I remember after practice going to Southport and walking by the sea. It was a very pleasant place.'

With Birkdale fast-running because of the heatwave – fire engines had to visit the course during the morning of the first round to put out gorse fires and play was held up for 30 minutes – Ballesteros's fiery swing could get him into plenty of trouble on what proved to be a capricious test. It was only his fifth time at playing links golf, too. His other four experiences – Carnoustie the year before, when he was hobbling, and nondescript performances at St George's, Sandwich and Turnberry – had not filled anyone with awe. But he began the Open in style with a 69.

His score, which earned him a share of the lead with Christy O'Connor Junior and the Japanese player Norio Suzuki, might have gone largely unnoticed in the media, but Seve was already proving popular with the crowd. His glittering smile and a carefree approach to the game appealed to the Birkdale gallery, who were used to seeing golf played in an entirely different way.

Some of Seve's new fans spotted him out in Southport after the first round and congratulated him. It was all a bit of a mystery to Seve, however:

'I didn't speak any English at the time. I was speaking with my brother Manuel and Roberto, Vicente and Cabrera during the week. They spoke English, so that was my way of communication with everybody.

'In the evenings, when I was walking in the street, having been leading the Championship, the people approached me and talked to me in English, but I didn't understand. I used to say, "No comprendo; no comprendo. Ask my brother!"

'The connection between me and the spectators began straight away. Probably they saw a young Spaniard approaching the game in a very positive way and smiling all the time, playing all types of shots. They called some of the shots "miraculous". I think they were just seeing something new. I remember Peter Alliss saying, "This is a young man who is breaking away from the normal, with a different approach to the game."

'So we had a good connection, the crowd and me. And even though I didn't understand what they were saying, I felt that the people were supporting me. It was a very nice feeling and it helped me all week.'

It had been predicted that an American would win that week, but there was a slow start by the superstars from over the Pond. Johnny

Miller, at the peak of his career and an Open champion in waiting, lay three strokes behind the top trio. Jack Nicklaus was always going to be among the favourites, but he was all of five shots adrift of the lead.

If Seve didn't get any column-space to speak of after the first round, then the Birkdale greens did. There were several complaints from the top players that the heatwave had burnt the grass badly and rendered the greens unpredictable, to say the least. Seve says there were no complaints from him, though:

'In the first round, I remember playing very steady golf, very consistent. I was putting extremely well. I enjoyed very much the golf course. When you go to a place for the first time, either you like the golf course or you don't. For some reason, Royal Birkdale looked a very familiar place. I was very comfortable there.'

But while Ballesteros was comfortable, a certain well-known American from six years earlier in the Open was quite fazed by it.

'I caddied for my brother Manuel in the pre-qualifying and he played with Doug Sanders. Then, when I shot 69, Doug Sanders came into the locker-room. I was sitting there but he went up to my brother and said, "Hey, Manuel, well done; 69, a wonderful score."

'Manuel said, "No, no, it's not me; it's my brother," and he pointed down to me.

'Sanders said, "What? He was your caddie the other day!" He didn't know I was Manuel's brother.'

After following up with a second 69 to lead by two strokes, finally the press gorged on Ballesteros's talents. He still didn't have a clue about the questions being fired at him, but he knew he had got the journalists excited. Seve pronounced himself *'muy contento'*, and then let Manuel do the talking for him. All he could think about was letting his clubs speak for him the next day, when he would play with the man of the moment, Johnny Miller, who held second place.

'I'd had two very good rounds. The conditions were nice – not a very strong wind, only a light breeze. Another 69 and I was leading. I surprised everybody. To see someone so young and unknown. And playing a different way. It really caught the attention of the media.

The press asked me a lot of things. I didn't know what the questions were because I didn't understand the language, but my brother Manuel helped me by translating everything.

'Even though I was leading, I wasn't very nervous. I was quite *tranquilo*. But I was very excited. For me, it was like being on top of the moon because I'm leading the Championship and now I'm going to be playing with Johnny Miller in the third round. He was the star of the moment in golf.

'I really handled the pressure very well. When I normally played a round of golf, it used to be just a couple of my friends watching, then all of a sudden there are 10–12,000 people following the match. It was very special, very different from anything I had experienced before.

'The reason I handled it so well was because I just played it as another game, a game played for fun and pleasure. That was my only thought: "Just enjoy, have fun." I was just playing hole by hole. I never cared about having a game plan: "Must make four here; four there." None of that.'

Seve refused to bow to adversity. Time and again, he turned a potentially lethal tee-shot into a par with a wonderful exhibition of pitching, chipping and putting. His playing-partner was impressed, and so were the media again. The only reservation was, how long could Seve keep up his incredible Houdini-like escapes?

'I did hit some wild shots, but I escaped because I had an unbelievable day with the short-game.'

Miller nosed in front of his young adversary by the 10th but conceded the lead on the 11th. Both shot 73s to preserve the status quo at the start of the round. Ballesteros was really in unknown territory now. He led Miller by two shots. Nicklaus, hoping to claim his third Open as a special treat for his caddie, his 14-year-old son Jack Junior, still threatened. But a sensation really seemed to be on the cards the next day. While Seve's brother Manuel erred on the side of caution, typically his younger sibling did no such thing:

'After the third round, that night I could see my brother was worried. He was very quiet. I said, "Are you worried?"

'He said, "No, no, no."

'I said, "But are you OK? Are you relaxed? Are you *tranquilo*?"

'He said, "Do you think you can play good tomorrow and finish in the top ten?"

'I said, "No. I'm going to win."

'He said to me, "Do you know what you are saying? Win the Open?"

'I said, "Yes. I think I can win. I've seen Miller play and he didn't do anything that really impressed me. I think I can handle it. So why not win?"

'My brother shook his head.'

Although Ballesteros and Miller had both shot the same score, there couldn't have been two more contrasting rounds. And, with Miller getting an early night, there couldn't have been two more contrasting ways of preparing for the final day, either.

Stories of Seve – who was, after all, a young, handsome teenager, understandably keen to sample Southport's nightlife – dancing till dawn, though, are greatly exaggerated, he says:

'No. It's not true that I went to a disco. It has been said that I danced until the early hours of the morning, but it wasn't a disco. It was some kind of a pub with dancing. That's all. And I wasn't drinking any alcohol. At the time, I was drinking Coca-Cola or soft drinks. That is all.

'After we had dinner, it was still too early to go to bed, so we went for a walk and we saw this pub and went in. I did have a couple of dances. Some people recognised me; some didn't. I was in bed some time between 11 p.m. and midnight. But the next day, I was playing late, so it wasn't a problem. We'd gone out because we knew we had plenty of time. It was hot and it was uncomfortable in the room, so we went out. It was just a way of relaxing.'

When he did get to bed, Seve had no trouble nodding off, either, he says – no pacing the floor worrying about how he was going to handle the next day.

'I slept very well. It has always been one of my stronger points as a traveller. I've always been able to sleep well before a round. It's very important. If you sleep well, you're ready for the next day. If you don't sleep good, then you're not going to be at your best the next day.'

After nine hours' sleep, Ballesteros met his date with destiny. There was a huge crowd waiting to urge him on. An exuberant gallery expected more Seve sorcery. They were not disappointed at the 1st hole. However, sorcerer soon turned into salvager, and, on many occasions this time, there was no escape from big numbers for Seve.

'I went to the course with my brother and warmed up as normal. When I walked to the first tee, the reception was tremendous. The people were all cheering for me. I didn't feel that nervous, though, not really.

'At the 1st hole, I hit my one-iron to the left into the deep rough. I hit my second shot short of the green in the bunker and my third shot to 20–25 ft. I holed the putt for par. Miller dropped a shot. He made three putts from the back of the green.

'He gave me a look, Johnny. I could tell he was thinking, "Well, I may have more hard work to do today than I expect to beat this young boy." Then, all of a sudden, things happened pretty quickly. At the next hole, he made birdie and I made bogey.'

From there on, it was all uphill for Ballesteros and downhill for his score. Where he had been able to make unlikely pars, he dropped shots, and Miller forged ahead. The 6th, where shortly before Nicklaus's Open chances had gone with a lost ball and a double-bogey, was the focal hole. Seve found the same deep rough and bushes as the Golden Bear, and he, too, foundered fatally. To the chagrin of his now ample following, Seve's dream was over.

'At the 6th, I was in the middle of the big bushes on the right and all I could do was to chop the ball forward a little. It went into the bunker well before the green. I made a double-bogey and I probably knew then that it was not going to be my Open. I didn't give up, but it was hard from then.

'I made a double-bogey on number 10, a triple-bogey on number 11 and I disappeared from the scoreboard. Then I had to make a great comeback.'

With Miller now out of sight, Ballesteros's objective had to be to finish at least runner-up. Suddenly, his playing-partner seemed keen for him to do so, too, he remembers:

'Johnny Miller started speaking Spanish with me! Walking to the tee on the 17th hole, he said something like, "Come on. It's very important for you to finish well, because Mr Nicklaus is already in the clubhouse and you need to finish strong to catch him."

'I thought, "Shit! We've been playing together for two days, eight hours, and he speaks very good Spanish! He's started to communicate with me in Spanish now he knows he's going to win! Before, he didn't say anything!"

'I made a beautiful putt from the back of the green on 17 for eagle. I needed a birdie at the last to finish second with Jack Nicklaus.'

Then followed the shot that characterised a career. The hole was a par-five at that time, and after his second shot Seve found himself jammed behind two of the three bunkers that were guarding a flag that was hiding down a gentle slope on a fast-running green. There was very little room to manoeuvre. A chip over the bunker was sure to send his ball running at least 20 ft past the flag; short and he wouldn't even make the green. Seve's chances of at least matching one of his heroes and sharing the Open salver looked slim indeed. He can recall how he handled the shot with precise detail:

'I walked forward and checked out my shot. I knew it was going to be difficult to stop the ball, even if I hit a high lob-shot. There was no chance to stop the ball, because of the slope. I think it was a combination of my instinct, visualisation and aggression. I was determined to finish second instead of third. And if I went in the bunker, I would have to get out – two putts and maybe finish fifth. I saw the shot, visualised the shape – and did it.'

He did it by landing his ball on a spot in the middle of a path between the two bunkers no more than a yard wide.

'I knew there were only two ways: one up in the air, which gave me a small percentage to be close, or hit a little nine-iron punch and go through the bunkers. I chose the second. It was a very small place to land the ball, only about a yard, and there was a little hump running down onto the green. There was the path close, too. If I hit that, then the ball could have gone anywhere. It came out perfect and I found just the right place I had intended to land the ball.'

All Seve's hours of manipulating his three-iron on the beach at Pedreña had paid off. His shot was greeted with the sort of gusto that the Open champion could expect a little later. And the next day, Seve's finale at Birkdale brought as many accolades as Miller's exemplary display when shooting a 66 to win by six strokes.

'That was the start of the media's attention on me. Before that, I'd already hit a lot of shots like that. I'd learned how to do that. It was just playing the way I am. I like to gamble. I have tremendous confidence also. It's a combination of confidence, instinct and, obviously, I suppose, ability.'

Ballesteros was crushed that he had not won. He fought back the tears and allowed his lack of English to hide his disappointment at the closing ceremony. Then he couldn't believe what his brother Manuel told him:

'At the prize-giving, Johnny said to me, "Say something."

'I didn't know what to say, so I just said, "Thank you to you all." That was it!

'My brother was listening in to Johnny's press conference and, as we came away, I asked him what he had said. Manuel told me Johnny had said, "It was better for Seve to finish second than win."

'I said, "He doesn't know what he's talking about . . . finishing second is better than winning the Open Championship?" At that moment, I just didn't understand.

'Years later, I understood very well what Johnny meant, and he was 100 per cent right. It was my introduction to the golfing world, and I was able to play the following years without any pressure. If I had won, that would not have been the case.'

The wonderful rapport between Ballesteros and the galleries, especially British galleries, continued for three decades, all starting with his heroics at Birkdale.

'Since then, there has been a great feeling between me and the spectators through the years. One of the reasons I won three Opens and have been so successful is because the people always support me on the course, and that's very important, believe me – very important. If I didn't have that support, it would have been much harder to win.'

1976 TOP SCORES
J. Miller 72–68–73–66 279
S. Ballesteros 69–69–73–74 285
J. Nicklaus 74–70–72–69 285
R. Floyd 76–67–73–70 286

1977, TURNBERRY: JACK NICKLAUS

(The famous 'Duel in the Sun', won by just a shot by Tom Watson after four days of breathtaking golf)

'The one mistake I suppose I made was missing about a 6-ft putt at 17 for birdie and giving Tom the lead.'

IT SEEMS BIZARRE to bracket Jack Nicklaus as part of a group that 'could have' won the Open. The same, I suppose, goes for Tom Watson and Seve Ballesteros. And for Tony Jacklin, Ernie Els and Nick Price, who all did lift the Auld Claret Jug in triumph. However, there were years when these great champions saw the Jug slip from their grasps.

Nicklaus had plenty of second places in the Open. None were more spectacular, though, than in 1977, when the Golden Bear and the Kansas Kid fought tooth and nail at Turnberry in a thrilling and never-to-be-forgotten Open, now legendary as the 'Duel in the Sun'. Golf had never been seen in an Open like the fare Nicklaus and Watson served up, as the two best golfers in the world at that time played for the Claret Jug as if it were some kind of fencing duel.

At thirty-seven, Nicklaus was the older man by ten years. Watson had arrived on the scene ready to usurp the Golden Bear's crown as the top player in the world. By the time the dust had settled – literally, as the sun beat down on the west of Scotland links – Watson could rightly wear the crown in 1977. While Nicklaus would win more majors, the crown stayed firmly on Watson's head after the Duel in the Sun.

The pair had already had one showdown in the April at Augusta. Watson had shown he would be more than just a young pretender to Nicklaus's throne when he beat the Golden Bear in the Masters by two strokes.

Watson had arrived on the major scene two years before the Turnberry shoot-out, when, remarkably on his debut in the Championship, he beat Jack Newton in a play-off for the Open. Nicklaus was still pretty well in his pomp, although he had already claimed 14 of his 18 major titles when he arrived at Turnberry in 1977. The Golden Bear was ready to show his claws after also having to settle for second-best in the previous year's Open behind Johnny Miller. Watson had won the Western Open a fortnight before Turnberry and absolutely torn a Barcelona field apart on the eve of the Championship. They were the world's number one and two, although no one was completely sure which way around it was.

Both players looked to be in good form as they worked out how to play the Ailsa course at a Turnberry making its first appearance on the Open rota. To the delight of the crowds that packed into the Scottish course, the pair practised together. Watson, in particular, looked as though he was at the top of his game. If Nicklaus was appreciative of his expected arch-opponent's attributes as he steeled himself for the fray, he wasn't going to show it. The Golden Bear says his legendary single-mindedness came into play:

'I would have been concentrating more on my game and the golf course than someone else's game. That's always been my approach: to focus on the things I can control, such as my game. I have to concentrate on my game and beating that particular golf course.'

Watson, however, did take plenty of notice of his practice partner. Twenty-six years later, when both players took part in the Senior British Open at the same course, Watson admitted he had Nicklaus to thank for what happened in 1977 when the pair sat side by side in a press conference before the tournament:

'I watched Jack's swing. I've always felt when I watch somebody swing the golf club properly it makes me swing the golf club properly. Little did you know, Jack, I played so well because you helped me. I watched your swing!'

With Watson seeming to have slightly the better of the practice sessions, but Nicklaus having the pedigree, it was no surprise that the world couldn't wait for the mouth-watering clash to go ahead. The stage was set for an epic four rounds of golf. Nicklaus sets the scene:

'My head-to-head with Tom Watson became known as the "Duel in the Sun" because Turnberry was amazingly hot and sunny that year and the heat had baked the course and thinned the rough.

'Every time I'd gone head-to-head with Tom, it had been a pretty good match, and the British golf fans had convinced themselves that another 'Gunfight at the OK Corral' was imminent. I don't think we disappointed them. As a matter a fact, the crowd got so unruly at one point I remember Tom and I saying, "OK, we're stopping." We just sat there. It's never happened at a golf tournament before, but we did, until they could get the crowd under control.

'We were so wrapped up in what was going on. It was hot, dry, and the course wasn't playing particularly difficult, as far as we could see. We kept it going.'

At first, Nicklaus and Watson didn't command all the attention. As thunderstorms threatened to disrupt the opening round, the man who also caught the headline-writers' eyes on the first day was the leader, John Schroeder, son of the 1949 Wimbledon tennis champion Ted Schroeder. His 66 earned him a one-shot lead.

The opening forays by Nicklaus and Watson only heightened the hype around them. They were well up there, as expected – and they even shot the same scores: 68s. That vein was to continue right to the bitter and sweet end.

Mark Hayes, a contemporary of Watson's, proved to be the sensation of the second round, carving out a stunning record-breaking 63, which many had thought impossible on an Open course. He didn't lead, though, and neither did Nicklaus nor Watson. Roger Maltbie, another American, shot a 66 to hold a one-stroke lead. That was over the two favourites. To keep the kettle boiling, Nicklaus and Watson had equalled themselves out again, both shooting 70s. That threw them together for the third round. The golfing world was engrossed.

Parched fairways and burnt rough were a recipe for spectacular golf, and Nicklaus and Watson produced more than their fair share of that in the third round. Surely they wouldn't shoot the same scores again, though? When they both shot 65s, the tournament was at fever pitch. They held a three-shot lead. That was over Ben Crenshaw, with the next players five strokes adrift.

As everyone had hoped and expected, it was a tournament within a tournament. Nicklaus and Watson were playing absorbing golf and bouncing off each other. The rest? Well, they were playing something else.

Despite their domination of the tournament and monopoly of the crowd, though, Nicklaus remembers it was more strength of will that kept him on a par with Watson:

'"Playing badly well" sums up my game over the first three days. The driver gave me problems but with the rough being sparse there were usually opportunities to recover. By putting well, I'd been able to grab most of them.'

Thus, they turned it into a two-man show.

'There really wasn't anyone else in the Championship. So, really the Open came down to just Tom and me. With both of us rated one and two in the world, it seemed a fitting way to decide the tournament.'

The final round became cut and thrust from the off. Nicklaus, who had said the previous day that 'an exceptional round of golf' would be needed from him to beat Watson, fired the early salvoes. Although he missed the fairway at the 2nd, it was first – and second – blood to the Bear. Despite his driving still causing him problems, Nicklaus birdied while Watson bogeyed. A two-shot swing and the experienced campaigner was in the ascendancy.

When Nicklaus birdied the 4th to a par by Watson, he went four strokes ahead. Soon that picture changed completely. Three majestic birdies from Watson followed in the next four holes. They were level again.

It was all too much for some. With the crowd dazzled by the pair's wonderful cut-and-thrust golf, it was no surprise that a few in the gallery lost their heads. People were running around like headless chickens, trying to make sure they had a better look, kicking up dust at the parched course. The marshals did their best, but they were losing control. At one point, Nicklaus and Watson could not even locate where they had hit because the crowd had surged in front of them. The gallery were almost on their elbows at one stage.

At the 9th, Nicklaus had had enough and suggested to Watson that they stop altogether until the crowd were under control. The pair downed tools until some semblance of order was established. Nicklaus remembers the episode well:

'It wasn't that they were boisterous. It was that we could not control them. They were all over the fairways. I guess you might say they were, basically, unruly. You couldn't play because fans were running everywhere. Finally we stopped playing until they could get the gallery under control.'

When order was finally restored, it was Nicklaus who went on to take the upper hand again. Watson bogeyed the 9th after the debacle to go a shot behind. Then a birdie by Nicklaus put the Bear two strokes in front at the 12th.

That put Watson in dangerous territory: two behind with six to play. He gathered his resources. A birdie at 13 left him only one adrift.

With the gallery still pressing, craning to see every move from the modern-day duellists, Nicklaus and Watson took stock at the 14th, looked around at the expectant faces and acknowledged what an epic finale they were producing. Watson observed that this was 'what it was all about': their sacrifices for the game, the thousands of hours of practice for perfection. Nicklaus said that he could hardly have put it better. It was like two gladiators saluting each other, knowing that, no matter how hard to take it would be, one of them would have to come out on top, the other be toppled.

Turnberry's tough 14th brought no change. Nicklaus had the firmer grip on the Claret Jug, still a stroke ahead after both made pars.

And so it all came down to the final four holes of the Championship. At first, it looked optimistic for Nicklaus, but then Watson brought the crowd to a new level of hysteria. Nicklaus remembers being checked in his stride after Watson pulled off what was to be one of the two defining acts late on in the 1977 Open, both of them putts:

'When we reached the par-three 15th, I stood on the tee with a one-shot lead. The hole played two hundred and nine yards and we both went in with a four-iron. Tom's tee-shot finished on the left fringe, and my ball landed much closer to the flag on the right.'

Faced with a putt of around 20 ft and uphill, the odds were stacked in Nicklaus's favour. Watson was off the green, his ball lying on a flat piece of rough that wouldn't take a chip. It had to be a putt, and sharply downhill.

'I figured he would be fortunate to get down in two. He did not get down in two. Tom made a wonderful birdie putt from all of 60 ft to tie me when I missed my 20-footer.'

With the wonderful show at stalemate, the protagonists knew that, just like at the OK Corral, one false move could mean the bullet.

Either could have gone back in front at the 16th, but both had to settle for pars. Still all-square. It had been a matchplay-type scenario for hours. The second critical moment of the shoot-out was just about to come.

They both hit accomplished drives on the long 17th. Watson chose a three-iron to go in. He struck an imperious blow to about 25 ft. Nicklaus chose one club less. His ball drifted into wispy rough. It needed a deft chip to put Nicklaus back on terms. He provided it with a shot to just under 6 ft. Watson putted up. While his ball refused to drop for eagle, he duly mopped up the birdie.

Nicklaus now knew he had to hole his putt or concede the advantage at a crucial point. He missed, swayed by Watson's putt into misreading the break, as he admitted later.

Watson was in front. Only a birdie would give Nicklaus any chance. He went for broke. Hitting the driver as hard as he could to cut down on the rest of the job in hand, Nicklaus pushed his tee-shot and his ball looped very close to an unplayable lie in gorse. His chances seemed over as he forced his way through the seething mass that was the anticipating crowd.

'At 18, Tom had a good tee-shot. I hit my tee-shot, not through the fairway but right up under a bush. I could swing at it and I'll never forget what happened there as I hit my shot out.

'It's apparently a Scottish custom that people will come over and throw coins on the divot, wishing you good luck. People came over and threw piles of coins on that divot after I left. I didn't see that but I was told about it later. My ball went up to the edge of the green.'

Nicklaus had extricated himself from dire straits. It was now all down to how Watson played his approach.

'Tom hit a beautiful second shot. I don't remember what club he played, maybe an eight-iron. He hit it up to inside 2 ft from the hole.'

That appeared to be that. The shoulders of the Nicklaus supporters in the frenzied gallery sank. Their hero refused to concede defeat yet, however. If he could sink his putt of near 40 ft, at least he could put pressure on Watson, whose two-footer would then elongate mentally.

'Well, obviously I didn't think I was going to make it but had to give it my best shot. I had about a 35-footer across the green with a break. I knocked it in the hole.'

The crowd erupted yet again. Watson had to use all his powers of concentration, even with such a short putt. He made no mistake. The most exciting and dramatic battle between two of golf's leviathans was over. Watson had needed to birdie the last to achieve the most memorable of victories, shooting a 65 which saw him break three records: for the last two rounds (130), the last three rounds (200), and for his winning aggregate of 268, the best by no fewer than six shots. Nicklaus had done all he could to hold him, making the birdie at the last for a 66 that would have crushed a mere mortal. He had finished ten strokes better than the third-placed player, Hubert Green, and shared with Watson the record for an Open first three rounds – a measure of how close the duel had gone without needing an extra shoot-out.

Vanquished saluted victor.

'I went over and put my arm round him, and I can't remember exactly what I said but it was something affectionate. He smiled back and said he got me this time.

'We both played very, very well, and there really weren't very many mistakes made. The one mistake I suppose I made was missing about a 6-ft putt at 17 for birdie and giving Tom the lead.

'It was terrific golf from the both of us and it was the best I could do. I'm sure we've all missed shots. I missed mine on the 17th. It was fun and it was good. I think that's what is great about the game of golf. Guys beat each other's head in all day long and walk off the 18th green with arms around each other.

'To break the Open record by five shots and still lose is not exactly what you like to do, but I can only do my best. If somebody does better, then well done. You congratulate them. They just played better than you did on that particular day.

'Sometimes a golf tournament whittles itself down to a battle between one or two golfers, and when a major championship is at stake, there are few moments more memorable and enjoyable. Even in loss, the thrill of the competition and the moment creates indelible images that almost paint over the disappointment of defeat. Almost.'

1977 TOP SCORES
T. Watson 68–70–65–65 268
J. Nicklaus 68–70–65–66 269
H. Green 72–66–74–67 279
L. Trevino 68–70–72–70 280

1978, ST ANDREWS: SIMON OWEN

*(Owen led by a stroke with just three holes to go before
Jack Nicklaus took the title)*

'I hit this second shot and it felt perfect. It was just eating
the flag up. I thought, "Well, there you are. Here comes
birdie number six."'

SOME OF THE cynics were asking if Jack Nicklaus, at 38 years old, might be over the hill as far as winning majors was concerned. He'd lost the previous year's Open, and many said he wouldn't contend in the British major again. They were way out in their assessments on both counts.

Nicklaus's swing, though, had been suspect for a few months, and the portents for a third Open Championship title were not good when the Bear came to the Home of Golf, the scene of his triumph in 1970. Tom Watson, who had elbowed Nicklaus out of the Open the previous year at Turnberry, was the clear favourite for St Andrews.

No one cast even a shadow of a thought about a New Zealander winning. Since 1963, when Bob Charles lifted the Auld Claret Jug, and six years later, when Tony Jacklin wrested it from him, the Kiwi challenge had disappeared. However, 1978 saw the emergence of a 27 year old from the southern hemisphere who came within a whisker of providing the biggest upset in the game for many a year.

Simon Owen took on the world's best and, in the end, came desperately close to denying Nicklaus what proved to be a rather fortunate third Open title and his second over the Old Course. Just one cruel stroke of luck as late as the 69th hole of the Open ended Owen's hopes and stopped the Claret Jug's engraver marking the second New Zealand name on the famous old trophy.

Owen was to take his place in the '70s alongside Doug Sanders and Jack Newton: players who had more than glimpsed the promised land but didn't quite make it to golf's nirvana; players who never did get both hands on the Claret Jug.

At the start of the week, Owen and Nicklaus, of course, had no idea they would be thrown together by fate and the magic of the Open. Nicklaus would have had little idea, even, who Owen was. They'd never met. Nicklaus was at the top part of the world order, still not that far from the very top. Owen, while by no means unknown – he had already won twice on the European Tour – was rather in the lower echelons.

Both had had reservations over their games in the weeks before going to St Andrews, again at different scales. Nicklaus was then relieved he had seemed to put right a fundamental fault in his grip just in time for the Open. He had not contended strongly for once in the Masters or the US Open. Owen was having a see-saw season, winning back home and in Asia but then going quiet. He was lifted by a few weeks of hitting the ball well before making his first appearance at St Andrews, but was not exactly expecting what was to come.

The odd couple both had to go to pre-qualifying. Nicklaus, who was, of course, exempt, caddied for his son Jackie. Jackie didn't make it. Owen played in pre-qualifying. He did make it. Owen remembers how his never-to-be-forgotten week began:

'It was my first St Andrews Open, and that's a very special time in a golfer's life, playing at the Home of Golf. I had to pre-qualify. That was job number one that had to be put out of the way. It was a close-run thing, but I managed to scramble a couple of birdies over the last five holes at Lundin Links and just got in. I didn't have to go into a play-off, but, from memory, I was the last one at my course to just scrape in.

'So that was quite satisfying. It's never easy to pre-qualify for the

British Open. I know they do it a little bit differently these days, but it's always a relief to get in. Any pro will tell you that. In those days, there weren't too many spots up for grabs. It was good fun.

'I'd had a mixed time of it up to then. I'd won the New Zealand PGA Championship at the beginning of the year and then the Malaysian Dunlop Masters, but apart from that it was kind of an up-and-down season. My form didn't suggest I was going to be in contention to win the British Open, put it that way.'

While the Golden Bear put his thoughts to two main criteria – staying out of the golden sand and concentrating on his putting – it was all new to Owen, but he liked what he saw. He says:

'When I got to St Andrews, the course just seemed to suit my game. The greens were nice and fast, and in those days I was a good fast-green putter. And I was driving the ball particularly well at the time. So everything at St Andrews just seemed to set up well for me.'

The name of one of Owen's practice-round partners summed up how he was feeling going into the Championship.

'Practice went well. I remember having a couple of practice rounds with David Good [one of the Australian players on the European Seniors Tour nowadays], a good friend of mine, and we enjoyed the days. Form is strange, though. These kind of things, like that week at St Andrews, just happen.'

You can bet there was quite a difference in the way Nicklaus and Owen spent their time off the course before the Open began. While Nicklaus had several press conferences to attend and autographs to sign, Owen had his practice and then retired to a small hostelry away from St Andrews to spend a few quiet nights. On the eve of the Open, though, it was anything but quiet, and he found himself shooting from the hip. He recalls:

'My wife, Catherine, who's Scottish, and I, stayed with my mother- and father-in-law in a little village near Pittenweem. The night before the Open began, they had a "Gunslingers' Club" which used to meet up at this little hotel. They were all dressed up as true Western gunslingers . . . Colt 45s in holsters . . . they looked like real tough hombres! They had this gunslinging competition, sort of fast on the draw, and I had a go at it. I was ready for a bit of shooting!'

Owen and Nicklaus were not far apart after the first round and not far off the lead. A 70 by the New Zealander was one better than the Bear's effort. The Japanese Isao Aoki took a one-shot lead with a 68. Some well-known names shared second place: Ray Floyd, Seve Ballesteros, Tom Weiskopf and Jack Newton.

When the second round ended, Aoki kept his lead but now shared it with Ballesteros and Ben Crenshaw. Although Nicklaus stayed in touch, four shots adrift of the lead, despite cursing his 36 putts, Owen's brief challenge looked over as he carded a 75.

The third round, though, saw Owen re-emerge. His splendid 67 captured the press's imagination, although not as much as the hapless Japanese player of whose misery one caption-writer penned 'The Sands of Nakajima'. A quintuple-bogey nine when putting into the infamous Road Hole Bunker was to cost him his Open chance but earned the said Nakajima immortality.

Owen's fortunes were in direct contrast to his previous round and took him through the field as he showed great mastery of the Old Course's famous 'loop', the middle-ground at St Andrews.

'I guess the first round was just a solid sort of round, but I remember I struggled a little bit in the second round. Of course, I remember the third and fourth rounds a lot clearer!

'For the third round, I had the equal low-round for the Championship. Around the loop that day, I ran just red hot. I think I had six threes in a row around the loop. That set me up. I came home nicely and posted a 67. It was a little bit breezy that day and, in general, I don't think the scoring was that good, but I had a particularly good round and found myself up on that big yellow leaderboard!'

Owen's surge through the field took him to within just a stroke of the lead held jointly by the man now firm favourite to defend his title, Tom Watson, and Peter Oosterhuis. Owen and Nicklaus were now being drawn together, as with unlike poles. They were in a cluster of players on six-under-par in second place. When the tee-times were announced, Owen and Nicklaus became even more firmly linked. Suddenly the situation struck home to Owen. But he says he was able to take it in his stride:

'You always do feel pressure. I'd never been in contention for a major championship before. Then, of course, when the draw came out and I was playing with a chap called Nicklaus, it was a kind of daunting sort of a feeling, but at the same time I knew I was playing well. And I'm the sort of player when I'm playing well, I don't care who I'm playing with because I enjoy it. I know I can play as well as anybody in the field. Obviously there were a few nerves, but at the same time, overall, I had a feeling of confidence.

'I slept surprisingly pretty well that night – a lot better than some nights when I was in contention. I was pretty confident with my game, and that was the key. Sometimes you get up into contention in a tournament and you know deep down you're struggling. You might have holed a lot more putts than usual, for instance. But that week I was playing solid golf, and whenever I've played like that I've slept well. There was anticipation, that churns around in your guts, but everyone gets that.

'I'd never even met Jack Nicklaus, let alone played with him. It was kind of a big day for me. There we were on the first tee at St Andrews and I talked to Jack for the first time!

'Needless to say, I was a little bit nervous starting off, but I played the first couple of holes quite well. I had a couple of three-putts in the first half-dozen holes, though. I hit a couple of iron-shots on the green, but probably not quite as near to the hole as they could have been, and paid for it.'

With Watson struggling, Nicklaus and the surging Tom Kite shared the lead. In the Nicklaus–Owen match, the shouts of encouragement all seemed for the Bear. Owen caught the gallery's attention when he attacked the St Andrews loop, however.

'Jack was just playing pretty steady par golf at that stage. I think he might have picked up one birdie. But things turned around again for me once I hit the loop.

'I played 7 and 8 quite nicely, and then the fireworks started to happen. On 9, I had a good drive, got in a nice second shot and holed the putt. That seemed to spur me on. It brought back memories of the day before. I hit a big drive down 10, finished just beside the green, chipped it up and made another birdie there. I parred the par-three and then knocked it on the green at the par-four 12th. It was a fairly long putt but I two-putted it.

'So that was three birdies in four holes, and I was really in the "zone" by this stage. I still wasn't ahead. I was still one behind Jack at that point, but I was really going for it.

'I parred 13. I had a good birdie chance from about 12–15 ft, but I missed it. Then I birdied the long par-five [14th]. I made a nice birdie there, played the hole well. I holed, I guess, about a four- or five-footer. That put me all-square with Jack at that point.'

Nicklaus had birdied the 13th to edge into the lead, so Owen's birdie on the 14th saw him catch his playing-partner on six-under-par. Oosterhuis was a stroke behind. Floyd, home in 31, had set the target of five-under. Kite soon matched that.

The truly critical part of the 1978 Open was about to take place for Owen:

'Then came two holes that I'll never be able to forget all my life. At the 15th, I was down in the dip and had to think hard about how to play it. If I ran it too far, I would have trouble with the one back. But I didn't want to be short. I pitched up. It skipped into the hole. I was leading.'

That was the good news. Next came the bad.

'The 16th, though, was just the opposite. I'd just had five birdies and then I had probably the unluckiest hole I've played in my career, especially because of the major outcome. I hit such a good tee-shot down there, straight over those Principal's Nose Bunkers. I just blasted it straight over. I was in the perfect position. All I had was a sand-iron to the green.

'I'd been driving it the whole time with the driver on the back nine. Jack had been doing it differently. His game plan was different. He obviously knew the course better than I did. The wind direction was different that day as well. It was downwind on the back nine instead of into the wind, like it had been. It was all new to me, as far as wind conditions went that day.

'Jack had been hitting three-woods most of the time on the back nine, sticking to his plan. He hit three-wood on 16, and, to be quite honest, it was a poor tee-shot. He probably deserved to go into the Principal's Nose Bunkers but somehow his ball missed them. He was left with about a nine-iron to the green. He hit a beautiful shot in.

'His game at that stage, though, was practically totally irrelevant as far as I was concerned. I was so wrapped up in my own game at that time and I was on an extreme wave of confidence. I just felt unstoppable. I hit this second shot and it felt perfect. It was just eating the flag up. I thought, "Well, there you are. Here comes birdie number six." It was all over it.

'The pin was fairly well back that day. It was just adrenalin, I suppose. The shot went just a touch further than I'd planned it to go. But I couldn't have hit it better if I'd stood there for a month. It was just a couple of yards too strong. It pitched on the downslope just on the back of the green. It was only a little two-foot downslope on the back of the green. The cruel part about it was, if the ball had just pitched short of it then it would have rolled into the little valley, which was easy to get up and down from. Or if it had pitched another couple of feet, it would have stayed in the valley. But it pitched right on the downslope and it took off. It finished up on the 17th tee. Of course, from there, the chances of getting up and down were pretty slim. I didn't get it up and down.

'Jack, being the master that he was, took advantage of the situation and holed his putt. I went from one ahead to one behind.'

Crenshaw, the only man to birdie the 17th and finishing birdie–birdie, joined the waiting Floyd and Kite in the clubhouse on five-under.

Then Nicklaus's decision to practice hard that week on his putting, especially long putting on the expansive St Andrews greens, paid off. The Road Hole finally finished off Owen's remarkable and brave bid.

'When we played 17, Jack had a good drive; I had a good drive, just caught the left-hand rough, but I was OK. He hit onto the front edge, leaving himself a long, long putt. I was just trying to run it up onto the green.

'Once again, I played what I thought was a good shot, bearing in mind how tough the hole is. The ball just trickled through the green onto the road. It's always tricky from over there, of course. I played a pretty good shot, got it within par distance, about 10 ft away, I suppose.

'Then Jack, to me, played the best shot of the day. His shot of the day was his putt on 17. From where he was, you could have putted it anywhere, putted it into the bunker. He hit this putt from 90 ft, or whatever, absolutely stone dead. It was a fantastic effort.

'Unfortunately, I couldn't quite make my par putt. I didn't hit a bad putt, but it didn't go in. So now I'm two behind. It all seemed to happen so quickly in the finish.

'I played the last hole well. I hit a good drive; Jack hit a good drive. Jack didn't have such a good second. He left himself a long putt from the back of the green. I came very close to hitting the pin with my second, with a little bump-and-run through the Valley of Sin.

'Jack putted down to about 4 ft. I thought, "It's not over yet if I can hole this." I had about a 12-footer. But I just couldn't quite manage it. That was it all over. I was so near, yet so far. I just thought, "Jeepers. I didn't do anything wrong!"

'I'll never forget what Jack said to me afterwards when we had a chat. I said, "You know, I really thought I had you at one stage there."

'He said, "Well, so did I. There's only one thing I can say. This is the first time you've been in contention in the British Open. I've been second in this tournament six times!"

'I thought, "Fair enough; I think I know what you're trying to say." It's just a matter of being there on a more regular basis.

'It was a great day. I played some great golf that day and, in the final analysis, the ball just didn't run my way towards the end of the round. I don't know what it was: adrenalin, inexperience, whatever.

'I had mixed emotions at the end of the day. Obviously there was disappointment that I'd lost, but when I looked back and played the holes shot by shot again, I just felt I couldn't have played them better than I did. In that sense, I felt quite proud of my accomplishment. I didn't feel like I'd blown it. In my mind, I didn't feel like I'd hit any bad shots. A couple got bad results but they weren't bad shots.

'In that sense, I could rest easy with myself. I really thought I'd genuinely given it my best shot. It's the old story: there's only one winner. He's usually the guy that gets the right breaks at the right time. It just didn't fall into place for me over the last few holes.

'What it did for me was to get me into the World Matchplay a couple of months later. I was runner-up there and took a few good scalps along the way before I got beaten by Isao Aoki in the final. Andy North had just won the US Open and I beat him in the first round. Then I beat Seve in the second round and Graham Marsh in the third round, so they were good scalps. Then Aoki wore me down in the final round.

'You don't like to be remembered for coming second in tournaments, though. In fact, not many people are remembered for coming second. I think it was such a good shoot-out in the 1978 Open it just sticks in people's minds. It was a great day, playing with the man who had the greatest golf record ever and giving him a run for his money.'

1978 TOP SCORES

J. Nicklaus 71–72–69–69 281
S. Owen 70–75–67–71 283
B. Crenshaw 70–69–73–71 283
R. Floyd 69–75–71–68 283
T. Kite 72–69–72–70 283
P. Oosterhuis 72–70–69–73 284

1982, ROYAL TROON:
BOBBY CLAMPETT AND NICK PRICE

(Clampett led by five strokes after the second round and led by a stroke after three rounds but eventually finished tenth. Price led by three with six holes to go but finished second to Tom Watson)

'I was so pumped up, so fired up. As I walked up to the 13th tee, I said to Kevin, "They're not going to catch me now."'

THE GOLFING SAGES say you have to lose an Open before you win one. Nick Price only belied that adage in that he lost two before he won one.

Price didn't care much for golfing adages at the age of twenty-five, when the son of British parents, born in South Africa but raised in Zimbabwe, had been a professional for five years. He came to the 1982 Open filled with hope. His game had been changed dramatically by a teaching professional who was to become a guru not only for him but for a whole string of champions: Price's fellow-Zimbabwean David Leadbetter.

By the time Price left Royal Troon's testing links, he had belief that he could be a world-beater. That was anything but the case before the 1982 Open, he remembers:

'I struggled in '81 with my game, and in '82 I went to see Leadbetter. I spent eight weeks in the spring of '82 with him, working on improving the fundamentals of my swing. I then went back to Europe and played pretty unsuccessfully for my first four or five events. I played OK but nothing startling.

'Then, the week before the Open – we were playing at The Belfry in the English Open – I started to hit the ball well. My swing was starting to feel like I had something to depend on.

'Coming into the week of the Open Championship, I felt like I was going to play well. Obviously I didn't feel I was going to have a three-shot lead with five or six to play, but I honestly felt that I had a good chance to play well that week.

'My driving had been particularly poor, so I worked hard on my driving. It was adequate that week. I don't think I drove the ball as well as I was capable of doing, but at Troon that year there weren't a lot of driving holes, particularly on the front nine, apart from the par-fives, the 4th and the 6th. It was more three-woods and one-irons off the tee. My iron-play was sharp and my putting was good. I suppose the weakest point of my game that week was my driving, but I tried to play to my strengths.'

It was not the name Price on the gallery's lips, nor was it the one that filled the sports pages on Friday and Saturday morning. Bobby Clampett was a gift to the headline-writers. Clampett, at 22 years of age, was showing great potential by the time he made his debut at Troon, but only to the pundits over the Pond in the USA. In Britain, he was virtually unknown. By the time the weekend came around, however, the lanky lad with the blond Orphan Annie bubbling hair had everyone's attention. He remembers his Open debut:

'I'd finished fourteenth on the money-list the year before on the American tour and had four second-place finishes, but the British Open was all new to me. I really didn't know what to expect. I'd heard about how different the game was over there and I was really looking forward to playing where the home of golf was, playing where the game originated, knowing the history of it all. It was just an unbelievable feeling.

'I was very excited about it and worked very, very hard getting ready for the tournament. I really wanted to do well. I remember specifically doing a lot of extra practice.

74

'As far as the course was concerned, the game really doesn't change that much. You need to work the ball, drive it straight, hit good, solid iron-shots. For the execution, the game is the same, but what is really unique about links golf and the Open is judging shots and the distance that shots will travel once they land. Also the strategy of placement, with the firm fairways and the amount of bump, and also the shots around the green. The ground is so much firmer.'

Clampett had some expert advice while he practised, he observes. In fact, he could hardly have had two better Open mentors.

'Johnny Miller showed me a special "flop" shot that I used quite a bit there. It came in very handy when you needed to flop it over a bunker and stop it very quickly. Johnny and I played a lot of practice rounds together. Johnny was like my big brother. I played some practice rounds that week with Gary Player as well.'

Good advice or not, Clampett was a little mystified before taking on Troon in earnest.

'I remember being perplexed how volatile my game was. It was on one day and completely off the next. In practice, I shot 65 on Tuesday, playing with Johnny and Gary, and the next day shot 75, the day before the tournament. I just couldn't believe how much my game could change so much from day to day. I felt like I was making good progress but then, gosh, it'd just get a little off and wow! Ten shots a round. The same thing happened in the tournament.'

To follow that 75 in practice, Clampett went on the up, shooting an opening 67. He was able to excel, despite admitting to being full of awe when he began his first round:

'I was playing with my friend Chip Beck. We had a mid-morning tee-time; I think around 11-ish. I recall the feeling of standing on the first tee, hitting that opening tee-shot, listening to the sound of bagpipes. I looked up and saw the flags of all the nations represented in the tournament . . . I remember walking down the fairway with Chip – it was his first British Open as well – and we kind of looked at each other, drinking in the aura, the feel. It was just magic in the air. It was the feeling of returning to the home of golf, playing in the national championship of the home of golf. People had been playing golf on these grounds for hundreds of years, and here we were, part of it. It was simply a remarkable feeling, a feeling of almost overwhelming gratitude for having the opportunity to be there.'

Having drunk in the atmosphere in the first round, Clampett in the second round proceeded to feed off his brilliant short-game, in particular, to add a 66, the course record, to his 67. His aggregate was only one stroke behind the record set all the way back in 1934 by Henry Cotton.

'The first two days were very similar. The wind stayed the same all week. The front nine was basically downwind; the back nine was into the wind. So the front nine was where we tended to do our scoring; the par-fives were all reachable and we had nothing more than a wedge at any par-four. I think I shot three- or four-under on the front nine, and then on the back nine you really had to play some golf, because every hole was a potential disaster.

'I do recall one particular shot I hit on 10 on Friday to a back-pin location. I hit a three-iron into the wind, second shot, 3 ft from the hole. Of all the shots I hit that week, that is the one that stands out the most in terms of pure strike. As soon as I struck it, I said, "Ooh, that's the one!"

'I thought the Postage Stamp [short 8th] was a great hole. There is great strategy on that hole. It really makes the player think, especially when the pin is back. How much are you going to attack? It's all about feeling the shot, feeling the wind. It's a unique hole. I love holes like that. The 7th at Pebble Beach; 15th at Cypress Point; 12 at Augusta . . . and I think the Postage Stamp: all great holes in golf. It just goes to show that you don't need length to make a great hole.

'My strategy there was more "let's just play this in the middle of the green", because wherever you are in the middle of the green you're not going to have a long putt.'

Clampett doesn't have to remember too hard how he fared on the Postage Stamp in the second round. Like Jack Newton at Carnoustie seven years earlier, for his course-record 66 he was presented with a solid silver scorecard of his feat, with his scores inscribed in it. For the record, Clampett parred the Postage Stamp in the second round. But his birdies on Friday on the 3rd, 4th, 6th, 7th and 10th (that three-iron to 3 ft), 11th, 16th and 18th, with bogeys on 15 and 17, amounted, at that stage, to an incredible eight-shot lead.

'I remember hitting a great six-iron to 5 ft on 18 to make up for the 17th. The 17th killed me for the week. I did not play 17 well and made a lot of bogeys on it that week, so I was very pleased to finish well.

'When I left the course on eleven-under, the nearest player to me was only three-under, so I had an eight-shot lead. Then Nick Price ended up getting to six-under. But a five-shot lead . . . I was excited and anxious to get going on the weekend. I didn't consider the tournament anywhere near finished, and I just wanted to prove to myself that I could handle it.

'I had to stay pretty focused and business-minded, because there was a lot of attention on me everywhere I went. When I got back to the hotel room, there were about 30 messages waiting for me. I had three hours of press conferences. The media attention was remarkable. When I got to the restaurant, people would come up to the dinner table and ask for autographs. I had a week of feeling what Tiger Woods feels every week!'

While Clampett enjoyed the attention, he was anxious not to let it faze him.

'I don't know if I was really feeling that confident. You could see with the bogeys on 15 and 17 coming in on Friday there were certain shots I wasn't hitting as consistently as I wanted to. I was missing a lot of shots. My short-game, though, was just fantastic. So I knew I was optimising my scoring opportunities. You're going to have days like that but there's no consistency – that generally doesn't last for four days. You can get away with it for a day or two, when you don't have your "A" game tee-to-green, but it doesn't last. I felt my "A" game was right around the corner, but I wasn't firing on all cylinders in terms of ball-striking.'

That fact hit Clampett straight away on Saturday afternoon. He says:

'I bogeyed the 1st hole. It was a real turn of events. I hit a nice three-iron off the tee right down the middle of the fairway but the ball took a strange left-hand hop and went into one of the pot-bunkers. So it was rather an unnerving start. I felt I'd hit a good shot off the tee and got nothing for it.

'But then I came back with birdies at 4 and 5, got back to one-under for the day and at that point I had a seven-shot lead.'

The lad with a shock of blond hair looked as though he was on his way to pulling off a shock Open victory.

However, in 1920, Abe Mitchell led the Open by five strokes after two rounds at Deal. That year, George Duncan won. In 1933, Walter Hagen held a six-shot lead after thirty-six holes at St Andrews. Densmore Shute won the Open that year. At the halfway stage at Royal Lytham in 1963, Phil Rodgers was five strokes to the good. Bob Charles won. The 1968 Open was won by Gary Player, when Billy Casper led by five going into the third round.

Clampett's nemesis was the 6th hole at Troon, the hole that contributed most to him joining that unenvied roll. The five-hundred-and-seventy-seven-yard par-five 6th used to be the longest hole in Open golf. It has been increased to 601 yards nowadays, but still does not carry the honour any more of being the longest. That is now the 14th at St Andrews, measuring 618 yards. Clampett had birdied the 6th the previous day, but on Saturday it began a downward spiral for him. For the sake of a few inches of bunker-face, not once but twice, an Open was to be lost.

'The 6th was a real turning point. I pulled my drive a little bit and went into the bunker. I studied the lie and felt I could take a full sand-wedge and get it over the lip. I thought that was the play. I was trying to advance the ball at least 60 yards. That was the key distance I needed to be able to hit the green with my third shot. If I was going to hit it 60 yards, I was going to be happy.

'I went ahead and hit it, made what I thought was a pretty decent contact, but the ball came out a little low and hit the lip, stayed in the bunker. Then I was faced with almost the exact same shot. I still really thought I could get it over the lip with a full sand-wedge. The same thing happened. The ball hit the lip and came back in the bunker.

'Now I realise I can't get a full sand-wedge over that lip. I'm going to have to blast it out. So I blast it out. Now I can't get to the green with my next shot. I tried to hit it extra hard and hooked it even deeper in the rough. I ended up with a triple-bogey.'

Clampett's lead was reduced to one shot.

Price's opening two 69s had left him the man five shots behind Clampett, so the pair had gone out together for the third round. Germany's emerging talent Bernhard Langer and Irishman Des Smyth had started six shots behind. Tom Watson, who was a further stroke back with Sandy Lyle, didn't look as though he would be a force to be reckoned with this time. Price says he was happy to let Clampett take all the spotlight:

'The first two rounds were all about Bobby Clampett. It was rather convenient that someone else was taking all the heat with the media. I was playing solidly, and after the first two rounds I knew I had a chance to do really well. I don't know that I contemplated winning after the second round, but I remember feeling I had a chance to post a top-five finish. That was important for me at that stage, with my confidence being a little low and also not playing very well for nearly the entire part of '82 to that stage.

'What was giving me confidence was that all the bits and pieces I had worked on with my swing with Leadbetter were starting to fall into place. More exciting for me was that here I was playing well and . . . well, I wouldn't say I'd rebuilt my swing, but I'd refined my swing in such a short period of time, career-wise. In the space of four months, here I was with an opportunity to do really well in one of the major championships. That was very comforting.

'On the Saturday, it was windier than the other days and it blew from a slightly different direction, which always confuses players for a while. We'd played all the practice rounds and the first two rounds with an identical wind. It was great weather that week; I didn't wear a sweater all week, except for the third round when the wind got up a little.

'Everybody knew who Bobby Clampett was and nobody knew who I was. I was in an underdog situation. I liked being in that situation, where no one really expects anything of you.

'I didn't hit the ball as well as I had the previous two days and started badly with three bogeys, which put me seven shots off the lead.

'But when Bobby triple-bogeyed the 6th, that shattered the confidence he had. He just never recovered from that.'

Dropped shots at the 10th, 11th, 13th and 15th saw the Open net drag in on Clampett. He rallied at the end of the round but his confidence looked threadbare as he finished a third-round 78 to be only a stroke ahead of Price, two better than Lyle and Smyth, and three ahead of a now ominously placed Watson. Clampett explains how he felt after a trying day:

'My confidence was really shaken because I didn't play well the whole day. I hit a lot of bad shots, wasn't striking my putts like I did the first two days. My whole game just went. It felt like the momentum I had created over the first two days was gone.'

Clampett was not convinced he had got his bad round out of the way, either.

'I tend to study trends and shots and look at my execution. That's the only thing you can control. You can't control the bounces. If I had been getting bad bounces like I did on the first hole all day long, that's one thing. Sometimes that does happen, when you execute pretty well and you just get a series of really bad breaks and nothing quite goes your way. I did have, in all honesty that day, some of that. I hit a couple of really good shots that day, so it wasn't like I was hitting everything off the mark, but the consistency wasn't there. Even then it was a day where I probably felt like I shot a 72 or 73 and ended up with a 78. It was one of those days where I got a lot of bad breaks, but 72 or 73 is not a great round either. I really needed to buckle down and get my swing, get everything, in gear.'

While Price by no means played at his best, a 74 in the windy conditions gave him hope. Instead of just contending, with Clampett looking fragile now, Price says he felt there could be a bigger prize on offer:

'I didn't start very well, but my game picked up a little, and at the end of the day I still had a really good chance to do well. That was probably the first time I started thinking about winning the Open. Bobby Clampett had shown a huge chink in his armour and had let everyone back into the Championship.

'It was comforting for me, knowing I hadn't played particularly at my best and I still had a chance to win the Open Championship.'

That was what Price went to bed on. Clampett, after dinner with his pal Mark McNulty, tossed the next day over in his mind but relied on the usual tenets to prepare himself and get into an Open-winning mode.

'I knew what to do. Tournament golf is tournament golf, no matter what level you're playing, whether you're playing the US Amateur, on the PGA Tour or the Open. You go about it the same way; your strategy's the same. You're trying to get your game to peak. You go out to compete; you go out to win.

'That's all I was thinking when I went out Sunday afternoon. Yes, there's a lot of pressure, and when things aren't going that well you feel the pressure even more. The greatest remedy for feeling pressure is confidence. The recipe for confidence is performance. You go out and execute your shots, your confidence increases and that creates the defence against any nerves.'

For Clampett, though, it all fell rather flat.

'It was a very frustrating day. I never got anything going at all. I think I had maybe one birdie all day. I wasn't hitting a lot of quality shots, and the shots I missed I seemed to make bogey from. I just wasn't clicking.

'It wasn't a question of "Oh, he suddenly choked on the final round", it was a question of my game just wasn't up to the challenge. Mentally, I felt very good. Looking back on it, I kind of pat myself on the back because mentally and emotionally I handled the situation well. In terms of execution, I felt that my game was lacking – lacking the ability to pull it off. The consistency wasn't there. It was more of a mechanical thing rather than a mental thing. If I were to grade myself, I'd probably give myself an A for focus, concentration and mental preparedness and an F for my execution.'

Eventually, all hope went for Clampett.

'The key hole in the final round was the 13th. It was a hard par-four, and we were hitting three-woods into the green. I double-bogeyed and that was it for me.'

If 13 was unlucky for Clampett, it was to be chillingly the same for Price, who had leapt from the traps like a frisky greyhound.

'I had a great start, birdied the first two holes and went into the lead. I holed a really good putt on the 2nd, around 30 ft, and that just got my tail in the air.

'I played pretty solidly all the way through to number 9. I bogeyed that and Tom Watson had been making birdies, so I knew it was getting tight.

'When I stood on the 10th tee, I was one behind Watson. He was playing the 13th or 14th and I distinctly remember saying to my caddie Kevin Woodward on the 10th tee, "If I'm going to win this Championship, I'm going to have to do something now." I meant I had to do something at 10, 11, 12, because once you made that turn into the wind on 13, things got tough. That was the thing about that week at Troon. If you could play the last six holes one-under, or level-par, or even one-over, you'd have done well. The media had been writing that all week.

'I then proceeded to play my best three holes of the Championship. I birdied 10. I nearly eagled 11 – had a putt from about 25 ft which I hit just over the edge of the hole. Then I hit a five-iron on the 12th to about 2 ft and made that for birdie. I suddenly went from one behind to standing on the 13th tee three ahead. I was so pumped up, so fired up. As I walked up to the 13th tee, I said to Kevin, "They're not going to catch me now."

'I've always been a good front-runner in the game, and I felt comfortable getting to the front at that stage. It was inexperience more than anything else.'

Inexperience indeed. And when the pressure was on, coach Leadbetter's remodelling of his swing was only helpful if Price could keep his concentration. By his own admittance, Price had started to run before he could walk. He was not helped, he recalls, by a wicked deflection, however:

'I made a poor bogey on 13, but 15 was the back-breaker for me. I hit a poor tee-shot on 15, but then I hit a wonderful second shot. I did nearly everything right. All I did was I miscalculated.

'There was a ridge between me and the green, probably about 18 in. high, that ran at 90° to my target-line. My ball was sitting on this very dry piece of rough. It was a perfect lie, a good break after my drive, lying just nice and tight. I hit this four-iron and just absolutely flushed it, hit it absolutely just the way I wanted to. It hit this ridge and instead of going over this ridge, which you would expect it to, it went off at about a 25–30° angle into a bunker.

'It was the worst break I got the whole week. If the ball had just gone forward, straight, it would have finished on the green. It got this horrific bounce off this ridge. The trouble was, I hit this four-iron so well, the ball just didn't get up above it. But I didn't even think about the ridge until after I had hit it. You'd probably normally hit with a one-iron or a three-wood off a tight lie like that, certainly not with a four-iron, but I hit this four-iron so flush and it finished up in the bunker.

'Now I'm reeling. Now I've got to go sideways. I got it out but then I still had to chip on and I ended up making double-bogey-six.'

Price's double-bogey at the 15th meant that he was tied with Watson, who had not long before finished his round of 70 to set a target of four-under-par, a stroke better than Peter Oosterhuis. Everyone thought Watson was going to come up short. But Price's agony was not over.

'I wasn't that worried about it at that stage. The next hole is a par-five. I had a chance to make birdie but missed a 15–18-footer. Then I bogeyed the 17th, the par-three. I hit a two-iron but miscued it slightly. It was into the wind. I was unlucky, really, because the ball just pitched and died. If I'd hit it solidly, the ball would have released, but I didn't hit it solidly. It could have got onto the front edge if I'd got a favourable bounce.'

As well as not quite getting the strike he wanted, Price's ball also pitched in a sand-filled divot, according to caddie Woodward, and that made sure he would come up short. With Watson waiting, Price felt he had to go for broke.

'At that stage, I didn't want to go into a play-off because I didn't fancy my chances against Tom Watson. I tried to chip the thing in! I hit a really nice chip and my ball nearly went in. It ran an inch over the left side of the hole, but went 4 ft by. It was strange, because as the ball went past the hole it broke to the right. So when I hit my putt coming back, I aimed it on the right lip and it stayed out there.

'I felt I'd done all my work and hadn't played that poorly, but I'd made a bogey and now I'm one behind. I've got to birdie 18 to get into a play-off. I had a poor swing off the tee, another hook, but then I hit a really good four-iron for my second shot. I had about a 30-footer to tie him. But it was done by then.

'There were three or four things that happened on that back nine that were unusual, but it was such an emotional roller coaster for me. Having birdied 10, 11, 12, and being on such a high, suddenly, walking on to the 16th tee, I'm now vulnerable.

'It was such an experience, though. I often look back and wonder if I had won that time, would I have had the career I've had? I think the answer is no. I don't think I would. I think it was too early in my career for me to really appreciate how tough it is to win a major championship. My dear old mum always says things happen for a reason. Whoever was looking down on me, the golfing gods or whoever was looking down upon me, was saying, "It's not your time. You're a good young player. Just bide your time. It's going to come."

'I learned a golden lesson from that week: not to get ahead of yourself. This game humbled me in 1982.'

Price was not the only one who paid and learned. Bobby Clampett did so, too. His downfall did not come through getting ahead but getting into a bunker on the 6th in the third round – and then not having the experience to save himself.

Twenty-two years later, by now a commentator and pundit for CBS, Clampett had no problem getting out of trouble at the 6th at Royal Troon, as he explains:

'I learned a very important lesson on that shot. I went home and figured things out – if I ever faced that situation again, what would I do? I actually learned a new shot and I demonstrated it on TV when we covered the tournament in 2004 at Troon.

'I think I had a great learning experience all round in 1982. Just being there and having the opportunity to win the British Open wire-to-wire was a great experience. I learned about myself, my game, and I took a lot of positives out of it, even though I was greatly disappointed when my expectation was to have won.

'I don't look back with painful memories; I only look upon them as positive memories. There's only one winner of every championship. We start out as 150 players, or how many compete, and we expect to be that one. It's a challenging game and we keep looking for ways to be that one and to keep improving.'

1982 TOP SCORES

T. Watson 69–71–74–70 284
N. Price 69–69–74–73 285
P. Oosterhuis 74–67–74–70 285

———

B. Clampett (10th) 67–66–78–77 288

1983, ROYAL BIRKDALE: HALE IRWIN

(Irwin's notorious 'whiffed' putt in the third round proved costly, as he lost by a stroke to Tom Watson)

'I had a very sick sensation, that I knew that I had made an attempt to hit the ball. Then I tapped it in, and when we were walking off the green I told Graham, "That's four." He looked at me with shock on his face. I said, "I stabbed at that first one and I missed it."'

WHEN HALE IRWIN arrived to play the famous Lancashire links at Southport, little did he know he would that week provide one of the legendary moments in Open Championship history. While the man from Missouri had one of the most illustrious careers in golf, he missed a chance of holding the famous Auld Claret Jug for the sake of an air-shot.

Irwin, one of the main players in 1983 after victories in the 1974 and 1979 US Opens, had not played in the British major since finishing sixth four years previously. He says he was glad he had made the trip again:

'There wasn't any specific reason for not coming to Britain for three years. It had nothing to do with not wanting to play in the Open. It had everything to do with my family and our summer. Making the journey over for a couple of weeks never seemed to quite fit my schedule. But in 1983, everything fell into place, so I decided to try again.

'I felt quite good about my game going into the Open. And what

86

I really liked about that week was that it was quite warm. I suppose you might call it a heatwave in the UK! I very much enjoyed that. Rather than having the cold and the blustery winds that you might have on links courses, we had quite benign conditions that week. The warmth has always helped my game.

'I hadn't played Birkdale before, but, as with all courses, regardless of where they may be, you have to have a comfort level with them. Your target visualisation has to be there. That was always one of the more difficult things for me when it came to playing links courses. Let's say St Andrews, for one, because it's simply so open out there. You have to be specific with your target, but it's hard to find that target on a course like that. All you have is maybe the steeple in the distance, the passing cloud or the bird hovering over the bunker. I rather like the well-defined trees or the hole that might go around and through some of those dunes. That's what Birkdale had for me. It had better target visualisation.

'From the practice rounds, we knew that the ball was going to be pitching and running with the dry conditions. So I just felt it was very important to make sure the ball ended up in an area that gave you maximum opportunity to hit your second shot onto the green in the right place.

'I've always felt my preparation and practice rounds are pretty much my own. I didn't want to necessarily see what everyone else was doing because I wanted to make sure my game was shaped to my eye and the way I was comfortable playing each hole.'

Irwin was well set, then. With the sun on his back and his familiarisation with Birkdale complete, he made his bid for a third major title.

It was a fellow American eight years his junior who stirred the gallery, however. Craig Stadler, whose drooping moustache and hefty form had earned him the sobriquet 'Walrus', broke Neil Coles's 13-year-old first-round Open record by a stroke with a 64. If it's possible to envisage a walrus leaping out of the traps, that's just what Stadler did, and, unlike many outsiders before him, he stayed in contention right until the back nine of the final round. The two previous winners, Tom Watson from the year before and Bill Rogers from 1981, lay second on 67. Irwin was not fazed by being back in the pack in fifth place, also a stroke behind Nick Faldo.

'Craig really came out of the blocks. But, as I always try to tell myself, even though you find yourself after one round, or perhaps even two, maybe well back in the field, you don't have to worry about it. If you're playing steadily and you're playing quality golf, those fellows that are out in front are perhaps having their really good days and it's hard to carry those days forward for that many rounds in succession. So I didn't go into any panic mode. I just felt if I continued playing the game I'd been playing, I'd be there at the end.'

True to his gut-feeling, Irwin continued playing steadily and contending. A second-round 68 left him only three behind Stadler, two adrift of Watson and Lee Trevino and one in arrears of Nick Faldo, who was the only one to prevent a totally US Tour-dominated leaderboard. The sunny days were paying off for the men from the USA, notes Irwin:

'It seemed very much like an American tournament at the time. The boys that were at the top were primarily from across the Pond. The weather conditions were very much what we were accustomed to, so it didn't surprise me too much. It was very much an up-for-grabs event for us.

'Nearly all the Americans stayed in the hotel together. Perhaps only Nicklaus and Palmer weren't there. They, I think, had leased homes. Those of us staying in the same hotel spent a lot of time together. Our doors were all open, simply because it was so warm. Everyone dined together. It was sort of like a dormitory.

'I don't remember too much about the first two rounds, but I know we were all in very good spirits about how things were going.'

The weather changed dramatically for the third round. So did Irwin's spirit for a time. Two holes were to decide, in the end, whether he would lift golf's most coveted trophy.

'It cooled down a bit. The wind came up and the scoring indicated the blustery conditions. The first two rounds had been in perfect conditions, and the only difficult part had not been so much club selection but just making sure you didn't run the ball into the wispy rough. When the wind came up in the third round, it gave you an altogether different prospect that we hadn't seen. Now you were having to play the wind as well the dry conditions, and it became a bit more difficult to put the ball in those areas that offered the scoring opportunity.'

One scoring opportunity that was nothing to do with the wind was lost on the 14th by Irwin. Here, he made to tap in his ball from just a few inches for par, but, in golfing parlance, 'whiffed' the ball, catching the ground behind and playing an air-shot. If that was to prove costly, the few minutes after it were just as pivotal in whether the name Hale Irwin would be engraved on the Auld Claret Jug. Irwin explains how two fateful holes panned out:

'It was just carelessness, really. There wasn't, sort of, anger or anything of that nature. When you're in that position, as I was, playing pretty well, you don't want to be upset with anything. I just made an error of judgement.

'At that time, I was using a putter that wasn't necessarily a two-sided putter but the back side of the putter was flat as well. I was playing with Graham Marsh. I'd hit my first putt and it had gone up there, oh, I don't know, 6, 8 in. from the hole. Rather than going around, standing in his line, I just went around to the other side and went to hit it in left-handed. As I was making my approach to the ball, I was also sort of giving it the old tap-in while I was on the move. I just misjudged it. I stuck the putter right in the ground.

'I had a very sick sensation, that I knew that I had made an attempt to hit the ball. Then I tapped it in, and when we were walking off the green I told Graham, "That's four." He looked at me with shock on his face. I said, "I stabbed at that first one and I missed it."

'I was as dumbfounded, I suppose, as anyone else. But it really didn't bother me as much as the drive at the next hole, where I hit it pretty much down the fairway a little right-centre. The ball hit on the edge of one of the little mounds in the fairway and pitched over into the little ditch on the right side of the fairway. I thought, "Well, that's worse than what happened at the last hole." It was a par-five and I ended up making a six.

'I went careless bogey, unfortunate bogey on two holes in a row. If anything, that gave me a feeling of doom. I don't look at the air-ball so much as the major disappointment than I do at not birdieing the par-five. For that matter, not making five but making six. For me, that was the bigger turning point than the inappropriate decision on the previous hole.'

Those two dropped shots were to play a critical role in the 1983 Open. After he had signed for a 72, Irwin did his best to put his misfortune out of his mind. He could have been only two strokes behind the third-round leader, Watson. He could have been only one behind Stadler, level with Faldo and one in front of Trevino. Instead, he trailed all of them and lagged four strokes off the lead. To have any chance of success, he felt, the 14th and 15th holes had to be pushed to the back of his mind:

'I tried to put it behind me. The older I've got, the easier it has become. I tried to pay more attention to what I did well, rather than think about what went wrong. Certainly go over some of the mistakes made. There's always a plethora of those. But at the same time, I wanted to make sure I'd collected myself well enough to make sure I could continue trying to win. It wasn't that big a deal. I didn't really lose any sleep over it. I try not to do that. If you start gnashing your teeth over those bad times, then you've got some problems when something really important happens.'

True to his psyche, Irwin did shrug off his previous day's woes. His third-round playing-partner, Marsh, set the mark of seven-under-par as he scorched around Birkdale in 64. Irwin and the lofty Andy Bean then set the target of eight-under, both shooting 67s. It was an exemplary showing by Irwin after his previous day's misfortunes. It could have been even better with a little luck on the last. But there was to be little luck for Irwin that week.

'I hit the ball quite well all day, and on the final hole I hit a very good drive and a very nice second shot right on line and, with the wind and the way the hole was playing, the ball just ran through the green a bit. But I still had a reasonable chance, I guess 25 ft from the edge. I gave it a good run, but I had to settle for a four. Then it was a matter of watching Tom come down the stretch.'

With Stadler, Faldo and Trevino spent, Watson was the only other person who could win. He had moved to nine-under with just the formidable Birkdale 18th remaining – at four hundred and seventy-three yards, one of the toughest par-fours in golf and one of the most difficult finishes on the Open rota. Irwin and Bean waited in anticipation. Irwin's anticipation, he says, was of an 18-hole play-off the next day:

'We were both pretty much glued to the situation, hopeful that Tom would perhaps come out of that two-iron a bit and give us a chance, but he struck it really nicely. It was probably one of the better shots to finish an Open.'

It was indeed memorable. After splitting the fairway with his drive, Watson struck his approach with such authority over the two hundred and thirteen yards he had left in the 1983 Open Championship that he nominated it as 'the best two-iron of my life'. Watson had only 15 ft left to go in the 1983 Open. Two putts gave him successive victories and ended the hopes of Bean and Irwin. Would Irwin now think about his mishap on the 14th green the previous day?

'I can say it certainly crossed my mind that things could have been different. But I then put it at the back of my mind and the only time it was moved forward was when someone brought it up. It was just one of those inopportune times. It can be part of your success in the end. If you make a mistake, whether it be a large one or a small one, you try to learn from it – go forward with more positive thoughts – just say: "That was really stupid but now I'm going to birdie the next hole." Don't think about what was, but what could be. That's been my creed through the years.

'There were no regrets from the 1983 Open. I'd given it my best shot. I had a simple error of judgement. It wasn't as if I'd thrown it away out of anger or frustration. You can go through any number of situations like it in sport where people have done something relatively stupid. It wasn't because of lack of effort. It was just a mental breakdown at the time.

'Certainly, I look back and think, "What if I'd not done that?" Well, maybe I'd have done something else along the way instead. I can't change it. We can't assume that all the shots played thereafter would fall in that same sequence. And if they did, who's to say I'd have beaten Tom in the play-off?'

1983 TOP SCORES
T. Watson 67–68–70–70 275
H. Irwin 69–68–72–67 276
A. Bean 70–69–70–67 276
G. Marsh 69–70–74–64 277

1984, ST ANDREWS:
TOM WATSON, BERNHARD LANGER
AND IAN BAKER-FINCH

*(Baker-Finch shared the lead going into the final round with
Watson but fell away to ninth place after finding the Swilcan
Burn at the 1st. Watson, still leading with five holes to go,
finished runner-up with Langer after a fateful 17th)*

'What most people don't realise is that the ball ended up
on an upslope. They say, "He hit way too much club."
Well, I had to get the ball up in the air into the wind. . . .
Instead of trying to chase it in, I tried to fly it in, which is
the risky shot.'

SEVE BALLESTEROS MIGHT have conquered St Andrews in 1984, to
claim the title he so craved at the Home of Golf, but there were three
players that year who could have raised the Claret Jug, none more so
than Tom Watson.

Watson was trying to become only the second player, behind
Harry Vardon, to win the Open Championship for a sixth time, and
he was also looking for the hat-trick, three in a row, having lifted the
trophy in 1982 and 1983. He so nearly did it, and Watson's was, in
the end, the hand most agonisingly wrenched from the Jug. Bad
luck, a bad decision or bad judgement on the famous and infamous
Road Hole 17th in the final round finally decided that year's Open
outcome.

There has always been one intriguing question about 1984,

though. It has been a mystery to many over the years: why did Tom Watson hit a two-iron on the Road Hole in the final round, an act which was to cost him his chance of that coveted sixth Open victory?

Most pundits reckon he took at least two clubs too much. Many a theory has been put forward. By and large, Watson has been fairly reticent over his playing of the 17th in the final round. But now, in this chapter, he explains his thinking behind his decision and why he feels it was forced on him. He also tells why it wasn't so much his two-iron but his putter that cost him so dearly in the end.

However, Watson's was by no means the only might-have-been story that year. Bernhard Langer was only a stroke off the lead after birdieing the 1st hole, playing alongside Ballesteros in the final round. The German, who went on to win the Masters the following year and contend right to the death in the Open, too, only lost his grasp on the Open late on Sunday.

Also, a young Australian making his Open debut startled the world by leading with a round to go. Maybe, just maybe, but for a cruel stroke of luck at the very first hole on the final day, Ian Baker-Finch may have gone on to pull off one of the shocks of the era in the oldest major.

Baker-Finch, virtually unknown outside the Australasian Tour, came to St Andrews with stars in his eyes. He was not only playing in his first Open Championship but in his very first major. It was all going to be a great adventure. Baker-Finch certainly had no designs on getting his name etched on the Claret Jug. His first objective, he says, was to make the cut and put to good use advice he had been given by his role model and five-times Open champion Peter Thomson:

'It was my first British Open. I qualified by finishing top five on the Australian order of merit. I was a young Australian journeyman; journeyman meaning someone who you'd not expect to come in and win the British Open, someone who'd just come in wide-eyed and looking forward to just being there. I'd watched it for many, many years and read a lot about it and could hardly believe I was there, playing in it. One of my mentors had been Peter Thomson, who won it five times. It was "the" event for a young Australian . . . the Open Championship.

'I was in good form, so I was expecting to play reasonably well. I had a number of practice rounds leading up to the start, because I'd missed the cut the week before in the Lawrence Batley. I got there on the Saturday, played with Peter Thomson and Kel Nagle and Graham Marsh. I had a real good look at the course. I had five practice rounds.

'I played well right from the start. It was a fairy-tale story: a young kid, playing in his first Open Championship, practising with Thomson and Nagle, who'd won it. That was a dream beginning to the week.

'Then I shot 68 and 66, playing with Isao Aoki and Hale Irwin, to be leading. It became a bit more than a fairy tale.

'I then shot 71 on the Saturday and shared the lead after three rounds with Tom Watson. That put me in the last group with Watson on Sunday. He was going for three in a row and his sixth Open win to equal the record. On Saturday night, though, I slept great; I always do. I got in nine hours' sleep, slept from midnight until nine. It was exciting. There were a number of us staying in the one house, as the Aussies did all the time. We got as many in as we could, to share costs and have a good time. There was myself, Mike Clayton, Wayne Grady, Steve Fraser, a close friend, Mike Clayton's caddie at the time, Steve Williams, who's now Tiger Woods's caddie, of course, and who caddied for me for two years later on, and my wife, Jennie, who was my girlfriend at the time. We were about 20 minutes from the course. We had a few beers on the Saturday night, toasted the fact that I'd been playing well all week. It was an exciting time.'

Baker-Finch was the rank outsider, though. The Sunday newspapers all favoured Watson's chances of carrying off his sixth Open.

On Saturday night, Watson could not have been more upbeat about his game and his chances as he talked to the media about his third round:

'I played better than I have all season. My touch was very good. I put the ball where I had to. My distance was good all day. Yesterday was the second best I've played this season and I hope it continues to get better. Where could I have improved? I could have made some of those putts because I had the ball close to the hole most of the day. Can't be too greedy, though.'

His putting fortunes were to be echoed the next day. As fate would have it, Watson's chances of winning his sixth Open were to hinge around the greens and one hole in particular, the Road Hole 17th.

In the third round, Watson parred the 17th hole comfortably, and in his press conference he explained how he had done it:

'I had a better drive at 17. I brought it back with the wind, a little bit left and [took] a two-iron to the front part of the green, and two-putted from there [from] about 80 ft.'

Watson would opt for the same two-iron the next day, and it would cost him the Open.

On the Saturday night, though, the man who had kissed the Claret Jug five times in triumph stood on the brink of equalling Harry Vardon's record and, importantly to him, doing so at the Home of Golf. He said:

'I am honest when I say I am inspired when I am over here. It is different. I like the turf, the conditions we play under. And I like the crowds. I did not particularly like it at first: the bouncing type of hard course. I did not think it rewarded skill. I had played American greens, protected in front by bunkers and hazards, which needed to be hit by high shots. Then I realised the game of golf over here was the way it was meant to be played.

'Going into the final day, my thoughts are to go out and play exactly as I did today. My thoughts are about playing here at St Andrews, winning a sixth British Open and winning at the oldest course in the world.'

The next day, Watson and Baker-Finch met up on the 1st tee, and the experienced campaigner had a few calming words for his young playing-partner. Baker-Finch reckons he didn't really need his advice, though:

'I wasn't really nervous or even apprehensive or worried about it all. That was surprising, really. I was very calm on the 1st tee. I remember Tom, on the 1st tee, coming over and saying, "Hi, I'm Tom Watson. Nice to meet you." He then said, "Don't worry. It's the 1st tee in the last round of the British Open; if you're not nervous, you're not human."

'I think he meant it in a friendly sort of manner, like, "Don't worry, kid, you'll be all right." But I looked at my caddie and said, "Nervous? I don't feel nervous. I feel fine. Let's go."'

Away went Baker-Finch. Within a few minutes, his Open chances had plummeted, after his ball found a watery grave in one of the most famous streams in the world.

'I ripped a three-wood down the right side, found a perfect angle into the front-left hole location. I decided to go with a little nine-iron, so I didn't nip it too much; I've always been a high spinner of the ball.

'I landed it on the green and it spun back into the burn. It was terribly unlucky. That green is normally very, very firm. Everyone lands it just on to get it to stop on the green. My ball decided against it and came back and in the burn. I dropped on the other side of the burn, chipped up to three feet and made the putt for a bogey-five.'

It was an understandable jolt to his confidence, and even though he didn't dwell on it, the mishap proved to be a prelude to Baker-Finch's Open demise.

'I still wasn't feeling that bad. But from there on, I just couldn't do anything right. When I drove, I'd finish in the rough and in a bad lie, or I'd three-putt. Everything seemed to go wrong as we went along.

'I became nervous and out of my comfort zone as the round went on, because I played very quickly. I remember going to the 13th tee, by which time I was well over par – eight- or nine-over. As I walked back to the tee, I thought, "Hell. I feel as though I've just teed off." Everything had happened so quickly.

'Then I settled down. I played the last five or six holes a couple-under-par and finished top ten, but I shot 79. Obviously, I was disappointed with the finish. I remember going into the locker-room. I was pretty down on myself and emotional about how I'd finished. A couple of players came by and said, "Hey, look. You just finished top ten in your first major. You had a wonderful week. You led. You showed the world you're a capable player." They gave me all these positives, and after that I started to think a bit more positively myself about it all. Initially, though, it was a real downer.'

If it was a downer for Baker-Finch, then his illustrious playing-partner was to undergo similar feelings in the end.

Watson looked in control, even though Langer had edged within just a stroke of him with an opening birdie – a peach of an approach to just a few inches. The German player, though, could find no luck at all on the greens. It eventually became evident that it was going to be a battle between Watson and Ballesteros.

As the final quartet came down the closing stretch of the Old Course, the gallery's roars and groans gauged how the Championship was unfolding. First there were 'oohs' and 'aahs', as Ballesteros missed a great chance to birdie the 10th but three-putted. Then Seve's huge band of followers let their disappointment show as he missed a birdie chance on the 11th. Watson supporters, and the knowledgeable British fans, then let it be known to the pair up ahead that he had birdied the 11th to pull ahead again.

Several more key moments came up quickly. Watson took out the driver on the 12th, found gorse and it looked as though double-bogey was going to be the outcome, which would have allowed Ballesteros a stroke's breathing space. Watson, though, managed to salvage an accomplished bogey – 'a scrambling five', in his words – to keep the outcome on a knife-edge, with the pair locked together on top of the leaderboard. When Watson then immediately got the shot back, his supporters celebrated – a fact not missed by the group up in front. He was ahead again.

But then, at the 14th, Ballesteros fans could vent their delight as he finally holed a big putt, this one a 25-footer, to get back level with seemingly his only rival. Watson's group knew exactly what the cheers and applause up ahead meant.

The Road Hole 17th awaited the two chief protagonists. Ballesteros had not been able to master it all week, three times bogeying it. This time, though, he hit a powerful drive and then struck a fine six-iron to comfortably manage par.

By now, it was like a football match, with Ballesteros fans close to fever pitch and Watson's hordes, including the many American visitors to St Andrews, urging him on. Then came the most significant moments of the 1984 Open Championship.

Ballesteros assured his caddie, Nick de Paul, 'There's going to be a play-off,' as he went to the 18th tee. If Ballesteros had looked back, though, he would have seen what de Paul saw: Watson walking to the back of the 17th and to the wall behind the road that gives one of golf's most notorious holes its name.

Watson had first of all sent his drive so far to the right of the fairway that he had to enquire if his ball were still in play. Having found it was safe, he then had to negotiate the way to the flag, with the Road Hole Bunker guarding it jealously. His over-hit approach was also well right. His ball had finished up just over a foot from the wall. He could only stab at it to get it onto the green. His subsequent two putts left him a stroke behind Ballesteros.

Up ahead, Ballesteros still thought he would need a birdie at least, then hope Watson would only par the last. The crowd told the story in sound, though, and it was almost in stereo. A roar like thunder signalled Ballesteros's birdie putt on 18, drowning out the cries of anguish that had seeped up past the Swilcan Bridge and Grannie Clark's Wynd. Watson glanced up the fairway after missing his par-saving putt from distance, to see Ballesteros making the familiar arm-pumping salute that has become not only an abiding memory of 1984 but the Spanish maestro's trademark, his famous gesture nowadays even tattooed on his arm.

Already being tattooed on the Auld Claret Jug by engraver Mr Alex Harvey was, for a second time, the name Severiano Ballesteros. His playing-partner, Langer, could only look on and think what might have been if his putter had been even warm, never mind hot. He gives his view on how the final round turned against him:

'I really outplayed Seve from tee to green. I had so many more opportunities than he did. I should have won the tournament by two or three shots. He made the putts and I didn't. He made putts from far greater distances than I did, the ones that were makeable, and in the end he was two shots better. I really played well and gave myself plenty of opportunities, but I just couldn't make a putt. It was just a case of either misreading or mis-hitting the putts – not getting the ball in the hole. He got everything out of his round and I got nothing out of mine.'

If the final round was something that Ballesteros would savour forever, its final half-hour was to become a bad memory for Watson, who, after his trials at the 17th, knew he was all but beaten. An eagle on the last was not out of the question, but it proved beyond him. He made par and finished in a tie for second with Langer. Harry Vardon's record would not be equalled by the man from Kansas.

While everyone remembers the 17th hole as the turning point in 1984, Watson's chances were also inhibited by his putter. He says:

'I remember the day very well. It was a day of missed putts. I saw Bernhard Langer up ahead having the same problem. We both had our opportunities to make a lot of putts and we didn't do very well with the putter. I remember seeing Bernhard hit a lot of great shots and come away with virtually nothing as far as birdies were concerned. I felt very similar to that. Everybody has missed putts, but I certainly felt I could have had a better day on the greens. When I look back on it, the things I remember most were the makeable putts I missed. Then there was the 17th, where I had to play a shot off the upslope into the wind.'

Despite his lack of luck on the greens, Watson might still have matched Ballesteros were it not for the penultimate hole. While Ballesteros had hit a six-iron on, following a scorching drive, Watson, having much more distance to travel, with the flag to the left of the green and behind the Road Hole Bunker, after deliberating between a two- or a three-iron, finally chose a two-iron for his approach. That was after much thought and discussion with his Southport caddie, Alfie Fyles.

Watson explains the reasoning for playing the 17th the way he did and dismisses out of hand the notion reached by some pundits that the two-iron, which he had also used the previous day on 17, was his 'favoured' club. (He had fashioned his superb finish the previous year in the Open at the final hole with a deadly two-iron approach, and the club had played its part in his 1977 victory over Jack Nicklaus.)

'That's absurd to say that. You use the two-iron when you think it's the proper club to use. That was the shot I chose to play.

'What most people don't realise is that the ball ended up on an upslope. They say, "He hit way too much club." Well, I had to get the ball up in the air into the wind. Maybe I chose the wrong shot to play, but I didn't choose the wrong club to play the shot I meant to play. It's very tough to hit a low-running shot off an upslope. Instead of trying to chase it in, I tried to fly it in, which is the risky shot.

'I pushed the two-iron 30 yards to the right and the ball ended up on the road. It was a disappointment, as it always is when you have an opportunity to win and you don't see it through.'

1984 TOP SCORES

S. Ballesteros 69–68–70–69 276
T. Watson 71–68–66–73 278
B. Langer 71–68–68–71 278
F. Couples 70–69–74–68 281
L. Wadkins 70–69–73–69 281

———

I. Baker-Finch (9th) 68–66–71–79 284

1985, ROYAL ST GEORGE'S: BERNHARD LANGER

(Langer's ball brushed the lip at the 72nd hole but failed to drop and earn him the birdie that would have put him into a play-off with winner Sandy Lyle)

'There was a marshal standing only three or four yards left of the green on the hill and my ball hit his foot. It bounced left and stayed on the hill. If it had not hit his foot, it would have rolled around the bank and onto the green.'

MANY PLAYERS HAVE come close to winning the Open Championship but not quite made it. Several have deserved to win but have never lifted the Auld Claret Jug – arguably, none more than Bernhard Langer.

In 1981, Langer burst onto the Open scene for the first time. However, he was never really in with a realistic chance of winning the title and finished a distant four strokes behind Bill Rogers. None the less, it was the first of two second places in the Open for Langer.

For two years, though – 1984 and 1985 – he came agonisingly closer to achieving his ultimate goal. In 1984, he was never out of contention until the closing holes at St Andrews, when his disobedient putter finally ended his chances. In 1985, a thoughtless marshal could have been the difference between Langer lifting the Claret Jug and watching enviously as Sandy Lyle did so instead.

They were not the only close-run Opens for Langer, either. In 1993, he was third behind Greg Norman, and in 2001 only another bad final day with the putter denied him his chance of at least a play-off with David Duval. Even in 2005, after becoming Europe's triumphant Ryder Cup captain the previous year, Langer gave himself a sniff of a chance, belying his veteran status.

However, it is 1985, a year before he became the first number one in the inaugural official world rankings, that gave Langer the bitterest taste in defeat. He says:

'In 1981, it came as much as a surprise as anything to finish second behind Bill Rogers. I don't think I was mentally ready, even though I'd had a great year and played good all season long. I was pretty young and I was a little bit surprised to be in contention.

'There were other occasions when it was much more realistic that I could win. In 1984, I tied with Watson behind Seve Ballesteros, but I should have won. I outplayed Seve from tee to green but didn't hole the putts and lost by two shots. That was a far greater disappointment than 1981. I thought I had a chance in '81, but in '84 my chance was much greater.

'The year I had my greatest opportunity, though, was 1985. Looking back, that was the easiest British Open for me to win. They're never easy, majors, but that was my easiest chance.'

Langer went into the 1985 Open a confident man, still floating on a cloud of success from Augusta, where his wonderful finish had earned him his first Masters title. Totally at ease with his game and with none of the worries that were soon to affect his game periodically – a dose of the putting 'yips' that visited him 18 months later and a perennially painful back – Langer was at his peak. He went into the tournament at Sandwich, on England's south-east coast, with the 'favourite' tag on his bag.

He had not even played a round of golf the previous week, preferring instead to take time off at home in Augsburg and go waterskiing, play tennis and football. The German press were more interested in Boris Becker's win at Wimbledon, but they were also giving Langer a little coverage because of his marvellous win at Augusta, and the sportsmen in his country waited expectantly for him to deliver.

Practice was promising for Langer, who had his coach of ten years, Willi Hofmann, on duty. Langer trusted Hofmann implicitly and had paid tribute to his teacher when winning the Masters. The pair worked all day together during Sandwich-week, from hitting balls on the range in the morning, playing 18 holes and then chipping and putting while winding down.

As well as building up his confidence with his game, Langer felt that winning one major should, in theory, make it slightly easier when coming to try to win another.

'I'd won the European money-list for a second time the previous year but, more importantly, won my first major in the April, the Masters. I knew what the pressure would be like. At the Masters, I was able to handle it very well and concentrated magnificently. There were no bad thoughts at all. I was positive all the way, and that is why I probably played so well and scored so well. It is so much harder to win a major. Some days, you can concentrate for eight hours, feel great, and some days you don't sleep well or eat well and have your ups and downs.

'Three months later, going into the British Open, I was still on a high. Looking back, it was one of the best years of my career, and I was very much at ease with my game and myself going into the tournament. I was playing well; I liked Sandwich. I'd had a good experience there in '81. I looked at myself as one of the guys who would be considered favourites to win. If I played well, I might have a chance to win.

'In practice, I tried to avoid the pot-bunkers, as you have to do on Open courses. I tried to hit as many quality shots as possible, so that I would be in that vein when the tournament started.

'I remember practising one evening and I was hitting the ball so good it was scary. I was hitting all my clubs so well, even three-irons and one-irons. The ball was going exactly where I wanted it to go. To be honest, I didn't want to stop practising, it was so much fun. That doesn't happen very often. It was one of those experiences where you think, "I'm hitting it so good. I'm going to have a great week."'

But Langer could do nothing about the weather. It was going to take his best game to combat high winds and thrashing rain that whipped over the course for three days. Depending on which direction they came from, the squalls flattened some of the knee-high hay just off the fairways, secreting balls forever, but also raised some of it waist-high, tall enough to lose a caddie in, let alone a ball.

Langer's swing and his meticulous course-management were largely good enough to master the weather – and shrug off the ill luck of the lottery that can decide an Open.

On the Thursday, Langer did not get off to the best of starts, as he shot a 72, two-over-par – not the sort of score to get the headline-writers excited. For the most part, it was a battling 72, scored when the bad weather was often at its worst. And it could have been so much better. At the 15th, Langer fell foul of a bunker and ran up a triple-bogey by leaving his ball in the hazard. How that shot was to cost him dearly.

Dissatisfied with his start, Langer went to work on the range after his round.

'I was not greedy in the bunker. I played a pitching wedge, just hit a bad shot and did not get up. I hit a few poor shots, but your rhythm can go if you are a bit nervous in the wind and your grip gets tighter.'

It left Langer no fewer than eight strokes off the lead, held by Christy O'Connor Junior. The man from the Emerald Isle had, in direct contrast to Langer, had the luck of the Irish. Well, at least the luck of the draw.

O'Connor Junior led by four strokes from a group that included two players who would, like the Irishman, stay in contention to the death: Sandy Lyle and David Graham. Langer was frustrated but, in the cool, nay icy, manner that was already his hallmark on the course, took his bad luck in his stride and got on with it. Things would be better the next day, surely? Regrettably for Langer, though, as far as the weather was concerned, they weren't. He recalls:

'The way the draw worked out gave me one of the worst breaks I've had in my whole career in terms of weather. It was fairly calm on Thursday morning and I had a late tee-time, probably around three o'clock. The storm came in and the wind started to blow.

'Then, the next day, I had an early tee-time, and by lunchtime the storm was gone. It meant there were two extremes and a tournament of opposites. Half of the field played in windy conditions and bad weather and the other half played in fairly calm and benign conditions. Out of my half of the draw, I think only seven or eight guys made the cut.'

Langer's 69, scored when the card-shredding weather was at its worst, was lauded by many of the pundits as the best round of the week, as good if not better than O'Connor Junior's 64 on the first day. Most put the par for the course that day as nearer 75 than 70. Langer says he was delighted to now be in the thick of things:

'I didn't just make the cut; I was in contention. For my 69 in the second round, I just kept the ball in play. I just had to battle it out with the wind. The conditions were very difficult, especially the last few holes. I had my best birdie of the entire year on 15 [a stunning one-iron approach to 12 ft]. I remember hitting driver on 17 for my second shot! I hit driver off the tee and it was quite a solid drive, but the wind was so strong I needed another driver to get there. I actually hit the flagstick with my second shot. That doesn't happen very often. You don't hit many drivers off the fairway period, but it's very rare to then hit the flagstick.'

The veering gusts cost Langer bogeys at the 16th and 18th and subsequently the lead. But if he could shoot scores like he had done over the first two days, what could he do if he got some good weather?

He was not about to find out immediately. Going into Saturday's third round, Langer lay two shots off the lead, which was held by Lyle and Graham on one-under. O'Connor Junior and the American D.A. Weibring were a stroke in front of Langer, too.

All of them had taken to the course when yet another storm hit Sandwich. Play was suspended until 4 p.m. Then, at last, came the calm after the storm. Langer did show what he could do when conditions were better.

'My scores over the first two rounds didn't really reflect how well I'd played. The bad weather seemed to follow me.

'During the storm, I stayed in a hut which was dark and lonely, but a German friend staying nearby came over and asked us if we'd like to go to the house for a cup of tea. We stayed there for about 45 minutes.

'I struggled a little for the first five holes because I was a bit cold after the hold-up, but I then hit a lot of good shots. I could have made two or three more putts, especially on the back nine.'

Another bogey on the 18th cost Langer the outright lead, but his round of 68 took him into a share of top place with Graham, who also faltered late on in the gathering gloom. The Australian was the most experienced player of the two. He had won the 1979 US PGA Championship and the 1981 US Open and was looking for the third part of a grand slam. Langer was looking for a 1985 major double and says he was delighted to be a force at Sandwich:

'I was excited to be co-leader with David Graham. We were three shots ahead and I was happy that I'd played well enough in the bad conditions of the first two rounds to stay in with a chance.

'On Saturday night, I was a little nervous but at the same time thrilled and ready to go out and try to win the British Open for the first time. I'd had my chances and been in this position before, so I was looking forward to Sunday. I had just played three very good rounds of golf and I saw no reason why it should not continue. I was healthy. I was confident. I'd won the Masters, so I had every reason to believe I could do it.

'Obviously, I knew David Graham was playing just as well, and there were still a lot of guys in with a chance behind us.'

Those guys were Lyle and O'Connor Junior, still. Ian Woosnam and Mark O'Meara joined them in third place. At three ahead of the field, though, everyone fully expected the winner to come from either Langer or Graham. That was reckoning without the karma that is the Open Championship. Langer was under no illusions that winning necessarily depended on who played best, rather, who got the best out of the day.

'Sandwich is, maybe, one of the most unpredictable courses of them all, where you can get some bad bounces. A bad bounce can change the whole picture on a hole, even change the whole picture of a round. I went out on Sunday very aware of that. You cannot afford to be over-confident, even when you are hitting the ball as well as I was, because something could happen that is beyond your control.'

Exactly that was to happen – and happen fairly quickly after the start of his round. However, he admits an early upset was caused by his own hand:

'I missed a four-footer, something like that, on the 1st hole and it kind of shook me up a little bit. It didn't shake me to the point where I couldn't play, but it was a real shock because I'd been putting pretty good up to that point. I wouldn't let it worry me, though. I kept playing solidly. But another incident that happened on the 4th hole did upset me a little bit.

'I had a one-iron into the green for my second shot. You have to play it a little bit left and run it in. I hit a really good shot. There was a marshal standing only three or four yards left of the green on the hill and my ball hit his foot. It bounced left and stayed on the hill. If it had not hit his foot, it would have rolled around the bank and onto the green. It would have worked out a totally different shot. I ended up making bogey when I had a chance of birdie but most likely would have made par. The ball ended up in a horrible place, where the best I could do, pretty well, was to make bogey.

'He shouldn't have been there. Something like that can change the outcome of the tournament. Every shot is important. As it turned out, one shot would have been vitally important to me. We'll never know what might have happened if I hadn't hit the marshal. I wasn't happy about it, but I had to take it as rub of the green.'

It was an untimely incident. Another bogey followed immediately. The field closed in on both Langer and Graham, the latter similarly bogeying the 1st, 4th and 5th holes.

Soon, Tom Kite, four shots off the lead at the start, threw in a challenge. He faded out of contention with a six at the 10th.

O'Meara hung on right to the closing holes, but Woosnam lost his way early in the round. Peter Jacobsen was up there. However, it was not the Claret Jug handle Jacobsen was to grab at the end of his round. Spaniard José Rivero posted an early target of four-over-par. That was then bettered by a stroke by another American, Payne Stewart. The man who was to die in tragic circumstances when his private jet crashed some years later could have put himself into a play-off if his putt on the last had not pulled up 2 in. short.

The finale of the 1985 Open was about to be played out, with Lyle finally stamping an indelible mark on it. After a wayward drive at the 'Suez Canal' 14th, the Scot somehow fashioned a birdie out of the hole, smashing a two-iron third shot some 220 yards against the wind before sinking an outrageous 45-footer. When he birdied the 15th, too, Lyle was in the driving seat. His playing-partner O'Connor Junior was then left in his wake with bogeys on 15 and 16.

Then came the streaker, hurtling out of the crowd just as Lyle was playing the 17th. Jacobsen took great delight in tackling the man. Lyle, though nonplussed, gathered himself to make par. Behind, Langer had slipped three shots behind his playing-partner by the 10th, but clawed level with Graham at 15. Both were a stroke behind Lyle. Then Langer and Graham ran up what proved to be fatal bogeys on the short 16th.

Langer blames his passion to win for the blemish that was ultimately to end his hopes again in the Open:

'Things went against me early on, but I still set up lots of opportunities and I was still in with a good chance of winning with three holes to go. But then I hit a bad shot on 16, the par-three. I did the same thing Thomas Björn did a few years later. I hit in the right bunker and my ball was plugged. I tried to be cute and bump the ball into the hill to make it run up, but I left it way short. In fact, I only just got it out of the sand. I made a four and that turned out to be costly.

'That's the one place where you don't want to hit it when the pin is set on the right side. At that point, I was trying to force things, and that's never a good thing to do.

'I don't remember a whole lot about the streaker, just a lot of people running around. It didn't affect my concentration. My only thought was to make birdie and try and get into the play-off. I was totally focused on that, and not much could have distracted me at that point.'

After the fuss over the streaker had died down, Lyle sent off his drive and then missed the 18th green, pulling his six-iron approach just into the edge of the rough in 'Duncan's Hollow'. His attempt at making the crest of the green fell short. He sank to his knees. His putt for his fourth shot did gain the top layer of the green, and a successful two-footer ended Stewart's hopes. It left Langer and Graham with a target of two-over-par to force a play-off. Their only route to salvation was to birdie the last. Langer says he was fully aware of the job in hand:

'After Sandy bogeyed the last, I knew when I went to the 18th tee that I was a stroke behind. I knew I had to make birdie. I hit a pretty good tee-shot. There was some wind as I played a five-iron into the green. I didn't want to be short and I didn't want to be left. I had to hit the green and give myself a chance for a birdie putt. The ball leaked a little bit, though, and I missed the green on the right. I was pretty much pin-high, maybe a fraction long, on the right side, in the rough about 6 or 7 ft off the green. I knew I had to make this one. I took a sand-wedge, trying to chip in. It had pretty good direction but I hit the ball a little bit too firm. It actually touched the hole but went over the lip.

'Then I had a blackout, because I knew it was all over. I missed the putt and I wasn't even second. It was more out of disappointment than anything else, because at that point I knew I wasn't going to win.'

With Graham needing to hole his bunker-shot to force a play-off and failing, also dropping a stroke on the last, Lyle became the first British winner of an Open for 16 years. A desolate Langer had to settle for a share of third place.

'There might have been times when I'd be pretty happy at finishing third in a British Open but not that week. I felt it was there for the taking. There were too many mistakes on my behalf, though. I missed that short putt on the first. At the 16th, I was too aggressive and nearly left my ball in there. Then there was the bad break on four. I was bitterly disappointed.

'Looking back, I lost because I gave away shots that I shouldn't have given away. That's why I was so disappointed.'

1985 TOP SCORES

S. Lyle 68–71–73–70 282
P. Stewart 70–75–70–68 283
B. Langer 72–69–68–75 284
D. Graham 68–71–70–75 284
J. Rivero 74–72–70–68 284
C. O'Connor Jnr 64–76–72–72 284
M. O'Meara 70–72–70–72 284

1987, MUIRFIELD: PAUL AZINGER

(Azinger only lost the Open on the 72nd hole)

'My decision to hit driver on 17 cost me the Championship. If I had parred that hole, I would have been in command. There was no point in taking driver. It should have been a one-iron. I don't know what I was thinking.'

IT WAS THE year Nick Faldo established himself as a major player after two years of remodelling his swing. Faldo's maiden major success proved the launching-pad for six major titles and three Open Championships as he became the best British golfer in the modern era.

The 1987 Open will be forever remembered for Faldo's remarkable finishing round of 18 straight pars.

A willowy American, 27 at the time, will never forget it for another reason. Paul Azinger had the tournament in his grasp with just two holes to go. His hand was on the Claret Jug with just one hole to go. Then, cruelly, a second successive mistake at Muirfield cost Azinger glory and left him forever to wonder what might have been.

Faldo came to that year's Open having spent two years revamping a swing with David Leadbetter, who had been such a boon to Nick Price. While he had already had considerable success, becoming number one in Europe, winning eleven times on the European Tour and once on the US Tour, Faldo felt his swing was not complete enough to win a major. When Sandy Lyle beat him to it and became Open champion in 1985, Faldo turned to Price's fellow-Zimbabwean Leadbetter to help him become a major-winner too.

Two years' work had already paid off modestly when Faldo won the 1987 Spanish Open with his new swing, giving him optimism for the coming Open. While Faldo, who missed the Masters and US Open for two successive years as he went through his swing changes, was returning tentatively to the fold, the man who was to become his arch-adversary in the 1987 Open was on a roll.

Azinger, from Florida, was in the throes of a magnificent US Tour-season that brought him three wins and second place on the money-list. Despite being the current American money-list leader, Azinger was not being talked about as a potential winner. Favourites were the usual suspects: Jack Nicklaus, the surprise 1986 Masters winner; Tom Watson, only beaten by a stroke by outsider Scott Simpson in the US Open not long before and seeking a record-equalling sixth Open title; Open defending champion Greg Norman; and Seve Ballesteros, joint runner-up with Norman in the Masters behind Larry Mize.

In fact, on paper, Azinger looked to have far more chance of winning than the rehabilitating Faldo, even if the big Englishman felt his game was coming together just at the right time. Azinger, though, was making his Open Championship debut. Watson had won the first time he played in the Open. How would the in-form Azinger fare?

He had declined trying to pre-qualify the previous year like many Americans before him, because he couldn't really afford to make a long trip that might prove fruitless. Indeed, Azinger made a prophetic statement at the Open:

'I think it would be good if US players could qualify for the British Open in America and British players could qualify over here for the US Open. I didn't come last year because I had to qualify. This year, I would have come if I'd had to qualify. The difference? I have more money now.'

It was a good while coming, but Azinger's wish did finally come true.

Azinger's caddying arrangements for his Open debut were thrown into disarray when his normal bagman said he was unable to make the trip to Britain. And that may have played a vital role in Azinger's Open fortunes, as you will find out later from his temporary bagman, Zimbabwean Kevin Woodward.

Woodward had been on Nick Price's bag when his compatriot missed out at the death in the 1982 Open. A change of mind by another one of those strongly fancied to do well at Muirfield in 1987, Andy Bean, gave Woodward a chance to carry for Azinger.

'I went to Muirfield without a bag but had an outside chance of a job because Terry Holt, who was working with Andy Bean, had arranged to work with Paul Azinger if Andy couldn't make it. It was a back-up for Terry, because Andy had an injury and there was a chance he wouldn't travel to Scotland.

'Terry had spoken to Paul, who'd agreed that I could work for him if Terry didn't. Bean decided to play and, true to his word, Azinger took me on.

'I'd made a yardage book and walked the course seven or eight times to try to ensure that I knew Muirfield and could be of as much assistance to Paul as possible.

'I'd known Paul when I was in America in 1984 but not well, and I don't think he remembered me. But he was very easy-going and we seemed to get on well from the start. The thing that impressed me most was his attitude to everything going on around him.

'And I was very impressed by his demeanour. The weather was not great, he had a cold and he'd just arrived after a tiring journey from America with his family, but, despite all this, not once did I hear him complain – all week. On the contrary, he had nothing but praise for everything: the course, travel, hotel, everything. He just loved being at the Open.

'He'd had a great year so far in America and was leading their order of merit, but, despite that, not many people in Britain knew of him. They were about to find out.'

They hardly knew each other, but fate was already drawing Faldo and Azinger together after the first round. Rodger Davis showed a clean pair of plus-twoed heels to the rest of the field as he opened with a magnificent round of 64. That put the moustachioed Australian three strokes ahead of evergreen Lee Trevino, who was trying to prove, like Nicklaus the previous year at Augusta, there was life in the old dog yet. Faldo and Azinger shared third place with Mize after rounds of 68, the latter looking to prove his chip-in to beat Norman at Augusta was not just a fluke.

A second round of wind and rain ended with Azinger firmly establishing himself as America's chief contender. Faldo was in the ascendancy too. However, a second 68 by Azinger, to move to six-under-par, earned him a one-stroke lead over Faldo. That lead was earned, ironically as it was to prove, by Azinger at the 18th. It was watched by his caddie Kevin Woodward.

'Paul played wonderfully controlled golf over the first two rounds, and, in addition to wonderful ball-striking in windy conditions, he putted beautifully. I also witnessed one of the best bunker-shots I have ever seen. It came at the greenside "doughnut" bunker in the second round.'

Azinger's plucky save at the last hole caused the wheels of destiny to revolve perfectly, taking him into the third round alongside Faldo.

One thing that was far from perfect, however, was again the weather. Score-billowing squalls had relented just a little by the time the last group went out, but conditions were pretty awful for Saturday afternoon's play. The wind was so strong that the R & A were forced to shorten four of the holes. With the early-starters getting the worst of the wind and rain, it gave little chance for anyone to come through the field. An idea of just how bad the weather was early on can be gleaned from the fact that a third of the players in the first half of the field failed to break 80. Azinger explained at the time how he coped:

'It was just a struggle, but we had a great break with the tee-times because from about 8 a.m. to 12 p.m. the conditions were not very good. We had the best of the weather. In fact, I had the best of the weather every day up to then. I'd played in wind like it before but not coupled with the cold. I had a lot of clothes on!

'I wasn't nervous on the 1st tee. The bad weather kind of took the pressure off me. I knew everyone was going to have a hard time and that it would be the survival of the fittest.'

Nervous or not, Azinger was caught immediately when he bogeyed the 1st. But, with the poor weather testing everyone, he kept his cool and soon held the lead on his own again.

Three successive birdies from the 7th re-established his place on top of the leaderboard. Faldo hung on but only to Azinger's shirt tails as the American went two ahead. A mistake on the 12th, though, pegged Azinger back.

'It was really the only bad mistake I made in the whole tournament that far. I three-putted from 45–50 ft, missed a save of about 2½ ft. I think I made a rush at it a little bit, but also the wind was blowing. I made my share of putts. You are always going to miss putts like that in the wind.'

Azinger's confidence was high going into the back nine. He needed to be upbeat, as Muirfield's incoming holes had caused him problems in the first two rounds. He just didn't seem to be as comfortable over them as the front nine. Unfortunately for Azinger, that trend was never bucked all week.

His focus, too, was affected by a significant incident on the back nine. And it was nothing to do with the way he was hitting the ball, rather the way he and Faldo were *not* hitting the ball – quickly enough.

Faldo's caddie Andy Prodger explains:

'On the 13th, we were warned for slow play. It was like water off a duck's back to Nick. He hardly turned a hair. But I'm sure it upset Paul.'

Coming to the 18th, though, Azinger looked as though he might be able to take a two-shot lead into the final round. However, Muirfield's deadly finishing hole then halved his margin. It was the first of two blows by that hole that defined Azinger's fortunes in 1987.

'I wasn't nervous of the 18th, but it is such a hard hole. I hit a terrible tee-shot. A left-to-right wind got me and in the end I was pretty fortunate to make bogey. It was the first time of the week I was in a pot-bunker. I hit my ball in the face of the bunker, so all I could do was try to get back on the fairway. Then my four-iron was not very good and I needed a wedge to get on. I had to make it from 13 ft and I desperately wanted to make the putt. I was proud to make that and have the lead.'

Avoidance of a double-bogey finish for a round of 71 kept Azinger one stroke ahead of the field. Because Faldo also bogeyed the last, it had a marked effect on Sunday's final-round draw. Who knows what might have happened if Faldo and Azinger had played together again? As it was, South African David Frost, who had come surging up the leaderboard with a fine 70, would be the one to accompany Azinger under the 'first one in, last one out' rule. Faldo would be playing with Craig Stadler in the penultimate match out.

It was, of course, all new to Azinger. He said on Saturday night:

'No matter what happens tomorrow, I am going to be a better player when it is over. You cannot get this experience anywhere else. I am enjoying it. I am going to be nervous like anybody else. Anxious is a better word. I'm anxious to get going. This is the greatest place in the world to play golf. I am in the best position. If this is my time to win, then I'll win. If I don't, I have had a great year so far. Winning would be the icing on the cake. At the beginning [of the week], I just wanted to know what it would be like to be in contention in a major. I'm getting to know. I know I have a long way to go. I know how bad I can hit it at times. Win, lose or draw, I have a long way to go to reach my peak.'

On a murky day when the haar descended on Muirfield, by the time he had played the opening eight holes on Sunday, Azinger reached his 1987 Open peak, at any rate, charging into a three-shot lead. Only an indifferent pitch on the long 9th to miss out on a birdie denied him an even greater advantage. Up ahead, Faldo was parring hole after hole, unable to go up a gear and in danger of being totally overrun. Then, according to Azinger's caddie, Kevin Woodward, came the turning point. And Woodward insists on taking the rap for it turning against Azinger:

'I blame myself for encouraging him to use a two-iron for his second shot on the 10th, him having favoured his one-iron. Knowing how well he had been striking the ball, I didn't want him to overshoot the green. But I was wrong, and the ball ended up in the greenside bunker. It was a very difficult recovery-shot to a back pin. That resulted in a bogey.

'Paul's confidence and rhythm were temporarily eroded, and he followed up with a bad drive and three putts, his first three-putt of the tournament, and another shot was dropped.'

Suddenly, Azinger was losing ground, despite Faldo up ahead gaining none by his own hand, by continuing his par sequence. Two terrific approach-shots at the 12th and 14th holes, though, both to no more than 10 ft, could have left Azinger unassailable. It was not to be. They were only parred. Then, on the short 16th, he had another chance. He takes up the story:

'On the 10th, I should have hit a one-iron but I took the two-iron. When I went into the bunker, I had no chance of making par. Then, on the 11th, I let a ten-footer for par get away. It was the same distance on 12 and 14. If I had made those putts on 12 and 14, no one would have beaten me.

'On the 16th [par-three], I hit a fantastic shot with a three-iron to 15 ft, but I missed that putt as well.'

Instead of being out of sight, Azinger held only a slender one-shot lead coming to the penultimate hole. Faldo had had to scramble for par at times and had also watched birdie putts arrive and leave without calling. At this juncture, the 1987 Open reached its penultimate turning point.

Azinger selected a driver. It proved to be too much club. His ball came to rest in the one place that would not only almost certainly end his birdie chance but also restrict his chance of par: the infamous fairway bunker at 17. The lanky American's Open bid started to fall apart at this stage, and the repercussions proved costly indeed.

'My decision to hit driver on 17 cost me the Championship. If I had parred that hole, I would have been in command. There was no point in taking driver. It should have been a one-iron. I don't know what I was thinking.'

Woodward, though, begs to differ:

'It has been said by many, including Paul himself, that he should not have used driver off the 17th tee. I disagree for two reasons. He had, for five holes, hit the ball with tremendous authority, so why become negative and back off, make the second shot over the cross-bunkers more difficult? There was plenty of fairway and lots of space right of the fairway, because at that time there was no out of bounds.'

Whatever the pros and cons, Azinger had to chip out and couldn't make the green in three. A bogey-six went on the card. He was now tied with Faldo, who was just playing the final hole.

At the 18th, Faldo decided on a five-iron to go in – the correct club because it left him with a birdie putt. Just like the others, though, this one avoided the hole. Faldo set the target of five-under-par with his 18-par 71, a feat of which even the history books couldn't find a match at that time. Azinger needed to birdie the last to win: par to go into a play-off.

Fatefully and fatally, he also chose a five-iron to go into the last green. He not only found the greenside bunker but also a dreadful lie. Azinger pitched out short, took two putts and relinquished the lead for the first time since Friday. He also handed the Claret Jug over to Nick Faldo.

There was never so much as even a hint from Azinger that anything influenced him over any of his clubbing decisions. Remarkably bravely, though, caddie Woodward shoulders the blame for the closing, mortal bogey:

'I again blame myself for influencing Paul on his club selection. Again, I was worrying about going over the green. I convinced him that five-iron was enough club. Maybe he tried to hit it a bit too hard and he pulled it.

'It was such a pity that Paul's regular caddie had not made the trip, because I think that their understanding of each other would have resulted in less mistakes being made, and Paul would have had another major title.'

Another point that Azinger never dwelt on, though he could have, was the behaviour of a minority section of the gallery, who cheered when he found those bunkers at the end. The watching Andy Prodger, Nick Faldo's caddie, did not like what he saw and heard.

'To be frank, I was a bit upset with the way it finished. It was great to win, but I was disgusted with the way spectators cheered Paul's bad shots and when he went into the bunkers at the end. I spoke to him afterwards and apologised for the crowd – as if it was my fault. He just said, "Well, you can't help it. That's just life." But the R & A, or the Muirfield captain, remarked on it during the presentation, about the unsporting behaviour of some sections of the crowd. It was an unsavoury ending.'

There was eventually a major triumph for Azinger to savour, and the golfing world will know no greater battler. He was as good as his words after his distressing finish: 'I have proven to myself and everyone that I am a contender, and I am going to benefit from what happened.'

Six years later, Azinger, to become a fearsome opponent in Ryder Cups, won the US PGA Championship. His far-greater victory came shortly afterwards when he fought and beat lymphoma cancer in his right shoulder.

1987 TOP SCORES

N. Faldo 68–69–71–71 279
P. Azinger 68–68–71–73 280
R. Davis 64–73–74–69 280
B. Crenshaw 73–68–72–68 281
P. Stewart 71–66–72–72 281

1988, ROYAL LYTHAM AND ST ANNES: NICK PRICE

(Price was in contention right up to the final hole, before losing out to Seve Ballesteros)

'I was so focused, and I was so sure that I was going to stiff my ball in there. I was going to hit it so close, it was like a kick-in. I rushed it. I rushed it just a smidge and I pulled it.'

IN 1988, THE names being touted around as potential winners of the Open Championship were predictable. Nick Faldo was defending the title he had clinched in obdurate fashion at Muirfield the previous year. Sandy Lyle was the Masters champion after beating the best at Augusta. Jack Nicklaus and Tom Watson were still potent forces. Surely Greg Norman should be able to add to his 1986 Open success?

And there was Seve.

Seve was always good for a bet, certainly each-way. He had won the last time the Open was at Royal Lytham and St Annes – the 1979 'Car Park Open', so named because of his exploitation of a temporary car park that year. There were no temporary car parks near the 16th fairway this time, but Seve was still strongly fancied to pull off his third Open after also winning in 1984.

Nick Price, though, hardly caught the eye of the punters before the Open got under way. Price was a winner, true enough, and an experienced player. He had one US Tour title and three European Tour successes to his name by the time he turned up at the Lancashire course. But the starting price on this Nick showed long odds, even though he could easily have won his first Open six years previously.

It was an Open notable for a historic first Monday finish. Virtually a day-long deluge wiped out Saturday's play from late morning, cancelling early scoring and causing a restart of the third round on the Sunday. The R & A hoped to get both the last two rounds in on the Sunday, but with the course still waterlogged there was never going to be the chance of more than one round. So the 1988 Open went into a fifth day. For the Lytham crowd, that meant they had to return on a normal workday, but it was certainly worth taking a day off as the tournament came down to the closing shots on the closing hole.

For Nick Price, it was a first visit to Lytham, and he says he couldn't wait to get under way:

'I'd had a great chance to win six years before, and since then I'd become more mature by learning a lot more than I knew in 1982. I'd been in position to win majors twice since 1982. Played well but just didn't have the breaks come my way in the 1985 US PGA Championship and 1986 Masters, where I finished fifth both times. If I got in the hunt again, I'd be no stranger to it. I felt a little bit more deliberate.

'Unfortunately, I missed the qualifying for the Open Championship in 1979, when Seve won. It was one of the two Open Championships I didn't play in my entire career. So it was my first experience of Royal Lytham and St Annes.

'The stories I'd heard about the course were very mixed. Some guys had said it was a very tricky course, but a few said I'd like it. I couldn't wait. When I did get there, I loved it. There was a premium on driving the ball, and I liked the way it played.

'The thing that's different about Lytham and St Annes to all the other links courses is that the wind seems to blow across the holes a lot more, as opposed to straight down and straight back in. The wind invariably blows right to left, slightly helping going out. Coming back in, it's left to right and into you, slightly hurting. That was the difficult thing to work out. Nobody likes to play too many cross-wind holes.

'I really enjoyed it, though, and before the championship started I was playing better and better. David Leadbetter was there, and he kept saying to me, "I've never seen you swing better." He hadn't been saying that for two or three weeks, so I knew it was all there. My big question mark was "How well am I putting?" I had been struggling with my putting up until that stage.

'I'd battled with my putter since February that year, but I'd worked hard on the putting and I was optimistic, especially as the time of the year was normally good for me. I always play well around June, July, August.

'I putted really well all week. Not as well as Seve, though!'

Price's was one of the steadiest opening rounds of a Thursday notable for buffeting winds on the Lancashire coast. He did not have a blemish on his card until a bogey on the 12th cancelled out his birdie on the 8th. When Price holed a 20-footer on the 16th, he was on the leaderboard with a round of one-under-par 70, which, he says, was better than it looked on paper, considering the harsh conditions:

'The wind was relentless. It was so difficult to get the ball close to the hole, whether with the wind or against it. It was so difficult to control the ball. My plan was to make sure I always kept the ball in play and not to get too quick with the swing in the wind.

'With the wind 20 mph stronger than it had been in practice and moving to a different direction from the previous days, it made the finishing holes – 15, 16, 17 and 18 – really difficult.'

One name stood out from the rest when a hectic day's play finished: the favourite's. Seve Ballesteros just carried on where he had left off in 1979. Ballesteros was like a runaway train from the 1st to the 7th holes, picking up five birdies and scattering the field. On the 14th, he made an extraordinary bogey that in retrospect proved to be one of the paramount points of the week. This time, it was not a car park he found but a small spinney of dense gorse. After weighing up his options, Ballesteros took penalty and dropped 50 yards back near the 6th tee. He had a totally blind shot from behind trees and gorse but stroked a seven-iron clear of trouble and onto the green. It was somehow inevitable that Seve would then hole the 15-footer. He had fashioned a bogey-five when a seven would have left a mere mortal relieved. The salvage operation, which took a good 25 minutes, left the 300 spectators who had followed him into the jungle wide-eyed. It was another legendary Lytham feat that his opponents, particularly Nick Price, would live to regret.

Ballesteros had two penalty drops in the round, needing another after a wayward drive into the bushes on the right on the last. He still, though, produced an opening round of 67, which gave him a two-shot lead over Wayne Grady and Brad Faxon, with Nick Price sharing fourth place, three behind.

Friday was moving-day for Price, however, as he matched Ballesteros's first-round 67 to surge five-under and relegate the Spaniard to second place, a stroke behind. The battle between the two main players in the piece in 1988 was well under way.

Price began his assault with an eagle on the long 6th, ramming home a 35-footer. He proved his putting prowess was no fluke, too, holing out twice from around 15 ft for birdies.

Then came his important save after he had overshot the 18th green. Disturbed by a radio call, Price tried to ignore it and went ahead with his chip, but, with his focus not at its best, he scuffed up 20 ft short. When he holed the putt to save par and lead on his own, he really knew his putting had gone through a timely renaissance.

'It was a case of kicking into gear. I played the opening holes well every day, played the par-fives, 6 and 7, well all week. That was the case on Friday, and then I just held it together coming down the stretch.

'I lost my concentration on my little chip on 18. Someone had a walkie-talkie going and I heard it. I should have backed off. But my putting was really solid, and that was why I was under par, and that was why I was where I was. My putting had been poor, on and off, for about a year. I'd got close to winning the Open the previous year but I putted so badly it was ridiculous. I had three three-putts on the last day alone.

'All in all, I was happy with the way I struck the ball, too. I definitely worked hard and prepared hard for the Open. For three, four, maybe even five, weeks before any major I start tuning up for the course I'm going to be playing. If you win any other tournament, it's not the same as winning a major. You don't get the same satisfaction.

'After coming so close before, I wanted to feel what it was like to win one. I was into my tenth year as a pro. I had all the ingredients for winning a major championship. This was the thing that was starting to frustrate me a little bit. I had the maturity, the game, my strategy on the course was strong. I had everything going for me. It was just a case of playing smart and not making foolish mistakes, giving myself a chance to win. That's what the first, second and third rounds are all about in a major championship: jockeying for position and giving yourself a chance on Sunday to win. I was doing that so well that week.'

Well, it wouldn't come on Sunday, but Price had certainly set up the chance. However, as well as Ballesteros, who had again fallen foul of the 14th to record another bogey and lose his lead, there was an impressive array of players on his heels, just a stroke behind him. The previous year's Open winner, Nick Faldo, was two behind with the 1982 Masters winner, Craig Stadler. Andy Bean, runner-up in the 1983 Open, held fifth place, four shots adrift. Two more major champions, Bob Tway and Sandy Lyle, that year's Masters winner, were a further stroke back alongside Fred Couples, who had finished fourth in the 1984 Open. It was a quality leaderboard.

Even though he led, Price could still not beat the odds. Ballesteros was 2–1 against before the third round, Faldo 4–1 and Lyle 7–1. Price had to settle for being fourth favourite at 8–1.

After the third round, Price's odds stayed the same. That was because none of the fancied players even got onto the course. After heavy morning rain, play was halted just after midday and abandoned for the day, with the earlier scoring scrapped an hour later. Some 36,000 expectant spectators were left disappointed and trudging home or to digs.

That gave Price a whole day and night to muse over his position.

'I was so confident in the way I was swinging that taking a day off didn't even worry me. When you have that confidence in your ability, any kind of adversity can come your way and you can deal with it.'

While the R & A were keen to get both the last two rounds completed on Sunday, Mother Nature was not. By Saturday midnight, four fairways – the 4th, 7th, 11th and 14th – were under water. The concern then was that the third round would complete on Sunday. Several pumps and the 'waterhog' from Old Trafford ensured that play would be possible, but the final round would now have to begin on the Monday.

By the time he took to the course on Sunday alongside Ballesteros and Stadler, at least Price had moved up to third favourite. For some reason, Lyle's odds had lengthened to 8–1, too. A gallery of over 41,000 squelched around Lytham, and a good few of them watched as Lanny Wadkins holed-in-one at the 1st to get the important action under way.

Later on, Price began his round with a birdie to extend his lead over Ballesteros, but then played enigmatically, by his own admission. He was satisfied, though, to sign for a 69 that earned him a two-shot lead to take into Monday's historic final round.

'Even though it didn't affect my confidence, the blank day probably upset my rhythm just a bit. I didn't get an opportunity to hit some balls, and I felt I didn't play as well from tee to green as the previous days. It's always been a tendency of mine: when I get excited, I get a little faster, so I've always got to slow myself down. So what I had to do was to try and get that rhythm and tempo back into my swing. Sometimes that happens if you don't hit for a day, but it doesn't take long to come back once you know what you're doing. My short-game was in top form, though. Every time I got it close, I holed out. And I putted well. If I had not putted well, I would have shot 71 or 72.

'At the 15th, I hit probably the best two-iron I have hit in my life. But I didn't play 17 very well. It's one of those holes that is potentially a complete round-wrecker, being the penultimate hole.

There was a lot of trouble on the left of that hole. You could make seven, triple-bogey, so quickly. I kind of played it cautiously the whole week. That day, I pulled my tee-shot into the bunker and I had to lay up, chip on and take two putts.'

That was Price's only blemish and did not prevent him holding a two-shot lead that night.

'Now I'd had to sleep on the lead the whole weekend, which made it a little tougher, but, again, I wasn't worried about it. I was ready to go.

'The Monday finish was a little disappointing from the fact that there were not as many spectators as there would normally have been for a final round. There were still a lot out there, but you always want to finish on a Sunday for the atmosphere. When Monday came along, I was as ready as anyone.

'The only negative was that we were playing threesomes again. I always enjoy playing twosomes. You play a little faster and it's more flowing. Sunday and Monday, I was trying to slow myself down a little bit so I could stay with the pace of the threesome.'

Price played with Ballesteros and Faldo, who both trailed him by the two shots, in the final round. Out just before them, Lyle was three strokes behind. The tall Zimbabwean was taking on two men who had appeared in the cauldron that is winning an Open, triumphing in a major. Indeed, Lyle had not long before beaten the best at Augusta.

Lyle was still confident he could pull off an Augusta–Lytham double. He thought Price was the man to beat. In his post-third-round press conference, Lyle predicted that Price would have to shoot 'a 68 or maybe a 69' if he were to win. A lot of people made a similar forecast. A lot of people put their money where their mouths were, too. Price became the firm favourite at the bookmakers, starting at 2–1 compared with Ballesteros 9–4, Faldo 3–1 and Lyle 4–1. Betting slips would not be torn up until after the 72nd hole had completed.

At first, there was a charge from the tapes, with players coming up on the rails, like Fred Couples, who made eagles on the 6th and 7th. Faldo and Lyle gave chase and, for a time, the Claret Jug was swapping hands between five players, like pass-the-parcel. Price's putting again saved him on the 3rd. He remembers:

'I hit my second shot to the left and had a difficult chip up and made a really great save from about 30 ft. The weakest part of my game coming into the week had been my putting. To make that putt just gave me so much confidence and turned what could have been a difficult start around for me.'

After a run of pars, Price and Ballesteros produced their own exhilarating charges and turned it into a two-horse race. Losing Faldo (when the defending champion three-putted the long 7th from just under the green) left Price feeling he had only one man to beat.

'It shouldn't have been the end of him [Faldo]. He let that adversity get the better of him. He started complaining. Seve and I, when we saw that, both knew he was not going to be a factor that day. We'd made threes and he'd three-putted to make five, but, to be honest, he didn't hit a particularly good second shot. It was always favouring the left side, and you need to be right there. I hit in with a three-iron to about 3 or 4 ft, and Seve went in with a four-iron and nearly holed it on the way by and finished about 15 ft behind. From then on, it was going to be Seve or me.

'It was as well as I've ever played in a major championship. When I look back on the week, the most enjoyable part for me was when Seve and I separated ourselves from the rest of the field. That was when we pulled ahead of Faldo on number 7, when Seve and I both eagled. We went four or five shots ahead of the field, and the next eleven holes gave me memories I'll savour forever.

'That was because Seve knew, even if he was one of the premier players in the world, if he didn't play his best I was going to beat him, and even if he did play his best it might be a shoot-out. I was again very much the underdog, and Seve would have been among the world's top players, maybe top three. If they had had a world ranking in those days, I would probably have been about 30th, 35th.

'And it *was* a shoot-out: a punch and counter-punch finish. It was so enjoyable. I'll never forget those last 11 holes as long as I live.'

The pair went into one of the most exciting finales the Open has seen, with neither giving an inch. Ballesteros did not give 240 inches on the 9th, to draw level with Price by holing a 20-ft birdie putt. It was another case of Ballesteros hitting his opponent with his sublime putting touch, says Price:

'I might have putted well that week but Seve's putting was wonderful. But I didn't let it get to me. He holed a 15-footer on the 10th and I had to stay with him by making about a five-footer. His putting was just beautiful to watch.'

It seemed Ballesteros could not miss. At the 11th, he went in front of Price by holing another 20-ft birdie putt. Price missed from just inside.

The cut and thrust continued. Price didn't need the cut at the 12th. Ballesteros's thrust was wanting as he came up short of the green and bogeyed. They were level again. Then Price played a magnificent approach to the 13th that might have killed off a less-determined opponent, winging in to less than 2 in. from the flag. Unabashed, Ballesteros hit to 12 ft – and also made birdie to keep the two still level on top.

'Of course it was disappointing. It was up to him. I'd stiffed mine. He holed from about 12 ft. He seemed to make a lot of putts that day from around 10–15 ft and a bit longer.'

Ballesteros's most unfavourite hole of the week, the 14th, cost him his third dropped shot of the tournament when he chipped too strongly after coming up short with his second shot. Price could strike back with a shortish putt. It was not to be, though.

'I had a chance to go back into the lead on the 14th, where we both made bogey. He'd already bogeyed before me, and I had a three and a half- to four-footer to save and misread it, clearly.'

Four holes to go, with nothing to separate the two. Then, however, came the shot that subsequently did so, although Price was certainly not hoisting any white flag. Ballesteros had won the 1979 Open with his unorthodox playing of the 16th, using the BBC car park to angle himself into the green. This time, he took an orthodox route, sliding in his approach to 2 in., a stunning riposte to Price's earlier golden shot on the 13th.

'On 16, it was one of the prettiest-looking nine-iron shots I've ever seen him hit. It was beautiful: just a soft little nine-iron off a bit of an upslope. He nearly holed it. I pulled my sand-wedge just a little long and left. I had a difficult putt of about 15 ft or so. It was a putt that broke up and away, left to right. I missed it and I'm one back again.

'Because of the way we'd been punching and counter-punching, it certainly wasn't a killer blow. Some of the press wrote that Seve's nine-iron on 16 was the killer blow, but there's nothing further from the truth.

'We were trading punches. I knew there was still 17 and 18 to go. He wasn't driving the ball particularly well. I would have said that if we had been tied going into 17 and 18, I would probably have beaten him, because I was driving the ball better than he was that day.'

The gallery were almost incandescent with excitement. At the 17th, Price pushed his drive so far right his ball finished up close to the practice-range fence. He knew he had to avoid dropping a shot at all costs.

'I hit my drive right, into the wind, and a two-iron just short of the green but got up and down. I had to.'

The drama that was the 1988 Open finally unfolded – a finale that Price, and golfing history, will never forget.

'I will always remember the final hole vividly. It was his tee. The wind is now blowing left to right, into us. He fans his tee-shot out to the right. There's a pot-bunker out there about 260 yards off the tee. I swear I thought his ball had gone in that pot-bunker. If he's in there, he has only an outside chance of making par and it's almost definitely a five. I just felt if I could make three, I was going to win. If I made four, I was going to tie.

'You're thinking, "Play-off." But play-off's not so good for me against Seve. Everyone's going to be pulling for Seve, too.

'I just ripped my tee-shot. It was the best tee-shot I hit all day – absolutely split the fairway in two. When I got up there, though, I see that Seve had carried the bunker. He got an exceptionally good break there. Not only had he carried the bunker, but he'd also missed the really long grass. He had an opportunity to advance the ball down to the green.'

Ballesteros did advance, but sent his ball into the dip to the left of the green in wispy rough. Price recalls he was greatly encouraged by this, as he faced the shot of his life at that time:

'I'm standing over my six-iron. Of all the shots I've ever had in golf, that would be one I'd love to have over again. I saw him miss the green, and I had the perfect yardage for a six-iron – just absolutely perfect. I was so focused, and I was so sure that I was going to stiff my ball in there. I was going to hit it so close, it was like a kick-in.

'I rushed it. I rushed it just a smidge and I pulled it. I hit the ball two seconds, maybe a second and a half, quicker than I should have. It was because I was so excited. There was no anxiety, no fear, no nothing. All the fear had gone on the front nine. There was no doubt. I just had this total vision of stiffing this iron shot.

'I pulled it 30 ft left of the hole. To this day, I'm certain if I'd hit that shot inside 10 ft, it would have made that chip of his so much harder. I knew it; he knew it. But he's a magician.'

Ballesteros conjured up the most magnificent of chips, his ball coming out softly but firm enough to make the green, gracefully arcing over towards the hole, which it brushed before coming to rest right beside.

Price had only one salvation. He had to hole his 30-footer. He gave his putt every chance, but as his ball raced past and he then missed the one back to bogey, Ballesteros's tap-in ended one of the greatest battles of attrition in the Open of all time. It had taken a 65 with a flamboyancy typical of a Spanish maestro to beat the gallant Price, who remembers what those closing moments meant to him:

'That chip on 18 and the nine-iron on 16 were shots of a magician. Two shots like that in three holes is phenomenal. He putted so beautifully that last day, too. That's not sour grapes whatsoever. What stopped me from winning that Open Championship was that my putting was not as good as his.

'That was the turning point for me in my career, because from that point onwards I started spending more time working on my putting.

'You learn lessons in losing. The lesson that day, hitting too quickly into the 18th, I used when I played my best golf, in the '90s.

'But Seve knew it had taken something special to beat me. He was very gracious. I knew Seve pretty well at that stage, but I don't think he gave me much respect as a player. After that, he realised I was not a player that would back down, and he knew that I had determination and drive in me, too. It's just that I was a later bloomer than him.

'I hadn't given the Open to him. It was different to '82. He'd beaten me. I didn't give it to him. You can't feel bad when someone beats you. It did wonders for my self-confidence.'

1988 TOP SCORES
S. Ballesteros 67–71–70–65 273
N. Price 70–67–69–69 275
N. Faldo 71–69–68–71 279

1989, ROYAL TROON:
WAYNE GRADY AND GREG NORMAN

*(Grady and Norman lost in a play-off with Mark
Calcavecchia)*

'I hit out to about 20 ft. That was the best putt I've hit in
my entire life. It was in. But it didn't go in the hole. It was
the first time since Friday lunchtime I wasn't in the lead
on my own.'

THE 118TH OPEN Championship will go down as one with some of
the greatest imponderables. If Wayne Grady had not bunkered
himself on the 71st hole, he would surely have won. If Greg Norman
had not bunkered himself on the 62nd hole, he could have won. If
Mark Calcavecchia had not pitched in on the full on the 66th hole,
he, almost certainly, would not have won. If Tom Watson's 'spitting
snake' had not betrayed him on several holes, he might have won.

A great deal of ifs and buts surrounded the 1989 Open – which
was played over a parched Royal Troon – before the first American
in six years lifted the Auld Claret Jug, following the first four-hole
play-off in the Championship's history. It certainly will go down as
one of the most see-saw Opens of all time. While Calcavecchia gained
on the swings *and* the roundabouts in the end, inevitably it will be
looked upon as a roller-coaster Open at which Norman and Grady
didn't finish the ride.

For Greg Norman, it was yet another chapter in his own personal
copy of major mishaps. Two years earlier, at Augusta, he had already

seen Seve Ballesteros make the long march back to the clubhouse as the first to fall in a three-man play-off for the Masters title. With Larry Mize's ball nestling awkwardly down in the dip and him already safely on the green, Norman had understandably eagerly awaited the denouement before he prepared to receive the famous Green Jacket. Then Mize pitched in. In 1986, Norman had looked odds-on to be wearing the Green Jacket. Then a bogey on the 72nd hole handed it over to Jack Nicklaus. Then, in the US PGA in 1986, it was Bob Tway doing the dirty, holing his bunker-shot to deny Norman another major title. At least in 1986 the Great White Shark had not been bitten. His victory in the Open Championship was decisive. However, one major title out of four was not such a good average. And it was not going to improve in 1989.

Grady, with five years in Asia and five years on the European Tour under his belt before trying his hand in America, had no history of underachievement. In fact, even though he had already featured in three World Cups for Australia, he was just becoming a real force in golf when he came to a burnished Troon, having recently won for the first time on the US PGA Tour, the Westchester Classic. Grady remembers how he looked forward to making an impact for the first time in an Open:

'I didn't go there thinking I was going to win, but I'd never played an Open, at that stage, in such good form. I'd been playing three months' solid golf. My victory in the Westchester helped me feel the best I ever had, coming to the Championship, and made me feel a lot better about going to Troon. Every time in the past, I'd not been playing well enough. I'd played well at St Andrews in 1984 but missed the cut. The year before, I was one behind after the first round and finished 38th. I wanted to finish off better this time.'

Having made the switch to the American tour that year, Grady's results started to plummet. He missed eight cuts in eleven events before a lot of hard work reached fruition.

'It's easy to work hard when you're getting results, but it was getting harder and harder to work because I was not getting anything from it. I didn't know what I was doing. I did a little bit of work with David Leadbetter, but I'm a difficult person to teach. I listened to a few things here and there and then worked things out for myself. I didn't hit a fairway bunker all week. Whenever you can keep the ball out of the fairway bunkers in an Open, you have a chance of doing well.

'I played fantastically in the practice rounds. Jack Newton was out walking around one day and I know he was a bit surprised how well I was hitting it.

'I played the first two rounds with Peter Baker and I played really well. Peter and I have a bit of a joke about it every time we see each other because I played so well. He reckons I didn't miss a shot in two days. It was a pretty good, honest round.

'My irons were good. If you missed your iron-shots, you could miss the green by 50 yards because it was so dry and fast-running. Then you had your work cut out to get the ball back on the green.'

In a round containing five birdies, Grady's only blemish came at the short 17th. It was a hole that was to defy him for much of the week and, in the end, deny him his victory chance.

A first-round 68 showed that Grady could be a force. He sat in a large group two strokes off the lead held by another Wayne, this one Channel Islander Wayne Stephens. A 66 finished in gathering gloom kept the hacks working late, as Stephens, a pre-qualifier, became the latest surprise leader of an Open first round. Stephens enjoyed his morning in some of the newspapers, then left the stage.

The other Wayne certainly didn't go away. A second-round 67 by Grady projected him into a two-shot lead over Payne Stewart, who broke the course record with a 65, and Tom Watson, who was making yet another bid for that elusive sixth Open title that would put him on a par with Harry Vardon.

Four front-nine birdies and two straight after the turn showed Grady was waxing rather than waning. His only blemish came at the 9th. The 17th again proved a trial, but this time Grady escaped with a par.

'When I hit it into the trap at 17, I could see myself hitting the lip, coming back in and having to struggle. I was plugged, but I hit my sand-wedge to 20 ft and made the putt to save par. I worked hard for par on the last two holes. It would have been a shame to have let it go on the last two. I tended to get a little bit ahead of myself, trying to finish the round at 17, instead of playing a shot at a time.

'I drove the ball well and wasn't silly, not trying to hit it really close to the flag, just playing smart golf, not doing anything silly, being very patient. You don't try to take on the course too much – take a one-iron or even a three-iron off the tee sometimes. It was so dry, if you started attacking the flag and finished on the wrong side, you were dead. I played pretty conservatively over the first two days.

'It was a very nice position to be in – very interesting, never having had a good major championship before. I wasn't surprised to be there. I'd played nicely. Everything felt good.'

Grady was anxious to keep his good run going – anxious enough to not want to change his sleeping arrangements at that stage. It was a sort of feng shui, he explains:

'We'd rented a house with Mike and Debbie Clayton, and there were only two bedrooms. Mike and Debbie had the double bed, my wife Lyn was in the single bed in the other room and I slept down in the lounge. Mike missed the cut, and on Friday they went back down to London, so we had the house to ourselves. But I didn't move. I kept sleeping on the lounger for the rest of the week. I'm a little bit superstitious in those things, so I made sure I didn't move.'

As far as Saturday went, it worked. A bogey-free 69 saw Grady maintain the lead, with two birdies after the turn and another on the 16th.

'I chipped and putted well and drove the ball well, but my irons were suspect. Chipping and putting well was important. I made a good round out of a so-so round.

'At Troon, you make the most of the birdies chances over the first 11 holes and then try to hold on over the tough holes coming in.'

Again, he had to battle with the 17th, the hole that gave him the most trouble during the week. He once more missed the green but produced an inspired chip to less than 6 in. to save par. What he would have given to be able to have repeated that feat the next day.

His hard work, and maybe refusal to leave the lounge couch, left Grady with a one-stroke lead over Tom Watson, who was on the brink of equalling that long-standing record again. Payne Stewart was two shots behind. Tellingly, Calcavecchia, worried enough about his wife going into labour that he was threatening to down tools and fly home, was one of those three strokes off the lead.

However, despite leading, Grady didn't command too many headlines on Sunday morning. Most were saved for Watson's bid for that elusive sixth Open title. He recalls:

'I'd been reading one paper for 15 minutes before I knew I was in the lead! I thought it was very interesting. Tom Watson was obviously the one everyone was talking about. They wanted Tom to win his sixth Open, and I could understand that. I was no one. Every article in the papers the next morning was about Tom and very little about me.

'Tom's my hero. As much as Jack Nicklaus was the greatest of all time, Tom's my favourite. And here I was, going to be playing with him in the final round.'

That just added to the thoughts scrambling around Grady's head on Saturday night when he got his head down on that lounge sofa.

'I didn't sleep that well. I was never a good sleeper when I was playing; my wife will attest to that. When I was competing, I could get a little testy and uppity. When the heat was on, I was not the best sleeper. That was one of the biggest difficulties about that Open – well, most tournaments when you're leading. I tend to wake up very early. I was up at five o'clock every morning and then you're not hitting off until 2.30 of an afternoon if you're in the lead at the weekend. That leaves a lot of time to kill, a lot of thoughts going through your head. It amazes me to hear people say they went to bed early and woke up at 10 o'clock. I've never slept until 10 o'clock in my life. I just don't know how they do that.

'You're always worried, because it was my first time in that position. On the other hand, I was playing that well, and generally I can normally calm myself down and take things one step at a time when I'm playing well and thinking well. I just thought about using a little bit of common sense in the final round.

'As a sports person, the worst thing you can do is to get too far ahead of yourself. So I was trying to make sure I didn't do that: think about winning an Open. Waking up at five o'clock and not playing until 2.30, I had nine hours of trying not to think about what would happen if I won!'

At last, Grady could concentrate on warming up on the range for his final push. No one had given Greg Norman much of a thought to this point. At the start of the day, he was seven strokes behind Grady and seemingly out of the hunt. He began his final round over one and a half hours before the final group out. Then the Shark bit.

A breathtaking surge from the start saw him run in six successive birdies. The crowd waiting for the leaders to tee-off broke ranks and rushed out onto the course to see the spectacle as Norman's birdie feats finally caught the notice of the leaderboard operators.

After his magnificent run, Norman was now definitely in the reckoning. Having played what he called 'the pitch of my life' to capture his sixth consecutive birdie, the combatants that had begun their rounds in contention wondered just what he was capable of shooting. Would it all be over before they even got in?

At the 7th, Norman's blistering attack finally eased with a par. Then the Shark met his match, snapped back at by a minnow and given a wound that was to prove, in the end, mortal.

The 126-yard 'Postage Stamp' 8th is one of the Open Championship's legendary tests, a treacherously deceptive green surrounded by bunker minefields. Norman found one of the minefields. It cost him a bogey. It cost him the Open.

It took three more holes to get his impetus, and the shot, back. Birdies at the 11th and 12th gave him hope that he was going to do enough to win in real time. When he picked up another shot at the 16th and then holed out with his sand-iron at the short 17th to preserve a wonderful round of 64, Norman had to sit back and hope he had set an unassailable target. His remarkable record final round was pure Shark, basking in a confident, penetrative swing and sublime short-game. And it came after what some might call divine inspiration: advice given by a trio of golfing gods.

One of the gods, from the constellation of the great Bear, told Norman something that in the subsequent play-off he might have done well to remember.

'It was a pretty good combination: Nicklaus, Floyd and Weiskopf, plus me. They all gave me encouragement before I played the final round. Nicklaus said he was disappointed with the way I played 18 [in the third round]. I'd played it too aggressively. I was trying to hit too close. He said, "Think about it more and where to put it." Put brain in my game.

'Raymond Floyd said, "You need to shoot a good score – but don't try to force it."

'Tom Weiskopf called and said, "You are playing as good as your swing. Put a little finesse into your game, too." I did.

'I had a dream, seeing three threes, and that's a pretty positive thought to go out with. Once I had birdied the first three, I just knew I was going to birdie 4. I just told myself to get the ball on the fairway and I knew it would be another. I hit a shot in the middle of the 5th, and when I reached the green I could picture the ball going into the hole. At the 6th, I said, "It's a par-five. I'm going to birdie this."

'I thought I would birdie 7, but I got a bit clumsy with the tee-shot. When I bogeyed 8, I said, "That's your only mistake of the day. Leave it at that and it will be good."'

But it wasn't good. After getting a telephone call from Australian Prime Minister Bob Hawke, who said he was very happy that the Australians were up there, Norman then had a long wait before finding out he had come up one stroke short of outright victory.

First of all, that was because of two outrageous acts by Mark Calcavecchia. On the 11th, the roly-poly American found bushes on both sides of the course but holed a raking 40-footer to save par. Then, on the 12th, he committed the act that would eventually lead to the ultimate triumph in strokeplay golf.

By his own admission 'all over the place, even into the gallery' on the 12th, he hit what at first he thought was a woeful chip, thinning his shot from the rough 40 ft above the green. Calcavecchia said later he thought at that moment, already four strokes behind Grady when he played the hole, his chance was gone. However, instead of shooting 30 ft past, his ball hit the flagstick like an incensed ram, then dived neatly into the cup for the spectacular birdie that would subsequently catapult him to unimaginable fame – unthinkable even at mid-afternoon on Sunday, 23 July 1989.

Another birdie followed on the 16th for Calcavecchia – only one behind Norman's target. When he birdied the last, as he knew he had to, hitting in to only 4 ft, Calcavecchia's resultant 68 left him tied with Norman on 13-under-par.

By that time, Grady was coming towards the end of his round. His first task had been to shrug off the attention of a five-times winner of the Open. The Queenslander says he was surprised to find his hero not at his best:

'Tom was out of it pretty early. He didn't present much of a challenge because he struggled on the last day, so he wasn't the player I was worried about. I could see from the leaderboard that Greg had birdied the first six holes. It wasn't until later that I heard what Calcavecchia did, but I saw from the board that he was a threat later on, too. I was trying to take that all in my stride.'

Showing admirable calm outwardly and plenty of acumen, too, Grady moved to fifteen-under-par after eleven holes, which was two shots better than the subsequent targets of Norman and Calcavecchia. The first of Troon's last two par-threes, though, confounded Grady. He feels his bogey there proved even more significant than his error three holes later:

'I didn't get on very well at the 17th for the week, which is understandable because it's one of the hardest par-threes around. But the 14th, the par-three, is what really killed me. I hit a six-iron on the green to about 35 ft, right of the flag. It wasn't a really good tee-shot, but it was on the green. I hit it down to about 3 ft and missed the second putt. That left me only one in front.'

Grady could not afford any more mistakes. Royal Troon, though, proved a bigger foe than any opponent over the closing holes.

'I hit a great second shot on 15, but the ball just caught the downslope and leapt forward. Instead of being a foot away, it finished 30 ft behind the hole. On 16, I hit 12 ft left of the hole with a nine-iron. Then I hit the second-best putt I hit all week. It didn't go in.'

His playing-partner Watson, too, got nothing from the course, and his slim chance of that sixth Open title disappeared at the 16th when his solid 25-footer looked as though it would drop but failed to do the honourable thing for such an Open doyen.

Troon's final short hole, the 223-yard 17th, protected by breeze, bunker and bounds, finally undid Grady's bid to win in real time. His tee-shot left him 30 yards short of the green in the forward trap.

'I hit one of the worst tee-shots I'd hit all week, to go in the bunker. I hit out to about 20 ft. That was the best putt I've hit in my entire life. It was in. But it didn't go in the hole. It was the first time since Friday lunchtime I wasn't in the lead on my own.'

A bogey left him needing a birdie on the last to win, or a par to meet up with Norman and Calcavecchia. Considering the disappointment of the penultimate hole of the Championship, Grady did well not to drop a shot after hitting through the back of the 18th green.

His dream could have been over there and then, but his courageous par left him sharing a historic finale. The play-off to decide the 1989 Open was the first to go to a four-hole shoot-out, the R & A having deemed this the best way to decide a tie. Grady had to regroup quickly. The pendulum had swung away. He recognised the play-off advantage might not be with him:

'I was trying to calm myself down. Greg and Calc had been finished for a long time. All of a sudden, they're happy to be in a play-off. I'd given them the chance. I was still thinking I could win but also saying to myself, "Right. Settle down. Let's get stuck into this play-off."

'I'd like to say, I think the R & A showed great initiative in introducing the four-hole play-off. Sudden-death is too quick, and 18 holes is logistically too difficult.'

Holes 1, 2, 17 and 18 provided the play-off arena. Whereas it had been Grady's tournament to win and all the focus had been on him, when the play-off began the Claret Jug was passed over to Norman for temporary custody. A birdie at the first put the Shark in the ascendancy. Grady and Calcavecchia, who needed to hole a six-footer to save, only made pars.

Calcavecchia briefly caught Norman by holing a 30-ft birdie putt on the second extra hole. The Shark's ten-footer, though, saw him go two-under and stay one shot ahead of Calcavecchia, two in front of Grady, who admits his head was spinning, rather:

'Everything happened so quickly. All of a sudden, I was out of the lead I'd held since Friday. It didn't affect me going straight out. That's just the way it is. Some people come straight off the course and go well in a play-off. But maybe I was expecting to try and ease my way into it, instead of saying to myself, "Come on; we've got to go. And we've got to go hard."

'I said to myself, "Hang on, I'm in trouble here. I've got to do something about this." Then we went to my "favourite" hole, the 17th.'

There the Claret Jug changed hands for the final time. On the 17th, Grady found the sand again. Norman's tee-shot was just a little too strong. His ball overshot and went into the semi-rough behind the green. A pitch, also too strong, left Norman with a 12-footer. He missed. Grady recovered expertly to 8 ft. He also missed.

One hole to go in the play-off and then sudden-death if necessary. Norman and Calcavecchia were one-under; Grady one-over.

On the fourth extra hole – the deadly 18th with its tight fairway, lurking bunkers and out of bounds behind the green – Calcavecchia sprayed his drive badly right. The 29-year-old Nebraskan's luck held, though. His ball glanced back from press photographers kneeling in front of the gallery, when it could have bounced another 25 yards into heavier rough. He found a decent lie in trodden-down, spiky hay.

Norman, fatally, reached for his driver. He launched a typically piercing drive – too penetrating. His ball faded in, took a huge leap forward and hurled itself into a greedy cross-bunker. With houses adjoining the course only a few yards from the right of the fairway with their windows open on a sultry early evening, the words of commentator Peter Alliss drifted down next to the fateful bunker, explaining the Shark's possible doom. He was not going to be able to reach the green now. Norman turned angrily to his caddie in frustration and apprehension and said, 'Dammit, the guy's telling me how to play the shot!'

Before Norman had a chance to make what was to be his last throw of the dice, Calcavecchia produced an incisive and Open-winning five-iron shot to just 7 ft. Norman tried in vain to find the green, only to see his ball dribble into another bunker well short. Grady hit on. His chances were gone already. Norman projected his ball out of bounds and, after being reminded it was not matchplay and he should hit another, turned to Calcavecchia and said, 'Carry on. If you happen to four-putt, I'll hit another.'

With no pressure then, apart from worrying whether he might have a 'double-hit', Calcavecchia slid home the putt to leave Wayne Grady, Greg Norman and Bob Hawke three very disappointed Australians.

Norman took defeat with dignity but cursed the scorched 18th fairway, blaming a cruel forward-bounce for costing him his second successive Open Championship.

'Unfortunately my ball landed on a hard patch. I had 318 yards to the bunker.'

As he later told Lauren St John in her book *Shooting at Clouds*:

> To this day I would not have hit another shot. I still believe, if that ball had landed six or eight feet left or short of where it landed, it would never have reached the bunker, because that bunker wasn't in play all week.
>
> 'Now you'll read where people say that bunker was in play; it's always been in play. I know exactly how far I hit the golf ball, but it was just one of those things. I've watched the

replay and slowed it down. It landed right on top of a hard mound and skidded.

'But, you know, that's seaside golf. That's the way the game crumbles.'

Grady tried to hang on but admits he had seen his chance crumble too. He endorses Norman's theory:

'It wasn't over until Calc hit that shot into the 18th. Then it was.

'A lot of people have criticised Greg for his tee-shot, but in the final round I hit a great tee-shot there and I was 25 yards short of that bunker. He hit this big, high cut down there, then bent down and picked the tee up, thinking it was perfect. I did, too – bent down and teed my ball up. And then we could hear the oohs and aahs of the crowd. We knew then the ball had gone in the bunker. No one had got anywhere near that bunker. It was just one of those adrenalin moments. Everyone criticises Greg for taking the driver, but realistically no one could have thought he could get to the bunker with a driver.

'Calc hit a great shot. He'd hit a great shot from there in the final round. It was quite ironic: when we were at Troon in 2004, I went over to see him. He was practising flop-shots over a bunker. As I walked over to him, he flushed one straight over the green. I said to him, "Yeah; it's a shame you didn't do that back in 1989 on the 12th! It would have saved everyone a lot of heartache."'

Grady could find little consolation in sharing the runners-up honours. A golden chance to add his name alongside those of Peter Thomson, Kel Nagle and, indeed, Greg Norman had gone. He says, though, that right there and then he made a vow that defeat would not bow him:

'I'm not a great player. I was a good player who worked his bum off. Not too many people get a chance to win a major championship, so it was quite gut-wrenching, to be honest. But I made a promise to myself that wouldn't be the end of me. I'd make sure I kept going and tried to win one. That's the only thing that kept me going, to be quite honest.

ABOVE: Hats off to Jacklin. But it was Lee Trevino (right) who won when the chips were down at Muirfield in 1972. (© Cleva)

LEFT: Both hands on the Claret Jug for Jack Newton (left), but Tom Watson was the winner after a play-off in 1975 at Carnoustie.

ABOVE: *No comprendo*! A 19-year-old Seve Ballesteros shares a joke after receiving his runner-up's cheque in 1976 at Royal Birkdale, without knowing what it was about. Johnny Miller may have helped with the translation.

BELOW: Round on the rocks at Turnberry: Jack Nicklaus (left) and Tom Watson sit out a storm delay in 1977, the 'Duel in the Sun'. Later, they had to sit out some unruly crowd behaviour.

One hand on the Golden Bear: Simon Owen (left) congratulates Jack Nicklaus on his 1978 victory at St Andrews.

It's all going right for Nick Price at this stage in 1982 at Royal Troon.

Bernhard Langer in action at
Royal St George's in 1985.

Paul Azinger finally loses
his hold on the Claret Jug
at Muirfield's 18th-hole
bunker in 1987.

ABOVE: Costantino Rocca on his knees after a 'vision' comes true in 1995 at St Andrews. Michael Campbell can't believe his eyes.

BELOW: Darren Clarke (right) and Jesper Parnevik battle it out at Royal Troon in 1997. Both had to settle for second best.

ABOVE: Jean Van de Velde preparing to lower himself into the Barry Burn at Carnoustie in 1999 – minutes too late.

RIGHT: Ian Woosnam disposes of the 'fifteenth club', the extra driver, at the second in 2001 at Royal Lytham and St Annes. Referee John Paramor shows sympathy, while caddie Myles Byrne looks rueful.

ABOVE: Thomas Levet splashes out of the fairway bunker on 18 in sudden-death, before finally losing out to Ernie Els in 2002 at Muirfield.

BELOW: Finger of fate: Thomas Björn's ball has rolled back into the 16th-hole bunker for a second time in the final round of the 2003 Open at Royal St George's.

All over now: Ernie Els (left) congratulates Todd Hamilton after the American had clinched the play-off in 2004 at Royal Troon.

Full Monty: Colin Montgomerie happy at running Tiger Woods close for a while in 2005 at St Andrews.

'When you talk to Doug Sanders and ask him if he thinks about 1970, he says on a good day he goes about five minutes without thinking about it. If I hadn't won the PGA the next year, I might have been the same as Doug. I made a concerted effort not to let it rule me, losing that play-off.

'It was only that that helped me win the PGA, because it was exactly the same scenario. I'd been in the lead since Friday lunchtime when I lost it on the 12th. I remembered all the disappointment for my family and friends when I lost the Open after almost having it, and I stood on the 13th tee thinking, "Here we go again." I started thinking about everyone at home watching on TV at four o'clock in the morning and I said to myself, "Don't be an idiot." I gave myself an uppercut, said, "This is not over yet," and I finished up winning.

'But it was losing the Open the year before that helped me win the PGA.'

1989 TOP SCORES
M. Calcavecchia 71–68–68–68 275
W. Grady 68–67–69–71 275
G. Norman 69–70–72–64 275
(Calcavecchia won four-hole play-off)
T. Watson 69–68–68–72 277

1990, ST ANDREWS:
GREG NORMAN AND IAN BAKER-FINCH

(Sharing the lead with eventual winner Nick Faldo,
Norman's victory chances were ended by a third-round
76. Baker-Finch lost his way in the final round again)

'I just putted terribly. I had a couple of bad breaks on the
12th and 13th and that was the end of my day.'

EVEN BEFORE THE 1990 Open began, it was billed as the
Faldo–Norman roadshow. They were the two players most talked
about before battle commenced, and they were the two favourites,
with little to choose between them as to who was chief favourite.
Maybe Faldo just had the edge.

Faldo had won his second successive Masters just over three
months before. Norman was aching to go one better this time after
his crushing disappointment in the Troon Open the previous year.
The Great White Shark, remembering back to his 1989 play-off
demise, refused to be downbeat when tackling his latest Open.

'I have good memories of last year, especially my 64 in the last
round. I was disappointed, but I really felt I didn't play badly at all.
Unfortunately for me, on the last play-off hole my ball landed on a
hard patch. I had 318 yards to the bunker. To this day, I would not
hit any other shot off the tee than the one I did.'

It was not just the previous year, though, that Norman wanted to
try to forget in getting on with his latest challenge. There was 1986,
when his wayward approach at the last cost him the Masters. Then

146

there was Bob Tway. Then there was Larry Mize. Norman quite rightly felt the majors owed him. Now was the time to cash in. He was enjoying a splendid season. All facets of his game were good, he reported. And he loved St Andrews, a course where his renowned penetrative driving could whittle down par-fours and reduce par-fives to par-fours. All he had to do, he surmised, in his pre-tournament press conference, was to hit the ball the way he had done all season, stay out of the bunkers and putt well all week.

Putt well all week. Some of that projected plan was to go terribly awry.

By the time the first two rounds had unfolded, there was still nothing between Faldo and Norman. They were locked on top of the leaderboard together. However, even if they had swapped blow for blow as far as scoring was concerned, they had not locked horns. After they did on the Saturday, there was a good deal to choose between them. There was to be no repeat of 1977, when Nicklaus and Watson duelled in the sun. As in days of yore, one knight carried on with his colours high; the other was left to tend to his wounds.

Then others rose to challenge the champion. Paul Broadhurst, with a St Andrews record, and Ian Baker-Finch, trying to put right at the Home of Golf on the Old Course what had gone wrong six years before, both put a loose grip on the trophy. So did Payne Stewart, another one trying to get it right after just missing out in 1985. Another Australian, Craig Parry, was also in with a chance.

Faldo's play-off victory over Ray Floyd in the Masters that year had left him ambitious to do the double and pull off his second Open triumph. However, it was his victory at Augusta the previous year that caught the headlines before the first round. Faldo and Scott Hoch, the man defeated in the 1989 Augusta play-off by the tall and imperious Englishman, were drawn together for Thursday and Friday, and that was rather unfortunate in one way. Several newspapers had gone with stories about Hoch disliking Faldo, whom he was just dying to better in a major after the American's failure in the Masters by missing that two-footer in extra time. Hoch denied all quotes when he met up with Faldo on the tee, but the brouhaha that was caused took some of the steam out of the much-awaited bids by the two chief rivals.

Blistering starts by the pair, though, soon had the headline-writers hard at work projecting something more positive and less subjective than any spat between characters.

Norman was delighted with his score, a flawless card containing six birdies which ended with a fifteen-footer on 18 for a six-under-par 66 to ensure he shared the lead with American Michael Allen. It was a just desert for the ultimate in preparation by Norman, who observed:

'I thought any score in the 60s would be good to start with. The breeze came from the opposite direction we had been practising all week. I had started to play the course in my mind before going out. Having played in the Dunhill Cup, I knew what to expect. I then took advantage of knowing the direction of the wind and played well. The wind is more difficult playing downwind on the back nine than into it.

'Every time you go out in a major, you look to shoot a good score. It is tough, though. I took advantage of every situation I was given. You have to accept what you get given. I try the best I can every time, but sometimes it just doesn't work out. It all goes in a cycle.'

Norman's cycle had swung in his favour. It was going to need a big finish from his chief rival to keep on his shirt tail. Faldo had that big finish. A pitch-and-run from forty yards out after favouring his two-wood off the tee took Faldo's ball into the cup for an eagle-two to leave him only a stroke behind Norman in third place on his own. The gauntlets were down, as Faldo signed for a 67.

By late afternoon the next day, the gloves were off. Norman came in with another 66, his round founded on a string of four successive birdies from the 7th and fashioned spectacularly by a shot even more sensational than Faldo's finale the previous day. On the long 14th, Norman used his renowned chief weapon, his ball-spin, to suck back a seventy-five-yard approach into the hole for an eagle-three.

With Norman sharp-shooting like that, it called for something equally flamboyant from his chief opponent. Faldo did not disappoint, outscoring Norman with a brilliant 65, stitching in seven birdies on a perfectly embroidered card.

Faldo and Norman had plundered St Andrews, thus far, for twenty-three birdies and two eagles. On twelve-under-par, they held a four-shot lead over Payne Stewart and Australian Craig Parry. The inevitable Nick Price was five behind in a group that also included England's Jamie Spence, who had briefly led in the morning with a splendid round of 65.

The top pair were fully aware of what the third round was going to mean – a head-to-head between the two best players in the tournament.

Norman, recognising fully what lay ahead, said on Friday evening:

'I definitely feel I can win this week. That will be my approach: to go for it tomorrow. I am not really that excited; I feel happy and comfortable and feel relaxed in my position. I am enjoying the game and I am not charged up or excited. If I don't come out and do something spectacular tomorrow, I will still be in a good position come Sunday. St Andrews is a place where we all want to win. As for a shoot-out with Faldo, it doesn't matter to me who I play with. Faldo and I grew up together in Europe. We've been together for over a decade since 1977. We know each other very well. We are friends. I bear no ill feeling towards him at all.'

An outwardly relaxed Faldo sounded as though he would relish the chance to take on Norman in what could be a fight to the death between them:

'We are all sailing along. Greg and I are playing well, holing putts and seizing opportunities. It's real good stuff. We are trying to chase each other. Tied at 12-under is a good position for both of us to be in. There's a long way to go and you have to play as hard as you can.'

The next day, Faldo was as good as his word. Norman, though, could not live with him. A 67 by Faldo took him five strokes ahead of the field. Norman's luckless 76 left him nine strokes behind, his dreams of a second Open title shattered. The Great White Shark's round was the epitome of Murphy's Law, which states that 'When a slice of bread and butter falls to the floor, it will always land butter-side down.' Norman just could not do a thing right. At the second hole, for instance, he missed a three-footer after Faldo had trundled in his birdie putt from all of 18 ft. Was it nerves? Was it the presence of Faldo? Was it just Murphy's Law? Whatever the reason, a series of three-putts and a couple of balls diving straight into bunkers instead of skipping holewards left Norman choking in Faldo's dust.

'I just putted terribly. I had a couple of bad breaks on the 12th and 13th and that was the end of my day.

'I lost my rhythm with my putter. The putt I missed on the second hole, I guess, was a very makeable putt, but I just hit it too hard and hit through the break. Then the next putt I missed a couple of holes later I hit too soft.

'So now I'm second-guessing myself on the line and speed. As time goes by, I'm getting myself worse and worse. I'm the one in the hole – in the way I feel about my putting.

'Then I hit a good drive on 12, which I thought was perfect, and it [the ball] trickles into the bunker. I hit a drive on 13, which I again thought was perfect, and it rolls into the bunker. And that's where, to me, the whole tournament changed: the tee-shot on 12, where the ball fell into the bunker. I lost my momentum. I lost it even though I was only a couple behind Nick.

'Nick putted extremely well the whole week, there's no question about it. He was making everything he looked at and he had a lot of confidence. And he kept the momentum going. That's what happened. It was the ebb and flow of the momentum.'

Faldo, no doubt inwardly happy to see his arch-opponent vanquished, but outwardly sympathising with Norman, said at the time:

'Greg didn't have the run of the ball. His putting hurt him. Every time he was not getting the breaks or getting the ball close, three-putting was absolutely killing him. He had a really tough day and handled it well.'

Norman had fallen by the wayside. In his stead, another

Australian picked up Faldo's gauntlet – a player who had good reason to want to get his own back on St Andrews and get something out of this Open after a major disappointment in 1984. Ian Baker-Finch had shared the lead going into the final round that year. This time, he shared second place with Payne Stewart, five shots behind Faldo. Parry was on eleven-under, in fourth place. Broadhurst's magnificent 63 left him a further stroke back.

Baker-Finch wondered if he was good enough to keep up with Faldo, his playing-partner in the final round. He says he found out the hard way:

'I felt I had a chance to redeem myself in 1990 after what had happened the last time at St Andrews, and I was playing really, really good. By that time, I'd won on the US Tour, which I was playing full-time, and I was in really good form.

'I had a good start with a 68, then a modest 72. Nick Faldo was playing really, really well, but I thought I could stay with him. Then I shot 64 in the third round. I actually three-putted 17. I was ten-under going to the Road Hole, with a good chance of going really low. I hit a four-wood onto the green at 17 and three-putted. That took the steam out of me a bit and I only parred the last for a 64. It put me in the last group, though.

'So there I was, on the first tee at St Andrews again, in the last group. That, in itself, was a pretty good thing for me.'

That was about the last time Baker-Finch felt completely at ease. Soon, Faldo was even further ahead, making a birdie at the first hole with a mere three-foot putt. While others did get closer to Faldo – Stewart closed to within only two shots at one time and Zimbabwean Mark McNulty came surging through the field to challenge – Baker-Finch rather lost his way in the final round. Not as early as he did six years previously, but still finishing well back in sixth place, seven strokes adrift.

Faldo's total of 18-under-par broke the Open record, as the newly acclaimed 1990 major double-winner finished five strokes ahead of Stewart and McNulty. Baker-Finch says he knew he had to return to the drawing board:

'Faldo was too good and I tried too hard. I putted poorly, took 37 putts. I just couldn't get the ball in the hole. It happens sometimes at St Andrews. You hit a lot of greens and have a lot of long putts. Nick was untouchable. He broke the record that year. I tried too hard. Had I been aiming to run second, I would probably have shot a much better score. But I was trying to beat Nick. Playing with him, I knew I had to do something special, and I just couldn't do it.

'But it was, once again, good experience for me. I got to see Faldo win first-hand and see how he did it. It showed me how focused he was in winning. Everything seemed to be bothering me. The greens were bothering me; there were a hundred television guys on carts; whatever. St Andrews is the worst venue for being crowded by cameramen and photographers, because there is nowhere to go. Everyone's in the confines of the course, so it's always horrendous with carts, media and cameras. At crosswalks, there are thousands of people trying to cross the holes . . . it just got to me. I thought, "Damn. How can I concentrate with all this going on?" Whereas Faldo just kept the blinkers on.

'I think that helped my chances the next year when I came back and won. I redeemed myself for the two chances I'd had. Getting my hand on that trophy means more to me than anything else. It is "the" Open. It was something I'd always dreamt of.

'In '84, I didn't go there thinking of winning. I was just proud to be part of the field. Then I learned a lot from Faldo in 1990. I served my time. After that, I believed in myself enough to feel I could do it if I had the chance again.'

And how did the man who was supposed to be Faldo's arch-opponent that week feel? Greg Norman had to take another setback on the chin, having to settle for a share of sixth place with his compatriot.

Like Baker-Finch, though, Norman came back. And in 1993 his putting this time complemented his magnificent long- and short-game that week. Faldo had to take second-best on that occasion. It was a case of Norman taking all the positives out of the brickbats thrown at him in previous majors, instead of sitting back and cursing his bad luck. As Norman told Lauren St John in *Shooting at Clouds*:

> 'If somebody beats you, heck, he beats you. He's better than you on the week. You've got to say to yourself, "Well, I'll go out there and work harder and beat him next time." Sure, your confidence can go down very quickly. It's happened to me over the years. But you know deep down in your gut, it's just a superficial deal. Three months will go by and you'll be bouncing back into the game. You'll then think, "What went wrong?"
>
> 'It's always going to happen, because of the mental and physical parts of your game. Your mental fits your physical and vice-versa. It's an amazing contrast of passions.
>
> 'Your mind is so strong. And if it's strong on the negative side, then you'll never play great golf. But if it's strong on the positive side, then you're going to be around for a long time. No matter what people do to you.'

1990 TOP SCORES
N. Faldo 67–65–67–71 270
M. McNulty 74–68–68–65 275
P. Stewart 68–68–68–71 275
I. Woosnam 68–69–70–69 276
J. Mudd 72–66–72–66 276
G. Norman 66–66–76–69 277
I. Baker-Finch 68–72–64–73 277

1992, MUIRFIELD: JOHN COOK

(Cook led eventual winner Nick Faldo by
two strokes with just two holes to go)

'On 17, I thought I had made the first putt. As the ball
went past the hole, it was starting to break. My second
putt was probably about $2\frac{1}{2}$ ft, and I thought it was going
to break a little bit to the right. I did not put a very good
stroke on it.'

THERE WAS A good deal of déjà vu about the '92 Open, flashbacks to
1987. As with Paul Azinger five years previously, an American came
to the Muirfield course on a crest of a wave and returned across the
Atlantic beaten by Nick Faldo. And, just like Azinger, he was beaten
when he had led with just two holes to go.

John Cook could have made his second Open a triumphant one,
whereas Azinger was making his debut in 1987. However, Cook had
little experience of the Open, having missed the cut in his only other
appearance in 1980, when he had been a pro for only two years,
although that was also at Muirfield.

Like Azinger five years before, Cook won three times on the US
Tour that year and was certainly not considered a rank outsider for
the 1992 Open. The 1978 US Amateur champion, talked of at that
time as the 'next Nicklaus', had finished fourth in the US Open as far
back as 1981 and, at 34, despite his Open Championship
inexperience, had the ability to be the latest American player to
make his mark in Britain. Just like Azinger, in fact.

Several years of niggling injuries, especially to a wrist which had been operated on three years before, had held Cook back. But 1992 looked like being his red-letter year.

It was. But it turned out to be more blue than red in the 1992 Open.

As far as Faldo was concerned, he had gone into the 1987 Muirfield Open with no 'favourite' tag attached. He hadn't even been sure if a two-year swing renovation would work, and Faldo had never won a major until prevailing against the flagging Azinger.

This time, Faldo was a strong favourite to collect his fifth major title, to go with his Open successes of '87 and '90 and wins in the '89 and '90 Masters. He was in his pomp. Like Cook, he had won on his home European Tour before contesting the Open. And, as Azinger found five years before, having 90 per cent of the crowd on your side could be worth a couple of strokes.

Having enjoyed plenty of success at US Tour level, with two titles under his belt before he arrived on the east coast of Scotland, Cook decided it was time to move up a level.

'My game had got to the point where I needed to do something in the major championships. But my experience was so limited [in the Open] that I didn't know what to expect. I knew I was playing well enough to win, though. I felt I was right.

'I'd had some injuries in the past. They started in the early '80s, and I had part of a bone extracted from my right hand in '89. It had kept healing then breaking. It got to the point in '89 where I just could not hold my hands together. It started to move under the index finger and the joints were all disintegrating. I took three or four weeks off every year because I felt it was about that time to do so.

'It meant I was never very consistent. It got so frustrating that I had to get something done if I was to get to the level of the game I wanted to get to. I had surgery on my hand in March '89 and hit my first balls then in October. I went from wondering if my career might be over to having a new lease of life.'

While injury was not something Cook now had to worry about,

he did have one other problem that held his practice back a little. His clubs went missing somewhere between checking in over in America and arriving in Scotland. He had to wait a day until they were located. He took it in his stride, though. Cook was no stranger to losing his favourite weapons. In 1987, his clubs went missing during a flight from Tampa to New Orleans. They didn't turn up until three years later. They were discovered in a pawn shop in San Francisco, and he had to buy them back for $300!

That was just one of the stories Cook had to tell before the championship got under way. Another was that he had an old schoolfriend on the bag instead of his regular caddie. When the vital club selections came along, though, would the lack of his regular caddie prove a critical one? The same sort of question that sprang to mind about Azinger and 1987. More déjà vu.

Cook had missed the 1984 Open because of injury, and several more because he couldn't justify the expense. His only other excursion to the Open had resulted in two rounds of 75 and a missed cut when he qualified for the 1980 Championship on a US-amateur exemption. He intended to do much better this time.

'I was very excited about playing. I didn't come over to beat the world or anything, but it had been a good year and I wanted to play well in the British Open, play well in all the majors. I'd played decently in the other two.'

This time, Cook was to play far better than decently. A first-round 66 was better than decent, for a start. It wasn't good enough to lead, however. On a day of low scoring, veteran Ray Floyd and Steve Pate, the man who had missed the singles in the Ryder Cup the previous year because of injury and sparked controversy in America's win over Europe at Kiawah Island, led with rounds of 64.

The Faldo forces were at work already. Floyd, never a bosom pal of Faldo's anyway, had lost to the Briton at sudden-death in the 1990 Masters. After the first round at Muirfield, he led Faldo by two strokes. And he also led Cook by two strokes.

Floyd, only six weeks away from his fiftieth birthday, was enjoying an Indian summer to his career. He had won twice on the

US Tour in 1992 and finished second again in the Masters, this time to Fred Couples. It was, though, to be Floyd's last hurrah in the Open, in majors, and the next day he began the fade that eventually left him well down the field. Pate, though, stayed in contention right until Sunday afternoon in the final round.

The top pair led by a stroke from 1991 Masters winner Ian Woosnam and Gordon Brand Junior, with two more now-big names sharing fifth place with Faldo and Cook: Ernie Els and Lee Janzen, both soon to be US Open champions.

With little wind for the first round, Muirfield, the sergeant-major of Open courses, had little bark, let alone bite. No fewer than 35 players shot in the 60s. Pundits said it boded well for an American victory if the weather stayed clement.

There are two significant facts from the first round: Nick Faldo struggled over the closing two holes; John Cook had just the opposite sort of finish. While Faldo bunkered himself on the long 17th and settled for par, then had to hole a six-footer on the last to avoid bogey, Cook ran in an eagle putt on 17. Significant facts if you fast-forward to the final round!

Stronger winds greeted the players on the Friday, and in the second round Muirfield was at last able to bare its teeth. Floyd, suffering with his putting, gradually slid off the leaderboard in the morning, while Cook, again playing alongside Davis Love III and Rodger Davis, benefited from a spectacular eagle early in his round to replace the veteran first-round front-runner.

At the long 5th, Cook, having done his share of scrambling beforehand, found himself in the greenside bunker after powering a three-wood approach against the strong wind. He pitched in from 50 ft away. When he birdied three of the next six holes as well, Cook moved to the top of the leaderboard.

Bogeys on the 12th and 13th holes held him back, but again he mastered the penultimate hole, almost adding his second eagle there and his second of the day. His putt from 30 ft brushed the lip of the hole but stayed out, leaving him a tap-in to briefly hold the lead until his nemesis Faldo took over.

A round of 67, though, took Cook to a share of second place. Faldo roared into a three-shot lead on twelve-under-par by shooting a 64. Faldo's 130 for the opening two rounds broke the Open thirty-six-hole aggregate by two strokes. Joining Cook in second place – a stroke better than Steve Pate – was Gordon Brand Junior. Cook was happy to have beaten the Muirfield gusts and delighted his form had swung back.

'If the week before had been any indication of how I was going to play in the British Open, and not only that but be nine-under after two rounds, I would have called anyone who predicted it crazy. I'd never found the middle of the club the previous week and missed the cut.

'It was difficult driving the ball in the wind, but I hit a lot of good shots. The wind was coming in at an odd angle. But I managed it well. When I did hit into the rough, it was just two or three yards in, not in the parking lot. I could always find the ball and play it.

'I was in four bunkers and got it up and down three times. And I holed out with one of my visits to a bunker. So I had to be pleased. On the 1st hole, I hit one of the best bunker-shots I have ever hit, and that kind of set the stage. The fifth was a real bonus.

'When I teed off, I knew it was going to be a difficult day because it was 8.45 a.m. in Britain and my brain was in bed at just past midnight! So first of all I just wanted to get the ball airborne. In the first round, the wind didn't come into play at all, but when I set off for the second round I knew it was going to.

'The course does give you options. You can either knock the ball down or hit it in the air. I knew this was a day to keep the ball down.

'I learned a little bit more about the course in the second round than I'd known before.'

One man who already knew plenty about Muirfield, of course, was Nick Faldo. After breaking the Open record, Faldo seemed to be at ease with the world. He teased the press, never his favourite people. He was up there, he said, because of a new putting stroke, brushing off questions about his method by saying it was all a secret – with the codename 'Basil'!

Faldo certainly was sweeping along on a crest of a wave. The gallery were with him and it looked as though it would now be a formality, just a question of by how many shots he would win.

When Faldo celebrated his birthday, as he invariably does at the Open, the new 35 year old increased his lead the next day in the third round, shooting a 69 to move to 14-under-par.

Alongside Faldo on the Saturday was John Cook. Playing with the crowd favourite could have affected the American. The British public really only had eyes for one man in their group. Cook, however, rode the tide of support for Faldo and stayed well in contention with a round of 70 that kept him in second place with Steve Pate.

There was another eagle for Cook to savour, this one coming at the par-five 9th. Here he again pitched in, this time from around 90 ft away, with shades of Mark Calcavecchia in 1989 as his ball rattled the flagstick at about the same velocity as a headmaster dealing out a caning. Realising his ball would have travelled at least 20 ft past, Cook fell backwards in delight and acknowledged the crowd's appreciation from a prone position. The gallery might have been highly partisan, but that didn't stop Cook getting his just deserts.

And Cook was again in credit on the 17th. He picked up his fourth shot in three days there by comfortably two-putting from 30 ft. Little did he know how luck would desert him the next day on that hole.

There was no thought of that on the Saturday, though, as Cook gained a good deal of pride from more than surviving alongside the British public's great hero.

'My round wasn't real pretty, that's for sure. I hit a lot of really good shots and some not very good ones. I knew I had to drive the ball a little bit better in the final round. But I hit my irons really solidly and played some pitch shots well. I was excited to be in the position I was in.

'I'd been looking forward to playing with Faldo to see how I would react. There were a lot of people out there but I enjoyed it. I felt far more comfortable out there than I thought I was going to feel.

'I learned that the British fans know golf. I was impressed by the comments as I was walking to the tees.

'I lost concentration a couple of times, but I wasn't disturbed by the crowds rushing away. I never had a problem with the crowd. I wish we could import them home!

'Nick and I talked a little but not much. That's the way he is. If he doesn't want to talk, then that is OK. I'm not a big talker on the course either.'

So Cook had had a dose of 'Faldo Fever' and not been badly infected. He was greatly impressed by Faldo, however. At the time, he said:

'Nick is playing so well you just cannot see him making a bogey anywhere. I know I have got to make some birdies and drive the ball a little better to have any chance to get the lead. Nick is swinging and putting well and he is kind of tough. But strange things happen out there. Nick can be beaten. Golf is such a crazy game.'

Cook's closing words there were to prove prophetic.

Having suffered strong gusts for a couple of days, the course was now subjected to the same conditions as the last day in 1987: misty and drizzly by the time the last two groups went out. Faldo was partnered by Pate. Cook went out in the penultimate group with Ernie Els, who trailed him by two shots. Els shared fourth place with another American, Donnie Hammond, and Brand.

With Faldo looking so indomitable, the bookmakers had him at a staggering 7–4 on for the title, but some urged an air of caution. Already that year, and not that long before the Open, Faldo had come a cropper at the French Open to lose when he was a street ahead, and he had made a meal of the Irish Open when holding a clear lead.

No such frailties were really expected this time, however. As Cook remarked before the final round: 'If there is anyone who doesn't beat himself, it is Nick Faldo.' And as Pate said: 'I don't know anyone I would want to give a four-stroke lead going into the final round of a British Open and least of all Nick Faldo.'

Faldo erred immediately, though, bogeying the 1st and giving his playing-partner Pate a glimmer of hope. Unfortunately for Cook, he bogeyed too, keeping him stationary behind Faldo for the time being.

As the drizzle turned to heavier rain, however, Cook did make headway. After picking up a shot at the 3rd, once again he eagled the 5th, sending a fifteen-footer home on the soaking green like a kid on a water chute, after an admirable five-iron approach. He was only a stroke off Faldo's lead.

Faldo had slipped into neutral and went into a run of pars, in much the same vein as 1987. A bogey on the 7th stopped Cook's momentum, bringing him back to two behind Faldo. Then the 9th hole, which had been so kind to Cook the previous day, took what was to become a dreadful toll on him, as destructive as the mistakes he would make later. He drove out of bounds and ran up a double-bogey. Cook's Open chance looked to have taken flight there and then. It ballooned him back to four strokes behind Faldo.

Faldo's pressure was coming from his playing-partner Pate and from a charging José Maria Olazabal. Then, suddenly, Cook was his foe as well. While Faldo bogeyed 11, 13 with a three-putt, and 14, Cook birdied 12, 15 and 16.

The leaderboard showed a new name on top, that of John Cook. Cook was in Azinger land. He was now two shots ahead of Faldo with just two holes of his own to go. Faldo was in never-never land. He had allowed a four-shot advantage to turn into a two-shot disadvantage. Faldo told himself, 'I'd better play the best four holes of my life now.'

He came close to doing exactly that, beginning by finally finding his first birdie of the day, spearing in a shot that was to prove as crucial as it was exquisite in touch. As Cook played the 17th, he heard ecstatic cheers behind him as Faldo holed a mere three-footer on the 15th after his trusty five-iron had landed his ball in just the perfect spot to allow it to release up to the flag.

That still left Cook a stroke ahead. His response to Faldo's birdie was incisive, as he slammed his three-iron shot into the penultimate green with great aplomb. Cook had eagled the hole once and birdied it twice. It looked as though he would again mug the 17th, as his ball settled around 30 ft from the flag. An eagle would surely win him the Open. A birdie would keep his hand firmly on the jug.

The engraver got out his tools.

Muirfield does not have the reputation for being one of the most capricious finishes of all the Open venues for nothing. And you will only have to remind yourself of previous chapters of this book to know how the 17th and 18th holes have played a major role in deciding whose name the engraver stencils in on the Auld Claret Jug. Remember 1972 and Lee Trevino's chip-in on 17 to snatch the Open from Tony Jacklin? And there was Azinger, bunkering himself on the final two holes to hand the trophy to the very same Faldo.

John Cook found that the last two holes turned their back on him as well.

At first, though, the gallery, those not desperately urging Faldo on behind, thought Cook had struck a mortal blow as his putt headed for the hole. It caught the edge of the hole but failed to drop.

Behind, Faldo pulled off a great escape with a chip stone dead from over the back of the 16th green.

Cook's ball had seemed to veer fractionally as it approached the hole. From just over 2 ft away, he estimated the slight borrow and pressed the trigger on his birdie putt. Faldo supporters held their breath, fearing their hero still had too much to do. The ball gently kissed the cup. But it was of a lover ending an affair with a parting caress, because it again refused to drop. It was the first goodbye to John Cook's Open hopes.

He very nearly missed the next one, too. A three-putt for par left him only a stroke ahead of Faldo.

Within 15 minutes, the last Open goodbye came for Cook. As he drove perfectly well down the 18th, Faldo struck a stunning shot on to the 17th, his ball finishing only 20 ft from the flag. Two putts and the pair were level.

With the cross-wind playing tricks over the closing holes, Cook pushed his two-iron long and into the gallery. He failed to get up and down, just missing an 8-ft putt. Cook could then only sign his card in resignation, fearing the worst from the man he had practically called invincible the day before.

Faldo did not let his unexpected chance go begging, although he still had to fight for his honour when he sent his approach with his three-iron – the club that Cook wished he had opted for – through the green. A putt up to 18 in. ended Cook's lingering hopes. There was to be no play-off. Like his friend Azinger, he had let in the big Englishman at the death.

Faldo was so overcome he dissolved into tears. Cook had to fight hard to hold them back. He explained how it all went wrong.

'I was alive. I was dead. I was really alive. Then pretty much dead. I missed three shots, and that cost me a lot, to say the least.

'I'm pretty proud of the way I hung in there and didn't let the 9th ruin a lot of good stuff. I said to my caddie, "We can still win this one." I played the 10th through to the drive at 18 with some of the best shots I have hit in my lifetime.

'On 17, I thought I had made the first putt. As the ball went past the hole, it was starting to break. My second putt was probably about 2½ ft, and I thought it was going to break a little bit to the right. I did not put a very good stroke on it.

'The [second] shot at 18 was not a very good one. I was unsure when I got there, because I was in between clubs. I did not know what I was thinking about but it probably cost me. But if someone had told me after leaving the 9th green that I would have had a chance to win on the 18th, I would have said, "You are crazy."

'On 18, I had two hundred yards to the flag and a hundred and seventy-eight yards to the front, which is usually a pretty comfortable three-iron shot for me. But I had the wind in my face and decided on a two-iron. As soon as I hit the ball, I knew it was too much club. I tried to hit it real easy, but I knew it was gone as soon as I hit it. I should have given the club a little more thought, but I could second-guess it forever. Then my putt to save par I thought I had made, too, but I did not hit it hard enough. It just caught the lip and didn't fall.

'I don't think I have ever gone through so many emotions in one round. I was up early in the round, down after nine, up again after playing the back side so nicely, then way down again.

'Absolutely I gave away the championship. Nick made a couple of birdies, and that is what great champions are made of. I definitely let one slip away. I had a chance to win a major championship and I didn't take it. I was so excited and wanted to get things done. I might have been a little too fast.'

Faldo revelled in his relief and glory, thanking his perceived persecutors in the media from the 'heart of my bottom' and bursting into a rendition of 'My Way'. Cook took the runner-up plaudits and made for home. Hardly reckoning on such an outstanding but, in the end, traumatic Open, Cook had entered the New England Classic the week after the championship and he decided he would not withdraw, rather try to get a few demons out of his head.

It was hard to do so at first. On his flight home, they ran the highlights of the Open and the commentator talked about England's 'favourite golfing son, Nick Faldo' coming out on top and an unknown American blowing his chances over the closing holes. Cook had to bite his lip and try to blot out the bad memories.

When he arrived at Pleasant Valley Country Club in Massachusetts (where, to his great credit, he finished third), almost the first person he bumped into in the locker-room was Paul Azinger. The pair cast out the demons together.

1992 TOP SCORES

N. Faldo 66–64–69–73 272
J. Cook 66–67–70–70 273
J.M. Olazabal 70–67–69–68 274
S. Pate 64–70–69–73 276

1994, TURNBERRY: JESPER PARNEVIK

(Parnevik led by three strokes standing on the 72nd tee but finished second, a stroke behind Nick Price)

'But then I started thinking again. I had such a good momentum going. I thought, "No. Let's go for birdie. I've got to make birdie to win."'

ALL OPENS ARE emotional. Some are more emotional than others, though, and 1994 fits into that category. It was the year that the friendly Zimbabwean Nick Price made it third time lucky.

It was rather fitting that Price made up for his disappointments in 1982 and 1988 by winning at a course whose famous landmark is 'Brucie's Castle'. Price took on board Robert the Bruce's famous observation: like the spider in the cave, he tried and tried again.

If there is a success story, though, invariably there is a hard-luck story. That belonged to a young Swede: Jesper Parnevik. Swedes, by the very nature of their country, are not supposed to be that extrovert. Parnevik, though, was no archetype. He wore a cap with its brim lifted to show off his sponsors' name and wore drainpipe trousers, smoked huge cigars and ate lava-dust, to cleanse his innards, he said. His dad, a famous comedian, had encouraged him to take up a few party tricks, too, and Jesper often kept his fellow pros enthralled as a part-time magician.

For all but the final few minutes of the 1994 Open Championship, Parnevik looked as though he was going to conjure up a surprise victory and leave Price disappointed once again. It all came down to an outrageous putt and a wrong decision. Parnevik was the loser because of both. He sets the scene on what was to be a traumatic week:

'It was only my second major, my second British Open. I'd tried to qualify for the British Open for many years but had never been successful. I qualified the year before by winning the Scottish Open. I finished 21st in 1993 and that gave me the taste. I enjoyed the atmosphere and everything felt good at Turnberry. I didn't have any expectations, or anything like that, but I was certainly really looking forward to the week.

'I remember my caddie, Mick Donaghy, on the Wednesday, saying, "I have a very strange feeling about this week." I don't know where he got it from, but the draw was just about to be posted when he said it. When it came out, I drew Jack Nicklaus for the first two rounds.

'That was a big, big thing for me, to start off the week. I wasn't exactly a rookie, but I was a rookie as far as majors were concerned. I felt it added the pressure on a lot. You get nervous playing with certain players. I remember with Seve it was the same thing. I thought if I could just get through these first two rounds, I'd be OK.

'Jack was great to play with, and I played really well. He supported me the first two rounds and I just played better and better as the rounds progressed. I remember walking down 18 and posing for pictures with Jack. He had his hat flipped up just like mine. He showed appreciation for the way I'd played, and that alone would have made it a great week for me, just to play well alongside Jack Nicklaus for the first two rounds.'

Play well Parnevik did, opening up with a 68 at the par-70 Ailsa course, following up with an even-better 66 that left him only a stroke away from the leader, Tom Watson, who was again trying to equal Harry Vardon's Open-winning record. It was almost surreal to Parnevik, though. The gangly Swede was almost walking around Turnberry in a dream.

'I don't think I was really realising what was going on, as far as the larger scale of the tournament was concerned. That I was getting into contention to win the tournament and all that.

'When the Saturday draw came out, I drew Tom Watson. It was another huge thing that week. It meant I'd play with my two biggest idols, all in one week at a British Open I had a chance to win. I could hardly get my breath. It was the same thing playing with Tom. I didn't really have any thoughts about winning. I just didn't want to embarrass myself in front of Tom Watson, just as I hadn't wanted to in front of Jack Nicklaus.

'I kept on playing well. It was remarkable. I shot 68 in the third round. In fact, I shot every round in the 60s that year – something not many players had done before. Certainly not many players have done it and not won the Open!'

After the third round, Parnevik was still just a stroke off the lead, now held by Fuzzy Zoeller and Brad Faxon on nine-under-par. Parnevik shared third place with Watson, Ronan Rafferty – and Nick Price. As fate, through the finishes of the players on Saturday (under the normal rule of first one in, last one out) would have it, Parnevik was drawn with Watson again. Nicklaus, Nicklaus, Watson and Watson. But would the 1994 Open Championship have turned out differently if the timings of the finishes had thrown Parnevik together with Price? An imponderable.

'I was with Tom Watson again on Sunday, and, of course, he was playing really well. Now I knew it was just a bit more than playing with one of your idols. Tom played really steadily, but then his putter started to be very shaky. He started missing a few short putts, and I felt a little bit sorry for him.'

Double-bogeys at the 8th and 9th put Watson out of the race and once more ended his quest for that elusive number six Open title. As in 1984 and 1989, when he had also had golden chances to match Harry Vardon, the club that he said 'felt like an anvil' let him down badly again.

'I had 38 putts, and that really says it all. I three-putted 8 and 9 for double-bogeys and couldn't make any putts. It was the three-putts that killed me. It hurt, hurt inside. Very disappointing. This was my most discouraging moment.'

Parnevik, despite an ordinary start, shared the lead at the turn with Zoeller and Price. Now there was a serious chance the Open could see a surprise winner. At this stage, Parnevik knew how good his chance was, because, contrary to reports of how he didn't look at a leaderboard all the way round, for the front nine he reminds us he was, for a time, keeping a close check on other players' progress – or, as it was, non-progress:

'I wasn't really thinking of winning at that stage. Nothing was really happening. I think I started even-par for the first ten holes and nothing special was going on. But no one in front of us was doing anything. I could see that because I was keeping a good eye on the scoreboards at that stage. I was amazed I was tying for the lead.

'I remember putting on the 11th, the par-three. I had a 20-footer for birdie and I said, "Hey, if no one else wants to win, why shouldn't I win then?" I drained that putt and I took the lead. I kept on hearing roars on every hole, and at that stage I decided to get very focused.'

Getting focused meant Parnevik blotted everything out around him, including leaderboards, although he insists it was not a conscious decision to avoid looking at the scores. Having the blinkers on so tightly was what got him where he was down the closing stretch. But, in the end, his determination not to be distracted by anything also proved his undoing.

'I really shut everything out and I was in my own zone. It was all going right. I birdied the 12th with a great eight-iron to about 6 ft and I knew I must be still well up there. Then I birdied the 13th. This time, it was a nine-iron, I remember, real close, only about 3 ft, but I still tried to avoid thinking much about what was going on. All I was thinking was, "Birdie every hole and you'll be all right." That was pretty much the mantra I had in my head.

'I did get a bit anxious at the 14th, because I hit my birdie putt 12 ft past the hole. I holed it coming back for par. That was a relief. But I'd had trouble all week with the 15th. It was a pretty tough par-three. I hit my tee-shot right, and though I kept saying to myself, "Don't drop a shot, don't drop a shot," I did. I made bogey. And at the same stage, I heard roars, like you always do at a British Open. I was new to that situation, and, of course, I was thinking everybody else is making birdies. But I tried not to let it affect me. Once again, I said to myself, "OK. Birdie in from here and you'll have a good chance."

'I hit a great tee-shot on 16 and a great shot up there, 15 to 20 ft past the hole. I holed that one for birdie. Then I birdied 17 as well, so my goal of birdieing the last three was right on track.

'There was a huge scoreboard behind 17, but I was so focused that I didn't even see it. So I had no idea how I was doing. I was just thinking about making birdies on every hole, and I got a great momentum going that I didn't want to lose. It never really even crossed my mind to look anywhere, even. To miss the scoreboard on 17, you'd pretty much have to be blind. But I was so into my chip there and so happy when my ball rolled up there, only a foot from the hole, I just didn't see it.

'The 18th hole is a really tough tee-shot to keep in the fairway, but I went at it pretty aggressively. My ball went just through the fairway. I remember Tom Watson and I were only about 10 ft apart, just in the semi-rough, and we had pretty good lies. I think Tom tried to hit a nine-iron and he caught this huge flyer. He hit it in the grandstand over the green. The first thought that came into my mind was that I should try and hit a low, punched hook in there and kind of chase it up, to make sure I didn't get a flyer. Then try and hole from maybe 30 ft just right of the hole.

'But then I started thinking again. I had such a good momentum going. I thought, "No. Let's go for birdie. I've got to make birdie to win." So I took out the wedge and tried to hit a high, soft shot at the pin, but the ball didn't fly or come out as firm as I thought it would and ended up maybe 6 ft short of where I wanted to land it. It found a bad spot in the deep rough just on the left under the green. It wasn't a great chip, but I knocked the ball up to maybe 6 ft. I missed the putt. Then that was the first time I looked at a scoreboard.

'The only reason I looked was because Tom Watson came over to me and said, "Congratulations, Jesper. You have won the British

Open. Helluva fight today." Something like that. "You really deserved to win, the way you played today."

'I looked up at the scoreboard. I could see that I had been leading by three when I stood on the 18th tee. Then Nick Price birdied 16. If I had known the position, I think I would have gone for the middle of the green, then gone for one putt, or par. The way it turned out, maybe I should have played the last hole differently.

'When I had holed out for bogey on 18, I still had a one-shot lead. But, I bet you, within one minute of Tom Watson congratulating me and saying, "You've won," as we went to the scorers' booth, we heard a huge roar behind. So, from it seeming like I'd won the tournament, I felt something bad just happened. I looked up at the scoreboard. Nick Price had just eagled the 17th.

'I went from the highest high to the lowest low, virtually in a matter of seconds.'

Price, who had been looking at leaderboards, had fought valiantly to try to catch Parnevik, but the Swede had kept distancing himself. The Zimbabwean's fifteen-footer to birdie the 16th still left him two shots behind Parnevik and fearing he might be the nearly-man for a third time in the Open Championship. Then fate, lady luck, call it what you will, stepped in. Or was it acumen? Price purposely played for the flat part of the green to give himself a chance of making a putt. Not even the greatest optimist would have predicted Price would hole a 50-footer with about 6 in. of break, though. As Parnevik had feared, something bad had happened to his chances. When Price played the 18th conservatively and took two putts from 25 ft, his Open misses of 1982 and 1988 could be put well back in the memory bank. For Parnevik, though, his Open agonies had just begun.

'I suppose at the moment I knew I'd lost, I was a bit crushed, but I still wasn't totally down-hearted afterwards. I had felt that if I could only birdie 18, I would win. I know I got a lot of criticism for thinking that way, but the way it turned out, and don't forget it was a bit of a freaky finish, if I had birdied 18, I would have won by one. You can't compensate for someone holing a 50-footer.

'It was still a huge week for me. Playing with Jack Thursday and Friday, Tom on Saturday and Sunday, and to do what I did in the final round, make five birdies on the back nine, was something to remember. I thought I gave it all I could. The only thought I remember I had at the time was that I hoped sometime in my career I could hole the putts like Nick Price did. It must be the ultimate feeling in golf. To have a 50-footer go in when you need it must be fantastic. But I wasn't so shattered that losing was a blow to my career, that I wouldn't be able to play that well again.'

1994 TOP SCORES

N. Price 69–66–67–66 268
J. Parnevik 68–66–68–67 269
F. Zoeller 71–66–64–70 271

1995, ST ANDREWS: MICHAEL CAMPBELL AND COSTANTINO ROCCA

(Rocca lost a play-off to John Daly. Campbell led going into the final round and finished tied third)

'It was a sort of vision. I could already see the ball in the hole. When I set the ball off, it takes the same line as I had pictured in my mind, running, running, and into the hole. It was unbelievable.'

IT WAS THE year of the cookie and the pizza. In the end, two burly men went head-to-head in a play-off to decide who took the biscuit.

One was America's eponymous 'Wild Thing', John Daly, a man with a penchant for Coca-Cola and chocolate-chip cookies, which he scoffed periodically through his rounds. The other was the pasta man, Costantino Rocca, a former metal-box factory worker and caddie at Bergamo, whose iron-play alone had earned him a 1993 Ryder Cup place.

They finished up as the leading aspirants to the trophy, but there were several others who could have lifted the Claret Jug in a finale of extraordinary twists and turns.

The week began with a four-way tie for the lead – Daly, Tom Watson (making yet another bid to add that elusive record-equalling sixth Open), Ben Crenshaw and Zimbabwean Mark McNulty leading the way by a stroke on five-under. Rocca was three-under.

Round two saw Arnold Palmer make his farewell appearance at St Andrews and Daly stay on top. This time, Daly shared the lead on six-under with Brad Faxon and the first Japanese to play full-time on the European Tour, Katsuyoshi Tomori. There was a whole gaggle a stroke behind, including Rocca and Mark Brooks.

At this stage, there was not much of a hint that a young New Zealand Maori, Michael Campbell, was about to be the surprise package of the whole week. For 26-year-old Campbell, playing in his second Open after missing the cut the previous year at Turnberry, the only mentions in the newspapers he got were in the southern hemisphere – a young near-rookie with little prospect, who had at least gone a little further this time. A great-great-great Saturday changed all that. Campbell rewinds on the week:

'I had no experience of St Andrews at all, so I purposely went for those who had when I did my practice. I went out with Raymond Floyd, Greg Norman, Nick Price, Ian Baker-Finch and Craig Parry. I made sure I picked their brains, particularly where to play, because there are a lot of blind shots. I learned a lot from them. I got there Sunday, too, so I played Monday, Tuesday, Wednesday.

'I shot 71 in the second round and it was like shooting 65, because I was nearly last off, conditions were tough and I finished late. I played great, but I was still only two-under and well off the lead.

'Then I really did shoot 65. On Saturday morning, I was off with Brett Ogle. The wind was blowing quite strongly, and I knew that if I could shoot low, I had a chance to get somewhere near the lead.'

Campbell's ancestor is Sir Logan Campbell, a Scot who emigrated in 1845, married a Maori woman and became mayor of Auckland, a man who was revered by his people enough to have a New Zealand landmark, One Tree Hill, dedicated to him. Now, 150 years on, another Campbell had returned to make his mark in Scotland.

'Someone was looking down on me. My great-great-great-grandfather would have been proud of a great-great-great round of golf.

'The third round was the type of round where just everything fell into place. Because of all my practice sessions, it was my sixth round, but it was still pretty well all new to me. Sometimes it's kind of nice not to know where bunkers are. It makes you more focused on what you are doing. Sometimes if you think about every bunker, you forget to focus on where you are going. To not know the course that well is sometimes an advantage rather than a disadvantage. You're less fearful of all those pot-bunkers out there. You just aim for your spot and hit it there.

'I only went in one bunker: at the 17th.'

At the fearsome Road Hole Bunker, Campbell belied his years and his inexperience, protecting his seven birdies and a blemish-free scorecard with an awesome shot straight up the steep bunker banking to leave his ball just 18 in. from the hole. Campbell modestly reckons he was lucky to do that. But his insistence on covering all the angles in practice paid off too.

'It was a complete fluke! Although Craig Parry and I were in that bunker for five minutes in one practice round. We tried to somehow figure out how to play it and do it a certain way. In the third round, it came out perfectly. I couldn't go backwards, sideways, any other direction than just straight ahead. It just popped up and rolled. I could easily have lost three or four shots. Someone up there was smiling down at me.

'I just missed a ten-footer on the last for birdie or it could have been even better.

'Leading was a bit of a shock, really. I could hardly believe it. I was 26 years old and very inexperienced at leading ordinary tournaments, let alone major championships.'

Campbell, on nine-under-par, led by two strokes from Rocca, with Australian Steve Elkington on six-under. Daly, playing aggressively, pulling out driver nearly as many times as his chocolate muffins, was one of four players a further stroke back.

The inexperienced leader was still thinking about it all in the wee small hours, he admits:

'I didn't sleep much that night, for obvious reasons. My nerves were not too bad. I was just so excited. My mind was racing. I tried to play computer games, solitaire, minesweepers, until two in the morning. I had about four hours' sleep and then got up at seven. You tee off at 2.30 in the afternoon, so I had seven hours to kill. Those seven hours felt like seventeen hours. Every time I tried to watch TV, I came on the screen! I watched the news and I was even on that. I felt like I was surrounded by the Open. My mind, my thoughts were all Open. My expectations were high and I thought about the consequences of winning. I thought about too many things.'

When the last group went out in the final round, Campbell with Rocca, a strong breeze had whipped up until it was forceful enough to blow wheelie bins around the car parks. Campbell was trying not to get the wind up over his lofty position, but it was not easy.

'I got to the first tee, and my heart was thumping pretty hard, and my mind was racing a lot. I'd put too much pressure on myself. I was lucky for my first tee-shot that it was a pretty wide-open fairway. Any other fairway, I'd have missed it by 20 yards. I hooked it left but I made par, and, with the 1st hole over, I felt pretty comfortable.

'I managed to shoot par for the next three holes, and I felt I was more settled. But then I made some errors. The wind was gusting all the time, and that made club selection difficult. At the 5th, the par-five, I was 30 ft or so away from the hole with a nine-iron shot and three-putted, missing a three- or four-footer for par. Then, after a poor drive, I needed two to get on the green at the next and came up 40 ft away with another nine-iron.

'While it felt as though it was slipping away a little bit, I was only one shot behind and I think I was level after seven holes. John [Daly] was going well; Rocca had a chance, too. He was hanging around, playing great.'

Soon, Campbell was really in trouble, however, a little while after Daly had gone out three-under with birdies on the 7th and 8th. His playing-partner Rocca was still in the thick of things. It was going to need a big finish if he were to stay in contention.

'I was struggling after I bogeyed the 8th – I missed a six-footer there – and the 11th. Then I got it together a bit, but I dropped another shot at the 15th and I knew I then had to fight or I'd be nowhere. I could have had birdies but made par at 16, only 15 ft away, and 17, about 20 ft, and I thought, "I'm not giving in without a fight."'

The 1995 Open was reaching a thrilling climax. Steven Bottomley, an amiable, rather noisy and fairly blunt Yorkshireman, had been in a position to cause the upset of the century before he bogeyed the 17th. His round of 69, though, hauled him through the field spectacularly, and he led in the clubhouse on five-under-par. This time, it was more than just the *Yorkshire Post* wanting to interview him, after his birdie on the 18th enabled him to set the mark. Bottomley was just a little starry-eyed and mystified by it all. In the end, though, his dropped shot on the 17th, finding the dreaded Road Hole Bunker and missing a 12-footer to save par, kept him out of the subsequent play-off.

'I think, in the circumstances, it was the best round of my life. If you look back to qualifying, I holed a 9-ft putt just to get into the Open. I'd made only one of the last nine cuts, so to finish that way was unbelievable.

'I tried not to think of it as the British Open. I loved it with the crowd. They got behind me. I was looking at leaderboards but I just tried to play golf and concentrate. My bogey at the 17th was my first there all the week. That was disappointing.'

The man who had been travelling in a mobile home to tournaments and whose best European Tour finish before his gutsy finish was tenth saw his hopes of a remarkable victory ended when Daly came in one better than him, with the new target of six-under after a 71.

Mark Brooks also fell a stroke short with a 71. His name sat proudly on top of the leaderboard after birdies on the 14th and 15th. Just one hole dashed his hopes: the 16th. There he took a double-bogey. Another birdie on the last proved too little, too late. His was another case of 'if only'. But for the sake of one hole, the name Brooks could have been the one the etcher marked on the Auld Claret Jug. He would have to wait until the following year for major honours, when he won the US PGA Championship.

'On the 16th, I drove into a pot-bunker, and I knew I couldn't do much more than just get the ball out. I was then on a hanging lie, and I came up well right of the green. I then three-putted. That was it. I was just a little disappointed! I felt I needed just one more good break.'

On a final day of mishaps like that, Daly, too, looked as though he would come up a stroke short. After going out three-under and then hanging on to hold the lead on the back nine, his bogeys on 16 and 17 left him only a single shot's leeway.

Having had an exceptional stroke of luck the previous day on 18, when he drove right through the green and up the R & A steps and nearly went out of bounds, Daly this time erred on the side of discretion and hit a one-iron off the tee. When he made par for a 71, to set the target of six-under, only Rocca and Campbell could better him.

For Campbell, though, time was running out, and only a miraculous finish would do. The young New Zealander recalls the closing moments:

'For some bizarre reason, the scoreboards were taken down before we got to the hole. They'd started taking it down before we got to the [18th] hole, so we had no idea what John was doing. I thought it was quite strange, because we had no real idea of what was going on. Rocca and I had no idea.

'Standing on 18th tee, I was thinking to myself, "If I can hole my tee-shot, I've won it." The wind was down-breeze, off the right, and the green was reachable. The pin was cut so that it wasn't impossible, so I just thought if I could hole out, I've won the Open. I wasn't actually kidding myself, either. I wasn't giving up. I was quite proud of how I had played the last three holes. In my mind, I had a shot to win the Open.

'I hit the ball pin-high left on the green. I still wouldn't give it up, even though I was 40 ft away from the flag.'

There was still the man from Bergamo to go. Little did Rocca know that he was about to produce some of the most memorable moments in Open history.

It had all begun fairly quietly for the affable and cuddly Italian, who was the first from his country to play in the Ryder Cup two years before. Even though he was a main player in the 1993 match, sorely maligned when made one of the scapegoats for Europe's defeat at The Belfry ('OK, I miss a putt; I don't kill anybody'), Rocca was by no means on the bookmakers' short-odds list at St Andrews. He had failed to qualify in six attempts, finished tied forty-third in 1991, tied fifty-fifth in 1992 and missed the cut in 1993 and 1994.

This year was different for Rocca, who knew the Old Course well. In 1990, he hadn't had the chance to play the St Andrews Open because of failing to qualify. But he'd played it four years running since then. He says he was happy to be on familiar territory:

'It was good for me that we were at St Andrews because I knew the Old Course well. I'd played in four Dunhill Cups over it, so it wasn't new to me and I knew quite a lot about it. How you need to miss a lot of bunkers. I knew there were no easy holes at St Andrews. The course can be completely different when it is windy. But I was aware it can be really tricky even without the wind. Some holes look very easy, and then you can make double-bogey on them. So, with practice, I was quite well prepared.

'I played well for the first round, shooting a 69. I was determined to make the cut again in an Open; that was the first target. Then we'd see how things went.

'I played even better the next day, even if I shot a 70. I didn't have to worry about the cut, but just check how far I was off the lead at the end of the day. It was good knowing I was going to play four rounds in the British Open this time.'

Rocca's second 70 in the high winds of the third round elevated him to second place. The man from Bergamo says he knew that he then had a realistic chance of becoming the first Italian to win the Open:

'I was hitting the driver much better than I had for a long time. I was happy to be in the position, more than nervous about it. I knew if I played well the next day, I'd have the chance of my life. I put it in my mind that this was my week.'

His daily and nightly routine at St Andrews didn't change, though. He had about twenty friends and fans camped in the area and on Saturday night cooked pasta for six of them. They discussed whether he was making news back home, where sport was dominated by football.

'Maybe if I won the next day, someone in Italy might know about it. Because of the Ryder Cup, sports fans had started to hear about me, and in my home town they knew me. But I didn't hold out much hope of anybody in Rome knowing what was going on. Even if I won, they would not recognise me in Rome!'

It started to look as though he would stay in obscurity, except for his loyal home followers, when Rocca dropped three shots in four holes from the 7th, twice three-putting, to drift down the leaderboard. His birdie on the long 14th gave him renewed hope, however, as he made the green in two, avoiding Hell Bunker. Safe pars on 15 and 16 followed. Then came the most pivotal moments of the 1995 Open. He flashes back to those unforgettable scenes:

'Coming to the 17th, the Road Hole, I could see I was only one shot behind the leader, John Daly. I knew 17 would be a very hard hole, but 18 you can make birdie. So I wanted to get away from 17 without getting into any trouble and then try and make my move on the last. No good going for the win by trying to force two birdies to finish. I told myself that.

'I hit two good shots on 17, but my second ended up with my ball on the road. I'd practised and practised with the putter from the road, and when I arrived at it I saw the ball lying in just the sort of place I had been practising for. There was no doubt in my mind that I should use the putter. I hit a great putt to only about 3 ft from the hole. From the road, that sort of shot is practically impossible to do, so I was very happy indeed to make a four there.'

With Daly waiting, Rocca knew his theory was working. A birdie on the last. He could be in a play-off. Whether it would be two-way or three-way depended on how the last two men out on the course played the 18th. Rocca says he was in no doubt what he must do:

'Now, the second part of the job. I had to make birdie on 18 to get into the play-off. I said to my caddie Mick [Doran], "I have to be on the green close in at least two shots." I hit a great drive and a really good second shot which was going straight to the pin. The ball got a bad bounce, though, and it dived left of the pin into a little gulley.

'When I walked up the 18th, the noise was deafening. But I am so concentrated. I can hear the clapping but I try to block it out. I am only thinking about what I have to do. I decided it was to be the sand-wedge. I was going to try to chip-and-run the ball. I knew I had to hit it perfectly. I wasn't frightened. Emotion didn't come into it. I felt good.

'Then I duffed it.'

Rocca's fluffed chip, which dribbled his ball only a few feet further forward in the Valley of Sin, left him with agony etched on his face. The engraver's tool was poised, ready to carve the name of John Daly on the Auld Claret Jug. He soon had to lay down his arm. Rocca had a vision. And Rocca's vision, he reveals, came true:

'I had been chipping good all week. I couldn't believe it. Where had this come from? I was chipping fantastically all day. OK, I was under pressure, because I'm trying to get into a play-off for the Open. But I was completely concentrated.

'A lot of thoughts started coming into my mind now, though. I had to blot them out and think about the putt. Suddenly, I could see the line of the putt. I knew exactly where it was going to go. It was a sort of vision. I could already see the ball in the hole. When I set the ball off, it takes the same line as I had pictured in my mind, running, running, and into the hole. It was unbelievable. Well, of course, it wasn't unbelievable because it had happened.

'I can say exactly how long it was . . . 17 yards. I had the pin position and knew to the inch exactly how far away I was. At that moment, I felt it was the most wonderful putt of my life, but because I had pictured it before and knew it was going to go in, it was in a way the easiest putt in my life!

'Of course, there was a lot of excitement. I was very excited and fell to the ground. I don't even remember banging the ground with my fists, but that's what I did, as I saw afterwards.'

Rocca's remarkable finish, one of the most spectacular in an Open Championship, was, of course, witnessed by his playing-partner

Michael Campbell, who feels unknown forces dictated how the 1995 Open would pan out:

'Even then, I had a 40-footer to tie Rocca and Daly. To me, I still had one hand on the Claret Jug. I took two putts and so that was it. If Costantino had missed his putt, then it would have put us all tied second. It wasn't to be. I said to him, "Best of luck for the play-off. Wish I was there, but there's always next time."

'When I think about it, it wasn't meant to be. The golfing gods didn't smile on me that day; they smiled on John. I remember watching the coverage of the third round and John hitting his ball up the steps on the last hole. He could have been out of bounds, but his ball rolled back down. To me, it's a sign. His name was already written on the trophy.

'The last time a New Zealander won a major championship was back in 1963, Sir Bob Charles, so it had been a long time between drinks! The folks back home got very excited when I was doing well.'

Those folks back home had their chance to get excited a decade later, when Campbell outdid Tiger Woods to win the 2005 US Open at Pinehurst. He did it just days after recording his thoughts on the 1995 Open Championship!

So Campbell was gone. Now to the business of the play-off. How could Rocca possibly gird his loins for the four-hole shoot-out with the imposing and daunting Daly? How could he mentally be ready to take on Wild Thing after that surreal finish? Rocca was ready, but was his body willing?

'People may think that the effort of that putt took too much out of me and I wasn't ready for the play-off after it, but it wasn't so. I was ready for the play-off, because I got my concentration back quickly.

'The only thing that made me a little bit nervous playing off was having to wait while they put the flags back in the play-off holes.

'At the first, I hit two good shots into the wind, I remember: a three-wood and a six-iron. I'm maybe six or seven yards from the hole. I have the wind behind me and when I brought the putter back and followed through to the ball, the wind pushed me and I passed the hole by three yards. I made three putts.

'Then, at the second hole, John holed a good putt, a long putt. I hit my putt just a couple of inches short. I'm now two shots behind.

'On 17, I know John is more nervous than me. He knows if he misses the driver on 17, he's dead. But he hit a perfect drive. He has only a wedge second shot. I hit a good drive. I'm two shots behind. I need to go for the pin. Because the wind is so strong from right to left, I need to hit 40 yards right of the pin. The ball pitched on the green and then falls in the bunker. I'm dead.

'He chips-and-runs onto the green. I can't do anything. I have an impossible shot. My ball's dead. So were my hopes of winning. I make a birdie on the last, but that was too late. It didn't mean anything.

'I was disappointed, but at that moment it all came back to me. When I started as a professional, I never dreamt I would have the chance to compete like I had done, for a major. It made me feel proud then. It also gave me a lot of confidence in the years to come, even if I'd finished second. If you win, you're there, but sometimes life gives you a little but not all. That was how it was for me.

'It was my greatest moment in golf. Well, my greatest moment on my own. The Ryder Cup was fantastic, because I love team competition, so I give my best all the time. I don't give 100 per cent; I give 150 per cent, because we're important for each other. But at the Open I was playing for myself.

'St Andrews is very special for me. Years later and the people might remember John won, but they remember my chip and my putt. For once, they remember who came second.'

1995 TOP SCORES

J. Daly 67–71–73–71 282
C. Rocca 69–70–70–73 282
(Daly won four-hole play-off)
M. Campbell 71–71–65–76 283
S. Bottomley 70–72–72–69 283
M. Brooks 70–69–73–71 283

1997, ROYAL TROON:
JESPER PARNEVIK AND DARREN CLARKE

(Five strokes ahead of Justin Leonard going into the final round, Parnevik was overhauled by the American and finished up second, three strokes behind, with Clarke)

'I was looking at the leaderboard all the time this time. When we walked off 16, I could see Justin had gone in front. Having missed that putt, that was when the air went out of me . . .'

AFTER THE DISAPPOINTMENT of 1994, when he finished a shot in arrears of Nick Price after leading the Open by three strokes standing on the 72nd tee, Jesper Parnevik bounced back in some style.

The tall and, some would say, unique Swede, with his flair for drainpipe trousers, flashy belts and upturned peaked cap (originally done so he could get a better suntan when he moved to Florida, apparently), set out to put the record straight and erase the bad memories of Turnberry.

For a long time, it looked as though the 1997 Open would be a battle between Parnevik and a big-hitting Northern Irishman. Darren Clarke, with two European Tour victories and a record-equalling round of 60 to his name, was carving out a promising career. Clarke made the early running in 1997 and might still have had a chance of pulling off his first major title but for one of golf's horror shots in the final round.

183

While contending strongly in an Open was a relatively new experience for Clarke, it was Parnevik's second stab at claiming the major title. His game had improved further in three years and the Swede felt he was a little more 'streetwise'. Certainly, Parnevik would be scrutinising leaderboards closely this time, if he got to the summit again. He explains how he went to Troon ready to make his earlier experiences count in his favour:

'Losing in 1994 at Turnberry did not spoil my career, and a little while later I had a great chance to win the [US] PGA Championship. I learned a lot from Turnberry. It was my first major, and I couldn't really have expected to be that lucky to win the very first time I played in a major. It gave me a great confidence boost, and I was pleased I could play so aggressively, even though it was a major. Then came Troon three years later. It was so different this time. At Turnberry, it never crossed my mind I was going to win until the last few holes, when I got on such a roll.

'With moving to play in America, my short-game and putting had improved a lot. That was because of playing on fast greens week in, week out. I didn't putt that well at Troon a lot of the time, though.

'The first few rounds, it was horrific weather, very windy. In the first round, I was one- or two-over-par going out, and it was supposed to be the easier nine then, downwind. I made a double-bogey on the back nine, but I shot two-under-par.

'I had a fantastic finish. On the 18th, I had this 50-footer with about 20 ft of break in it. I holed it and it got one of those roars you remember for the rest of your life. I kind of felt a bit like Nick Price must have felt on the 17th at Turnberry! That is the sort of thing that happens in the British Open. It almost makes your hair stand up when you play. Things like that you always remember.

'It was the toughest Open course I'd played. Nobody was even close to being under par on the back nine, so it was a great round of 70. My game and my putting had felt terrible, though, and I went to bed not knowing how I'd done it, especially shooting 34 on the back nine.'

Given the conditions, it was a sterling effort from a player whose swing was not at its best. Parnevik's 34 shots coming home bettered by a stroke the two joint leaders, Clarke and Jim Furyk. The leading pair did their best work on the front nine, as both shot four-under-par 67s to head Greg Norman, Fred Couples and, in the end significantly, Justin Leonard by two strokes. Parnevik was in the pack three off the lead.

It was to prove ironic. In the first round, Clarke birdied the 2nd hole in style on a day of disappointment for one of the favourites, Tiger Woods, and he also made a safe par at the small but perfectly formed 8th, the Postage Stamp. The Stamp confounded Woods, who bogeyed it. However, Woods virtually lost his Open chance in the first round that year at the 11th, arguably one of the toughest holes in golf, which flirts with railway lines and gorse. A triple-bogey-seven put Woods on the back foot and left him playing catch-up for the rest of the tournament.

Joint-leader Clarke, by contrast, built his Open hopes on the very same 11th hole, and his birdie at the four hundred and sixty-three-yard par-four, which his great strength helped him reach in two before sinking a putt of over twenty yards, was the highlight of his round. It ensured he would not be over par coming home and, like Parnevik, Clarke knew the value of mastering the incoming nine in the difficult conditions of Thursday.

'I played very well around the front nine, round the back nine not so well, but I made quite a few good putts for saves. On 11, I hit a driver, then a two-iron up to the front-right edge of the green and holed from about 70 ft. The back nine was playing unbelievably difficult, so I was very pleased to come back in 35. Par on the back nine was 39, probably.'

A 66 the next day earned Clarke the outright lead, two shots in front of the man who would haunt him later, Justin Leonard. Parnevik was a further stroke behind. Clarke had changed his tactics to suit Royal Troon. A little advice from Colin Montgomerie, too, went a long way. Montgomerie's father, James, was the Troon secretary for many years, and Monty, himself not playing that well, ironically, had passed on some of his local knowledge to Clarke.

'I played with Monty on Monday and Wednesday and he was very good to me. He gave me a lot of advice, because I hadn't played Troon before. It was about certain areas where not to go and certain holes, which shots to take on and what flags go here and what flags go there. What side to miss them on.'

Clarke's decision to keep the driver in the bag most of the time reaped dividends.

'I was taking the traps out of play. I was making sure I couldn't reach bunkers. As soon as you go into a fairway bunker, it's a penalty-shot straight away. There's no going forward; it's just a case of getting the ball out.'

Parnevik, despite not being happy with his swing or his putting, was somehow staying in contention.

'I wasn't playing that well that week, to be honest, so it was a case of hanging in there on the Friday. My feeling for the British Open and my passion to win it was such that I pretty much played on pure spirit. My focus was very good, and with my feelings for the British Open, which are different to any other tournament, I was able to stay in contention. My shotmaking was really good, so I had a good feeling about that year, even if I wasn't striking the ball all that well.

'In the second round, things were not so hit or miss, though, and I hit pretty much every green, if I remember. It was much easier on the back nine, and there were more birdie opportunities. Whereas I had been hitting three-irons in on some of the holes, it was now eight-irons.

'I had a good front nine after dropping a shot on the 1st. I'd changed putters, and the first thing I did was to three-putt, which was not very pleasing! I eagled the 4th, though, then made a couple of birdies before the turn and one soon after, and I never dropped another shot. There was no big finish this time. In fact, I had to play a good sand-wedge shot on 18 to save par.'

The next day, Parnevik finally hit top form to charge straight after Clarke early on. Two birdies at the first two holes left him brimming with confidence. He was so confident he was even moved to try something he had never done before, he recalls. That was to putt up the fairway following his drive on the 7th, to earn one of seven birdies:

'I felt just great. The two birdies really got me going and I felt like I could do what I wanted on the golf course. On the 7th, I hit a long drive, much longer than I thought, and I had about 50 yards to the front of the green, so I decided to putt it. It finished up about 15 ft short of the flag, but I holed the putt. I'd never tried that sort of shot before, putting on the fairway, but I couldn't come up with a better shot.'

It was Parnevik's finish, birdies on the 16th and 17th, that took him past Clarke, though.

'My main thought was to somehow get into the lead, because I didn't want Darren to get away and be too many shots ahead. You can kind of freewheel then. But if somebody cuts the lead, it almost feels like you're behind, even though you're leading. I knew if I could make some birdies coming in, I could put pressure on Darren.'

A second 66 that took him to 11-under-par put Parnevik to the fore on Saturday. Clarke slipped back to second place, two strokes behind. Sharing third place, five strokes adrift, were Fred Couples and Justin Leonard.

Taking the lead brought all the buzz of Turnberry 1994 back to Parnevik, he says:

'When you hole the putts, everything goes away. It feels like all the negative thoughts have gone. All you have in your mind are positive thoughts.

'I recognised all the feelings of '94 – the same rush every time you made birdie. You hear the same sort of roars from the crowd. Just amazing.'

Parnevik, who this time vowed he would be looking at leaderboards all the way round, was playing so well he felt he could hardly do wrong. The 1st hole in the final round did not change his view nor dim his optimism.

'When I teed up at the 1st on Sunday, I felt like it was going to happen today. I remember hitting a four-iron off the tee and then a wedge-shot that I thought I'd hit fairly good, but the ball ended up in a horrific spot in the front-left bunker. The pin was just over the left-front bunker. I was lying on a downslope. I had to go up a very steep bank, about 2 ft, and then it was downhill to the hole. I stood over the shot and thought, "Wow. I could be in here for the rest of the day! This is pretty much impossible." I hit this fantastic shot. It came out perfect, just hit the upslope, one bite and then the ball trickled down to just a foot from the hole.

'From that, I gained a lot of confidence. I thought to myself, "I'm going to do this. This is no problem."'

For Clarke, there was his biggest problem of the week. And it cost him any realistic chance of winning. On the 2nd hole, a 'shank' on the tee sent his ball out of bounds onto the beach. That effectively prised his hand from the trophy.

While Clarke's chances receded, his playing-partner stayed optimistic of this time getting both hands on the Claret Jug. The opening five holes gave Parnevik belief he could make up for his disappointment in 1994. Then came a mistake that he admits was subsequently to cost him dearly:

'Everything was going great until number 6, the par-five. I made what I'd say was the tactical error of the week. I'd hit a good drive and I was going to knock it on in two, and instead of taking the three-wood and kind of landing it up by the green, I needed to be a little bit long. I decided to hit a three-iron – the ground was very firm that week – and kind of chase it up there. I just never thought about the cross-bunkers about 40 yards or so short of the green. I ended up tearing straight into the bunker and found a bad lie under the lip. All I could do was blast it out. I then tried what I'd done the day before on the 7th hole and putted up the fairway, but I came up well short this time and I bogeyed the hole.

'It was at pretty much the same time as Justin Leonard put on his charge. He started birdieing every hole. From that stage on, I was fighting for my life. As I said, my game wasn't really there that week, but I somehow made pars on all the holes I felt I needed to. Sometimes I didn't know how I made pars.

'I then birdied the 11th and went back two shots ahead again. The

11th was a really tough hole, especially with the way the wind was. The OB was right of the green and the pin was tucked in the right side. It was a great birdie, but whereas before I had been thinking nothing else than I am going to win, all of a sudden it turned into a kind of "chasing" mode for me, even though I was still in front. I was trying to hold on as good as I could.

'Justin kept on making birdie after birdie, but I hung in there all the way to 16, and there I hit this great shot 3 ft from the hole. I'd putted really nicely all week, but the putt was just one of those putts I just could not get a good feel for. My caddie and me looked at the line a few times, but we couldn't really figure it out properly. It was a big left-to-right break outside the hole, or was it inside and go firm? I heard a big roar from up ahead at the 17th, where Justin was. I knew all about big roars, but I tried to ignore it. I couldn't see Justin putting, and the roar might not have been for him. I got my head together again, went for inside and firm. It broke really hard. I missed the putt.

'I was looking at the leaderboard all the time this time. When we walked off 16, I could see Justin had gone in front. Having missed that putt, that was when the air went out of me a little bit.'

Parnevik knew the worst. The roar had been for Leonard, who had holed a 15-footer at the penultimate hole to move to 12-under-par, a stroke ahead of Parnevik. It was a dagger-thrust similar to Nick Price's outrageous putt on the 17th at Turnberry three years before. A deflated Parnevik could not rally this time. Soon, his second chance of an Open Championship drifted away altogether.

'It was all going wrong, after I had been so sure I could win. I hit a bad tee-shot on 17 and I bogeyed. That left me two shots behind Justin. To catch him, I had to make eagle on 18, which was a four-hundred-and-fifty-yards par-four. No chance, although I did try, but my energy was completely gone. I was drained. Pretty much all the fight and focus I had all week just went out of me. I hit a pretty awful tee-shot on 18 and made bogey.'

That left Parnevik sharing second place with Clarke, who, by contrast, had a good finish. The pair finished up three shots behind

Leonard. Having started five strokes behind Parnevik, Leonard's was the record biggest catch-up in latter-day Open history – a record that would, though, only last two years.

For Parnevik, this was much worse than 1994, when he had made that wrong decision at 18 to be pipped by Nick Price. This time, his hand had been more firmly on the Claret Jug, he feels:

'That was much, much more disappointing than Turnberry, because I really felt like I would win this time. I remember, some journalist told me afterwards that I'd seemed in such a daze – well, more in shock, I would say – that I walked around with my glove still on my hand, to the press conference, everywhere. I was just kind of lost. I couldn't really understand how I could have lost that one.

'I guess there was a lot of pressure on when Justin started his charge. Darren was pretty nervous, too, especially after the shank he hit on number 2. I thought then it was pretty much up to me to win the tournament. Then Justin started making birdie after birdie. Of course the pressure builds up when someone does that, because you're not really in control of the situation any more.

'It was the biggest disappointment of my career, because I really felt I was in charge. I never really even considered someone was going to come from that far behind and shoot a 65 and catch me.'

1997 TOP SCORES

J. Leonard 69–66–72–65 272
J. Parnevik 70–66–66–73 275
D. Clarke 67–66–71–71 275

1998, ROYAL BIRKDALE: BRIAN WATTS, JUSTIN ROSE AND JESPER PARNEVIK

(Watts lost a four-hole play-off to Mark O'Meara. Rose led briefly and coloured the final round with a memorable chip-in to finish tied fourth, only two shots away from the play-off. Parnevik might have won but for a gust of wind and an ill-timed hooter)

'If someone would have told me I would have been in a play-off for the Open Championship, I wouldn't have believed them. But you have to be disappointed when you know you had the opportunity to win.'

WHEN THE 1998 Open Championship began at Royal Birkdale, no one, apart from aficionados of Asian and Japanese golf, had heard of Brian Watts. By the time an often-turbulent week had finished, the whole golfing world knew about the man born in Montreal who became an American when he was 16 years old.

The age of the surprise Open winner was not quite upon us, but Watts, and young British amateur Justin Rose, very nearly brought its dawn. It was another year, too, when Sweden's best hope at that time for a major title, Jesper Parnevik, again placed a hold on the Open trophy.

The man who came closest, however, was not even well known in America, and, even though he had already made several visits to the Open, he was anonymous in Britain. However, Brian Watts was an institution in Asia.

The thirty-two year old had had only a fleeting glimpse of professional golf in the USA, to where his English father and German mother moved when he was just six months old. Raised in Texas, Watts played college golf successfully at Oklahoma State, where he won the NCAA Championship.

Although he played in the same college team as established US Tour players Jeff Maggert and Scott Verplank, Watts could not find the same success as his contemporaries when he joined the paid ranks in 1988. After an indifferent three years or so in America, he decided to ply his trade on the Japanese and Asian circuits, where he had won several titles – five in 1994 to tot up $1.4 million – by the time he arrived at the Lancashire links with an Open exemption.

He had already played in the previous five Opens, qualifying in 1993 from the Asian Tour, the rest of his visits to Britain coming from his Japanese Tour finishes. Watts had had limited success in the British major. After he practised at Birkdale, which had undergone a complete revamp of all its greens following criticism during the 1991 Open, he was not optimistic about his chances this time either.

'My previous Open record was OK. I missed the cut in '93, then, in '94 at Turnberry, I finished 55th. I was in twelfth place after two rounds on that one. That was my best go up to then. At St Andrews in '95, I finished fortieth, but then I missed the cut the two previous years to Birkdale.

'Before I got to Birkdale, I was playing quite well. Unfortunately, though, Sunday, Monday and Tuesday didn't give me any belief in the world that I could even make one birdie at Birkdale.

'I played very, very poorly Sunday, Monday and Tuesday – probably lost two balls a day. That's two too many. One of the photographers from Japan actually found one of my balls and gave it back to me the next day!

'I worked a little bit on my golf swing on Tuesday afternoon and Wednesday, and then I started hitting it better. My caddie helped me out. My shoulders were lined up well to the right, because I was hitting so many "punch" shots. I was having a bad time until Tuesday on the back nine.

'But I really had no expectations whatsoever, which was probably a good thing.'

A memorable week for Watts was coming up, though. If he walked down the street in Tokyo, the older generation of golf fans would recognise him instantly. He had won 11 times in the East, so he was quite a star in Japan. That week, he was to eventually become a household name in America and Britain, too.

Before he started to look like a potential Open champion, though, Watts enjoyed his hours off the course. As he spent a great deal of his time in Japanese hotels, while his wife, Debbye, and then one-year-old son, Jason Bradshaw, stayed in Oklahoma, Watts at first treated his Open week as something of a much-needed holiday with his wife. Unnoticed by golf fans, they dined out – Far Eastern food sometimes on the menu – at night in local restaurants. As Watts climbed the leaderboard, though, the week became more serious.

After an opening 68, when everyone played in near-perfect conditions, nobody was yet talking about Brian Watts. Tiger Woods was one of the names being touted as a potential winner, after a blistering 65 in the first round. Mark O'Meara, who had sunk a huge putt on the last to clinch the Masters title and finally end his long wait for a major triumph, was another player in the news. O'Meara's 72, though, in clement weather, was only a modest start by the Augusta champion.

Woods shared the lead with John Huston. Huston was something of a surprise co-leader, but the players tied for third place offered no surprises: the 1994 Open champion Nick Price and major runners-up Loren Roberts and Fred Couples. Couples was second behind O'Meara at Augusta in April and no stranger to Open leaderboards. Watts, meanwhile, had bettered his 12th position in 1994, because he lay tied 11th after the first round, but he and Debbye could still enjoy their egg foo yung that night without fear of interruption by autograph-hunters.

While the players enjoyed benign conditions in the first round, the weather and Birkdale proved spiteful the next day and the luck of the draw came into play. It all depended on whether you wanted the morning rain or the high winds that caused a 30-minute suspension of play in early evening.

For Watts, it was the worst of both worlds. He got the wind and the rain. That didn't prevent him adding a 69 to his opening 68, though, and taking the lead. It meant, for him, a rare English-speaking press conference. In Japan, he could only go through his shots in Japanese and always needed an interpreter when he had to speak to the media. Here, he was able to breeze through his press conference:

'Conditions were much different, very much British Open-style golf: very tough, with the strong winds on the back nine. The front nine, we had the rain for the first five holes and a steady wind, but the back nine it really picked up strong. Mentally, you want to enjoy them, but I can't say I enjoy playing in it. You deal with it as it comes.

'Japan has a quite different wind and it is different in Texas. Where I grew up in Dallas, the wind is very strong, but not like it is over in Britain. It is a "thick" wind. It is so strong – even if it is the same miles per hour as back home!'

Watts held a one-shot lead on three-under-par over Woods, Price . . . and the lad who was to become the young sensation of the week, seventeen-year-old English amateur Justin Rose.

Rose's wonderful round of 66 equalled the lowest in an Open by an amateur, matching Woods's feat in 1996 at Royal Lytham and St Annes, for one. Rose had only left school 18 months beforehand and wouldn't be 18 until the end of July. He was making his Open debut after failing at pre-qualifying the previous three years. His surprise position came after quite a disappointing time of it, before getting to Birkdale through final qualifying in wretched conditions up the road. As he said at the time:

'My aim was to have a good round and make the cut. The British Amateur had been one of my main goals for the year, and unfortunately I got knocked out in the first round. So to do this at the Open, you can't actually believe it.

'On the practice area at Loch Lomond [at the previous week's tournament], I began to hit the ball very well, and unfortunately nothing happened for me there. Then, at qualifying on Sunday and Monday, I began to play some good golf. My caddie and I were choosing the right shots. I was thinking clearly, hitting the shots I wanted to hit and then holing the putts.

'Playing in the awful conditions we did on the Sunday and Monday definitely helped me. It was quite gruelling. The winds were at least as strong, and in hindsight that was great preparation.'

Rose, the previous year at 17 becoming the youngest player to have taken part in the Walker Cup, had his role models. They were Ernie Els and Nick Price. He was now rubbing shoulders with Price – 'he gives everybody time; he's got a great sort of fighting spirit on the course; a true gentleman' – and he had left Els trailing by eight strokes. Rose had made light of the windy day and basked in his glory, rather than suffering too many Open nerves.

'To tell the truth, I was surprisingly relaxed all the way round. Coming up 18 is a fantastic experience, when everybody is clapping you up the hole. I did have a few nerves on the putt, but luckily it went in.'

That putt, a 20-footer for birdie, followed by an eagle on the 17th, meant Rose would go out on Saturday in the final two-ball. It was not a prospect that daunted the British teenager and it gave him sweet dreams, rather than nightmares.

'I'm a heavy sleeper. Maybe I dreamt about winning the Claret Jug! I don't know, but I slept pretty well.'

The wind had taken its toll on first-round joint-leader Huston. Roberts and Couples also struggled. But a new name now graced the mid-section of the leaderboard. Mark O'Meara had vaulted through the field with a fine 68, to be only three shots off Watts's lead. As Masters champion, there was plenty of interest surrounding the greying American. But not as much as for youngster Rose, whose face and name were in all the British newspapers on Saturday morning. He tried not to take much notice of his press, leaving his father, Ken, his mentor, to take in what the newspapers had to say about him.

'To tell the truth, I left that to my mum and dad. That's something I tend not to do: look at the newspapers too much. I knew there was a lot of attention on me, but I tried my best to block it out.

'A lot of the top players were congratulating me. You feel at home, almost.'

The fervour surrounding his Open bid did not die down when he went out onto the course, either, but that was to work in Rose's favour. He was touched by his reception from the Birkdale gallery.

'Tremendous. Starting the day, I didn't realise it would be anything like that. Every hole I walked up, I got an ovation all the way up the hole. It was incredible; people shouting my name. I almost sort of saw myself as Jack Nicklaus, for some silly reason. That's something. Every time he walks up the 18th hole, he gets a standing ovation. To get anything like that was just incredible. That pushed me on.'

It pushed Rose on to the lead in the midst of his round. With the winds stronger than they had been all week, scoring billowed. Rose began badly, bogeying the first two holes, but, with the crowd urging him on and others falling by the wayside, he briefly took control.

'It was around 8, 9 and 10. I obviously felt great. I wasn't uncomfortable with that situation either.'

Rose's lead did not last. A closing bogey for a round of 75 left him three strokes off first place, still held by Watts.

While Rose had moved into the limelight, Watts had stayed anonymous. The fans hadn't identified him when he had eaten out the night before the third round, but that didn't bother him. The leader of the Open did not begrudge Rose his glory and was happy for the youngster to take all the crowd salutes when they played together on Saturday.

'We had dinner with my caddie and his girlfriend at a Chinese place in Southport. I don't think anybody recognised me. I don't think anybody knew I was winning the tournament. That was actually nice.

'It was a lot of fun playing with Justin, because every time he came to the green or holed a putt the crowd was ecstatic. He's an outstanding player. He'll be holding the Jug some day, I'm sure.

'We had a really good time out there, a little chitchat here and there and complimenting each other. We had a lot of fun.'

Even though the gallery's enthusiasm for Rose never abated all afternoon, Watts went about his job. He was delighted with the finish to his day after an inconspicuous time of it. Being the front-runner in a major was something completely new to him, but he was growing into the role.

'The first time in the last group and I felt lots of pressure from the start. I felt I handled it pretty well. I was fairly nervous.

'I don't think I did anything special over the first twelve holes, as I was five-over-par. I was hanging in there fine. I finished two-under for the last six holes to turn a not-so-good round into a respectable one.

'It might have helped that nobody got off to a real good start. Jesper [Parnevik] and Jim Furyk had good rounds, I think. I was too busy trying to figure out if I can hit the green, how much wind to play, trying to stay steady on my putts. There was a lot going through my mind without looking at the leaderboard.

'It was so tough out there. There was no let-up. You don't have one time to kind of take a break, just kind of enjoy and say to yourself, "OK, there's an easy hole." You don't have one shot out there that's easy. That's why usually the strongest people mentally win major championships.'

With Nick Price blown away, Watts, at his press conference, thought Parnevik 'might have a little bit of an advantage, since he's been in this situation before'.

Parnevik had come through the field to sit in second place. The tall Swede was ready to make up for his disappointments when he had had the Claret Jug snatched from his hands first by Price and then Justin Leonard. He could have been in an even better position if he had not suffered a cruel blow in the second round, he divulges:

'The best golf I played at an Open was 1998, better than '94 or '97. I played unbelievably well, but I didn't putt very well. I didn't let the putting bother me too much because I was striking the ball awesomely well. I had this really nice, penetrating shot I seemed to be able to hit at will, and it was very necessary because it was really rough weather. It was probably the toughest British Open weather I'd played in. I remember in the practice rounds it was blowing 30–40 miles per hour.

'In the second round, the balls started moving around on the greens. I got a terrible break on number 9. I was standing in the fairway and the wind was howling. It was gusting between a downwind and a crosswind. I was in between using a six- or a seven-iron and I went with the six-iron. As soon as I hit it, the wind just took off behind me and my ball went 40 yards over the green into some bushes. Just as I hit the shot, they blew the siren and called play off. If they had called us in just a minute earlier, when I went back I would have had an easy shot with an eight-iron, because the weather was better.

'They were right to call us in, because it was unplayable at the time, but when I went back I could only chip on and I bogeyed the hole.

'It was terrible luck, but afterwards I really hung in there. I didn't worry too much about the rough, which was pretty bad, because I was hitting the ball so straight – off the tee and with my iron-shots.'

If Parnevik had suffered a cruel blow from the hands of time and fate, then, by total contrast, the clock proved to be on Mark O'Meara's side in the third round. For the sake of a few seconds, an Open was lost and won.

At the 6th hole, O'Meara drove into just about the deepest rough in Birkdale and had given up any hope of finding his ball as his five minutes' grace to find it, under the rules, ticked away. O'Meara went back to the tee. His ball was somehow found in the bushes and gorse. But, with less than 60 seconds left, being now so far away, he would not have had time to get back to identify it within the allowed five minutes. His caddie, Jerry Higginbotham, did so instead, within the rules. Instead of running up what could have been at least a triple-bogey, O'Meara, who had already double-bogeyed the 1st and bogeyed the 5th, escaped with just one dropped shot. He even had the advantage of placing after his ball twice rolled nearer the hole from his penalty-drop. From there, he didn't put a foot wrong and repaired half of his first-nine damage with a tidy incoming nine, to take a share of second place.

Watts was the only man not over par, holding a two-shot lead over O'Meara, Parnevik and Furyk going into Sunday's final round, with Rose a further stroke back. There was no Chinese restaurant this time for Watts. On Saturday night, it was a few groceries and dinner at his apartment. The much-travelled leader, about whose nationality many were still unsure ('Is he Canadian or American?' some reporters were still asking), would stay anonymous until he got out onto the course.

At last, the murderous winds had relented. The chief protagonists in the 1998 British Open went out in light breezes and occasional drizzle.

Honours were even for the two who were to become the chief rivals at holding the Claret Jug. Watts and O'Meara both went out in level-par. Furyk, Parnevik and Rose hung in. Tiger Woods came back into the reckoning. Scot Raymond Russell set the target with a blistering 66.

It was to be the closing holes that told, though, before the Open went into another four-hole play-off.

Parnevik was in the last group out. He knew where his chances died. The Swede remembers how another Open title went by the board:

'While I hit the ball so accurately, I still couldn't putt when it came to the final round. I had so many chances over the last nine holes. I couldn't get the ball in the hole, though, and I just couldn't convert it to a win. I played with Brian Watts in the final round and I was ahead of him all the time. I felt I was hitting the ball so much better than him but I just couldn't hole the putts.

'I finally did hole a putt on 17 for birdie and thought if I could also birdie 18, I might have a chance. I finished up two shots behind, but the way I'd struck the ball that week I felt I could have won by five!

'Even though it was not looked upon as a close call for me, with everyone focusing on the play-off and Tiger Woods making a late charge to get one in front of me, I had a great chance to finally pull it off in the British Open that week.

'It was almost like there were demons at the British Open acting against me. I could have had three Opens, and I have none. It was such a great experience, though: the crowds, the atmosphere. Not many people have had three chances to win the British Open. I thoroughly enjoyed all three occasions. Of course, I would have loved to have won one of them, but I wouldn't trade the three experiences for anything else. I don't hold any regrets. And I could still do it.

'I remember Nick Price's winner's speech at Turnberry, saying he'd had one hand on the Claret Jug twice. Well, I have had one hand on it three times and I'm still looking forward to many more British Opens to come.'

Rose's Open hopes lay with the unlikely prospect of a birdie–birdie finish, which was not to be. He did pluckily get half the job done. His chance may have gone by the time he played into the 18th. But the youngster still gave himself and his adoring crowd a wonderful memory to savour forever, pitching into the hole from behind a bunker to pick up the stroke on the last that ensured him a share of fourth place with Parnevik, Furyk and Russell.

'It was a tough shot, out of the rough behind a bunker, about 45 yards. I said to my caddie, "I'm going to go for the shot, try and get it close," because I could have bailed out. I had nothing to lose. It was one of those incredible moments. The ball got nearer and nearer and finally disappeared. I couldn't believe it.

'The whole week was really, really special. To finish on that note was in context with the whole week. I was put at ease by the crowd. The incredible support I had didn't give me time to be nervous.'

Rose, who would have pocketed a fortune for a teenager if he had been a professional, joined the paid ranks at 17 years old the following week.

Woods had set the target of one-over-par. O'Meara, who had had the better back nine than his arch-rival Watts, surpassed him by a stroke with a birdie at the 17th, despite a poor drive, holing a fifteen-footer. A par by O'Meara to close, around the time Watts was making birdie from 18 ft at the penultimate hole, left the pair locked together on top. A birdie on the last by Watts would ensure his anonymity would be ended forever.

At the 72nd hole, though, Watts had to perform a minor miracle just to get into a play-off with O'Meara, after his ball ran into the greenside bunker from his approach. It stopped on the back edge on a downslope. Watts had to play the ball with one foot out of the bunker and hope to pitch over the face and try to run out towards the hole. It looked an impossible shot.

Watts not only got it absolutely right – he nearly won the Open. Having arced high above the face, his ball dropped down like a plane making a mock stall in an airshow and skipped on to the hole. The crowd shrieked rather than roared, as it looked as though it must go in. It came to rest, agonisingly, 9 in. from the hole. The Claret Jug engraver would have to wait a little longer.

Even the waiting O'Meara applauded Watts's wonder shot, of which Watts said:

'I tried to create something in my mind and visualise a good shot. It came off to almost perfection.'

After the usual formalities, the pair set off for the 15th, 16th, 17th and 18th holes. In the play-off, extraordinarily, Watts needed the full miracle this time. Having missed out on two glorious birdie chances at the first two extra holes, he trailed O'Meara, who had holed from outside him for a birdie on the 15th, by a stroke going to the 18th for the second time that day. This time, Watts needed not only to coax his ball close but to hole it, when it had finished up in an almost-identical spot to the one he'd found about an hour earlier. Only birdie would send the play-off pair into sudden-death.

For Watts, though, the heroics were over. He bogeyed the hole this time. O'Meara made a safe par to add the Open to his Masters title.

The brave attempt by Watts gave him fleeting fame. He was no longer the anonymous Brian Watts. The spotlight now beckoned, even if he would, just a few years later, dogged by injuries, slip back into the wings.

'If someone would have told me I would have been in a play-off for the Open Championship, I wouldn't have believed them. But you have to be disappointed when you know you had the opportunity to win.

'But Mark is a class act. I said to him after he'd won that if it wasn't me, I was glad that he won.

'I never gave up, never. That's why I was so proud of myself.'

1998 TOP SCORES
M. O'Meara 72–68–72–68 280

B. Watts 68–69–73–70 280

(O'Meara won four-hole play-off)

T. Woods 65–73–77–66 281

J. Parnevik 68–72–72–70 282

J. Rose (am.) 72–66–75–69 282

R. Russell 68–73–75–66 282

J. Furyk 70–70–72–70 282

1999, CARNOUSTIE: JEAN VAN DE VELDE

*(Van de Velde could have made a double-bogey on the
72nd hole and won but he triple-bogeyed it. Paul Lawrie
won the subsequent play-off)*

'By the time I took my shoes off, the ball went from being
only half in the water to being completely submerged. If it
had remained the way it was – half out – it is nothing. It's
like a bunker-shot. I could play it any day . . .'

QUITE SIMPLY, THE 1999 Open provided the most-talked-about
finish since Doug Sanders's despair in 1970. Jean Van de Velde has
acquired legendary status for losing an Open. His final-hole
calamities turned him into a celebrity, remarkably mostly in America
– where they don't normally have much time for a loser.

Van de Velde is no loser. The congenial Frenchman saw lady luck
conspire against him around the Barry Burn at Carnoustie's closing
hole, where a wrong decision was never so bad that it should have
cost him so dearly. A 1,000–1-chance ricochet off the stands . . . even
the tide coming in at the wrong time: fate definitely had it in for
Jean Van de Velde in 1999.

That year's Open saw probably the worst rough of all time in the
Championship. It sometimes left some of the smaller players with
hardly a view over it. The fairways were the narrowest anyone could
remember. It blew most of the time – a recipe for high-scoring. And
high-scoring the R & A got. Several players (and a good many
pundits) cried 'unfair'. But it was the same for everybody, and like

they say, 'Someone will always fathom it out.' That someone, until the fateful 72nd hole, was a 33-year-old Frenchman. He takes us back to that unforgettable Open:

'I was playing very well leading up to the Open in 1999. At the Scottish Open the week before, my game was coming together, and I remember starting to putt very well. It was one of those weeks that lead to great putting performances for a while.

'I went to qualify for the Open at Monifieth and won the qualifying there. I was starting to play really, really good and putting even better.

'When I came to Carnoustie, I went for a practice round on the Tuesday but the weather was horrific: very windy, very tough conditions. The course looked a bitch. The rough was very high; the fairways were pretty narrow. I played 18 holes and had a good, good look at the course, seeing how I wanted to play it: where to hit the ball from the tee and what to hit off the tee. I worked out there and then what I was willing to do and what sort of risks I was willing to take.

'I wouldn't play on the Wednesday. My friends said, "Why don't you come and play?"

'I said, "I won't come and play because I don't need to be reassured that I can miss every fairway during 18 holes. I already know that, so I'm not going out there."

'I had no intentions of going out there and playing badly. I didn't want to realise you could shoot 90 out there if you weren't careful. I practised a lot around the greens, putted a lot, and left it at that.'

The Frenchman had an Open champion as one of his partners in the first two rounds: New Zealand's veteran left-hander Bob Charles. Charles won at Royal Lytham and St Annes in 1963, beating American Phil Rodgers in a play-off. Rodgers, was, of course, yet another who had one hand on the Claret Jug. But not nearly as firm a grasp as Van de Velde. His hard-luck story was about to begin its first chapter.

'Off I went on the Thursday. I played really well, but I remember having a disappointing finish. I was one-over and four to play and finished four-over. If I could have just hung on, I would have been in the top ten at least, maybe the top five. It all meant a lot, later on, of course, but you can't look back on it really and say that made a difference, because you don't know how the ball would have dropped in the next three rounds. A 75 was still a good score, but it didn't reflect the way I'd played. It was quite windy and it was a course that tired you out, especially because of the extreme condition it was in. You need a lot of energy to play a course like that, and I probably ran out of it over the last few holes.'

A 75 for starters was nowhere near as bad as it sounds. Well over a third of the field, fifty-five players, shot in the 80s, and there were two rounds in the 90s as Carnoustie and the R & A showed what some felt was a rather sadistic streak. Van de Velde was determined not to run out of steam in the second round, which he began in mid-morning this time. He had started his opening round just after three o'clock and finished not far off eight o'clock. Players finishing late on the first two days of the Open often do fade late in their rounds, when the galleries have dwindled and the dew starts to gather.

'I really focused twice as hard on the last five holes on the Friday, and luckily this time I shot two-under for them. I was pretty lucky. I ended up leading the tournament, because I shot a 68 in the second round. After two rounds, I was one-over. That showed how tough the conditions were. It was very tiring. You knew you had been in a fight, and after so much concentration on making sure I didn't lose my way at the end again, I was very tired indeed when I went to the locker-room.'

Nearly exhausted, but by the end of the day Van de Velde had earned a one-shot lead with his 68. Not so successful was the man who had led the first round with a 71. Australian Rodney Pampling, who could perhaps say he had a fingernail on the Claret Jug, became the first player in modern times to lead but then miss the cut, after shooting an 86 on the Friday.

Van de Velde led by a stroke from the burly big-hitter from Argentina, Angel Cabrera, with the perennial Open challenger Jesper Parnevik, again grasping after the Claret Jug, a further shot back. Three players were on four-over, and it's worth mentioning at this stage that Paul Lawrie of Scotland lay seventh on five-over, four strokes off the pace.

Early Saturday morning rain was replaced by sun and a fairly strong wind for Van de Velde's bid to hang on to his lead. He says he took a philosophical approach to his position:

'You're leading the Open playing the third round, but I didn't feel I had any pressure on my shoulders. First of all, I have to make sure I don't beat myself. Second of all, I have to try to play the golf course instead of all the many great players around. You just have to go out and play and try not to think about anything else.

'It was great playing with Cabrera. He has such a good temperament. That helped me a lot. But I had quite an amazing day. Sometimes, you can putt well throughout a tournament but there is always a day when you can still putt well but not make as many. I was making so many putts. It was incredible. And I had another great finish. This time, I birdied 14, 16 and 18 and shot a 70. Three-under for the last five holes at Carnoustie, you're doing pretty good.'

The golfing world was shaken. Van de Velde had been a 100–1 outsider even after the first round, but, five strokes ahead of the field on level-par, he was now in a position to become the second French winner after Arnaud Massey lifted the Claret Jug in 1907 at the Royal Liverpool Club, Hoylake.

Van de Velde was beating the odds and leaving the fancied players in his wake. The favourite, Tiger Woods, for instance, trailed by seven strokes, although he did share fourth place. One of Van de Velde's nearest challengers was the Australian they call 'Popeye' because of his brawny arms, Craig Parry. If Popeye felt he had one hand on the Claret Jug with a stunning early run the next day, it was to be cruelly whipped off by a triple-bogey uppercut that the cartoon character's chief adversary, Bluto, would have been proud of. Then, after clawing his way back, Parry was hit by another body-blow, this one a double-bogey, at the penultimate hole.

Justin Leonard, the winner two years previously at Royal Troon, was the other player sharing second place. Leonard would have a grasp on the trophy in the end, but have it wrenched off by Carnoustie's 18th hole, first in proper time and then in a play-off.

The third player in the piece on that unforgettable Sunday finale, Paul Lawrie, did not even rate a mention by anybody other than a couple of mournful Scottish newspapermen, noting that the man from Aberdeen, just up the road, lay ten shots behind Van de Velde. Curiously, although everyone marvelled at Van de Velde's feats, he didn't get a huge amount of press coverage on the Sunday morning, either. That included back home, where it would have taken something pretty mega-sensational to overshadow the Tour de France. By Sunday afternoon, though, Van de Velde had done the unthinkable: his feats at Carnoustie broke into the Tour de France coverage on French television.

Van de Velde admits he was in a bit of whirl when he took to the tee after a fitful night:

'Five ahead. I'm thinking, "What's going on?" That night in bed, I was like a slice of toast. You lie on one side for a while and then you turn over and toast the other side, and then you repeat it over again. I finally fell asleep around two o'clock in the morning, but then I slept OK.

'In the morning, I went through all my normal routines as if it was any day. Deep down, I knew it wasn't, of course. When we went to play the final round, the conditions were not as difficult. The wind dropped and it had turned the other way round. For instance, when we played 17, it was downwind this time. I remember hitting two-iron, four-iron, when the previous day I'd hit driver, three-wood on 17.

'I was playing with Craig Parry, and I went through a difficult start. Craig played really well at the start, though, and I think he was two- or three-under reaching the turn. I was two- or three-over, and Craig was one ahead through ten or eleven holes.

'Nothing was really happening for me. But I just thought, "Sooner or later, you are going to run into some difficulty on that golf course," and unfortunately for Craig it came at the 12th, where he triple-bogeyed. He was in the rough and couldn't even get the ball out. In fact, I think he had a fresh-air shot. He made double or triple and I made bogey. It was a very tough par-four, very long. The wind was blowing from the left.

'It gave me a bit of breathing space. I went from one behind to one ahead. I thought to myself, "If you can play these last six holes level-par, you're going to win this tournament." I "parred" the par-three – bogeyed it, that is – and then birdied the par-five, the 14th, hit on in two. I miraculously parred the 15th after hitting 100 yards right into the bunker of number 4 hole – got up and down from 70 yards. I made a good par on 16 and then hit a great four-iron on 17 but took the wrong side of the mound there. I hit a great putt up stone dead, though, so that was another par.'

Then, as they say, the rest is history.

Paul Lawrie had been half-tempted to make a start for home, but his was not exactly a long journey, and, besides, hadn't he better just hang on a little while? He might yet be needed for the prize-giving after surging through the field with a 67 – easily the best final round. His aggregate of six-over-par started to look really good, and it only improved.

Leonard looked as though he would better Lawrie's four-round target, but the American lost his chance of outright victory by finding the Barry Burn at the last and also finished six-over.

It was there for the taking for Van de Velde, who held a three-stroke lead with only the par-four 18th to come. Only the 18th. If only.

'On the last, I hit it straight right. Actually, I was pretty unlucky not to be in the burn. Because if I'm in the burn, I take a drop there. And, because of the angle, I probably would have had to drop it further back. I would then not be able to reach the green. So I would have had to hit it short of the burn, then pitch onto the green, probably make two putts and make a six.

'Unfortunately, as it turned out, I was perfectly placed when I got to my ball. The ball was sitting just in the kind of semi-rough of the 17th hole. It was like it was on a tee-peg. The fairway was diagonal to me, compared to where I came from. I thought there was one thing

I have to do here. That's to get past the water. Then, wherever I finish, it was basically, don't finish left. That was 50 yards off-line from where I was hitting, so I didn't worry about that. Even if it leaks a little right and you end up in the grandstand, it shouldn't be a problem. I've never seen a ball bounce off the grandstand out of bounds – or do what it did to me.

'I hit my two-iron. What happened was just freaky. But I couldn't see anything. I heard a big bang, a clatter, as the ball hit what I can only call "designer-fencing". It was a kind of arch to make the grandstand not look too ugly, I guess. Then I heard the crowd go "Awhhh" and then "Oooh" and then "Ahhh". I'm thinking, "What happened?"

'I walked up and found my ball 40 yards short of the green and about 25 yards short of the burn, and I am mystified. I thought, "How the hell did it come here?"

'Somebody said, "Well, you hit the grandstand."

'I thought, "Well, even if I hit the grandstand, how can the ball come all the way back here?"

'What had happened was, after hitting the grandstand, the ball went into the hazard. It's a stone wall, the hazard, with steps. It landed in the hazard, probably hit a rock or one of the steps and bounced back up again another 20 yards. It was in deep rough. The problem was not just being in the rough. That's a horrific break, to be honest. That kind of thing doesn't happen, only in a horror movie. But on top of coming back, the ball found a terrible spot. Because the wind had been blowing so hard from behind all week, on 18, all the grass was lying towards the green. My ball was lying embedded in very thick stuff. The grass was lying with me, but with the ball buried underneath it. I thought, "Oh, my God."

'If there was one shot I could take back, the next one would have been the only one. From being there in two, I was now not sure what to do. I considered chipping it sideways, but I thought, "I have no insurance I'll be on the fairway." I didn't know if I was going to make ten yards, or fifteen yards, or twenty-five yards, or whatever. Thinking about it afterwards, that was irrelevant. Ten yards and I'm likely to have a better lie than I've got. Then, from there, I could have a pretty straight pitch, 40 yards or so to the green, which is straight in line with me, because I'm gaining the angle. From there, I would have been very likely to have hit it onto the green.

'That's just history and speculation. I decided to go forward. I thought I could clear the water. I definitely didn't hit it hard enough. There's no doubt about it. I could have given it a big whack. But it's OB behind the green. The club-face shuts and you could go straight left and OB as well . . . You'd never know what was going to happen if you hit it too hard.

'I went in the burn.'

With that, Van de Velde took off his shoes and socks, rolled his trousers up past his knees and lowered himself into the Barry Burn. The time he took to do this probably cost him the Open. In taking care not to spoil his shoes and clothing, the dapper Frenchman lessened his chances of being able to hit his ball, which was sitting high enough above the waterline to get a stroke on it at first. Should he have ignored his instinct to always look his best? Holding the Auld Claret Jug aloft with squelching shoes and soaked trousers would have been a small price to pay. Easy to discuss in hindsight. In the throes of trying to win an Open, who does think straight? And, thinks Van de Velde, Mother Nature probably cost him dearly, too:

'When I went to my ball in the burn, it was very funny, because the tide was coming up. People don't realise what I was doing and they say, "What did you get in the water for?" But the ball wasn't under the level of the water when I decided I was going to take my shoes off. I don't know whether people know, but the burn is tidal. It can rise two metres in half an hour. It's amazing how quickly it was coming in.

'Craig Parry said to me, "Mate, if you wait for six hours, you could probably play it. There won't be any water there."

'By the time I took my shoes off, the ball went from being only half in the water to being completely submerged. If it had remained the way it was — half out — it is nothing. It's like a bunker-shot. I could play it any day, to be honest, if it had stayed the way it was. The problem then was not hitting it out; I was pretty sure I could hit it out. The problem was the face [of the burn]. If I hit it and leave it in, I waste a shot. So I thought, "I'm going to have to drop it behind."

'The rough was still very, very high where I dropped it, and now I had the bunkers straight in line. I have the flag I can go at, but it's a tough shot. I could have decided to chip maybe a little less, but if it goes a little quicker, maybe I hit it a little too hard, then I can release and go OB, because I am hitting directly in line with the OB as well. But I decided to go for the flag and see where it goes. Once again, I didn't want to hit it too hard, because there is trouble everywhere. I put it in the bunker.

'Craig said to me, "Let me get out of your way."

'He's lying 2 ft past my ball. He's got exactly the same shot that I have. From there, he played exactly the shot that I need. He holes it.

'I smiled, but my heart had sunk because what are the odds of me following him in? [Parry urged Van de Velde to do just that.] The guy tells me he's going to get out of my way, ends up missing the play-off by one shot, because he made six on 17 by three-putting from 20 ft, and he hits the shot that I need. I wondered, "What else is going to happen today?" Of course, I didn't follow him in. But I did make a good up-and-down with a putt of about 8 or 9 ft.'

And so into a four-hole play-off with Lawrie and Leonard, played over Carnoustie's formidable four closing holes. Van de Velde explains how he had to lift himself for the fray:

'It was very late, getting dark. To be honest, I wasn't in the best of spirits for the play-off, ending a tournament like I had. Afterwards, when I reflected on it, I either had not enough time or too much time. After I signed my card, I had half an hour before we went to play the play-off. Half an hour is a long time. I should have signed the card, got straight on the buggy and gone straight out. In that half-hour, you start to have all kind of emotions in your head. You have all these questions coming into your head and not enough time to answer them. You are in between the two. You are ready and you're not ready. I was definitely not ready to go and play four more holes, that's for sure.

'Then it started raining. And I wasn't fresh. You come out after an emotional stretch. It's difficult, no doubt. It was very hard to get back and concentrate on what I was supposed to do. It took me a couple of holes to get back.

'You can't take two holes to recover in a four-hole play-off. It was very damp, very late. I made a double at the first hole, 15. Everybody hit it left and got into trouble, but they both escaped with just bogeys. I hit a pretty good shot on 16, the par-three, but just caught the bunker. We all made bogeys. I birdied the 17th, so I could still hope, but Paul also birdied it.

'Then Paul hit two tremendous shots on 18. He hit a driver and a four-iron to only 3 ft. That was it, the end of the story.'

The end of the story indeed. Lawrie's second birdie of the day on 18, fashioned on a magnificent two-hundred-and-twenty-one-yard four-iron approach, saw the Scot win by three strokes and get his name etched on the famous old trophy. Triumph for Lawrie, and misery for Van de Velde and Leonard.

Van de Velde put on a brave face. He walked into his press conference and, when he saw all the sympathetic faces, said, 'What's the matter? Somebody died?' He had made the news and would go down in history as producing the biggest blow-up in the Open. And Lawrie had won. So what about Leonard? In years to come, the question might be: who was the other player who made up the three-man play-off in the Open of 1999? Who's going to remember Justin Leonard for anything other than 1997?

Leonard saw it this way:

'I lost the British Open twice in one day. That makes it twice as hard to take. When I played the 18th the first time, I pretty much thought I had to make birdie. If I was just trying to make four, I would have laid up. I thought there was a reasonable chance I could get the ball over the burn. Jean was on the green on 17, and I figured the worst he would do on the last was to make five, so I needed to make a three. I had about 229 to the front edge of the 18th green, which put me at about 216 to carry the burn. I tried to hit a three-wood. It didn't quite come out the way I'd hoped, and the ball ended up trickling into the burn. Then I got up and down for bogey. At that point, I didn't really think it meant a whole lot.'

While it launched Lawrie to celebratory status, Van de Velde would never be forgotten either for his escapade at Carnoustie's closing hole. Would he have played it any other way?

'Well, you can rewrite history! Why did I need to hit a driver on the 18th when I could have got down to the burn with a couple of irons? People need to check the hole before they criticise. It's over 480 yards, a bit into the breeze when we arrived at the tee. It's 185 or 188 to carry the burn; the burn opens up at 240, so you can see taking a driver is the best option – if you can hit a good drive. Even if you hit it into the bunker, it doesn't matter. You hit it forward from a bunker, from the rough; you hit it short and then you hit it on.

'I hit the ball OK – not on the correct fairway, but I was perfectly placed. The argument is "Why didn't you go left? Why didn't you come back on the fairway?" The answer is because I was coming at an angle. If I was in the middle of the fairway, straight in front, then maybe I would have decided it was a little bit risky. Maybe then I'd have played an eight-iron short and then a wedge or a sand-iron. But I was coming from an angle, so I thought I'd got a good chance to get over. And I had such a good lie.

'That's the way it goes. I suffered from a freak rebound. I'd say 999 times out of a thousand you couldn't have been that unlucky with a ricochet.

'But that week, it showed me that if I play well and putt well, I can compete with anybody in the world. You always have that in your head, but you have the confirmation when it happens.

'Having your name on the trophy would have been nice and, of course, good for your ego. Everyone dreams about it. But, at the end of the day, with the reaction I got, I was pretty proud anyway. I had so many messages, and so many people in my country, all over Europe, in America, said to me, "You know what? You've made me love golf. You've inspired me to start the game."

'If you can make people dream, that's priceless. That made me feel a lot better about not having my name on the trophy.'

1999 TOP SCORES

P. Lawrie 73–74–76–67 290

J. Van de Velde 75–68–70–77 290

J. Leonard 73–74–71–72 290

(Lawrie won four-hole play-off)

C. Parry 76–75–67–73 291

A. Cabrera 75–69–77–70 291

2001, ROYAL LYTHAM AND ST ANNES: IAN WOOSNAM

(When leading straight after the start of the final round, Woosnam suffered a two-stroke penalty for having one too many clubs in his bag and finished tied third behind winner David Duval)

'My caddie said to me, "You're going to go ballistic."

'I said, "Why?"

'He said, "We have two drivers in the bag!"

'It meant we had fifteen clubs – an automatic two-shot penalty.'

SEVERAL PLAYERS COULD say they had a loose grip on the Claret Jug in 2001 before David Duval lifted it. Colin Montgomerie, Ernie Els, Bernhard Langer, Darren Clarke and Alex Cejka were in contention either early on or over the closing holes. One player, though, stands out as the biggest 'if only' of the week: the pocket battleship Ian Woosnam.

The stocky little Welsh veteran had already rolled back the years to produce the sort of form that won him the Masters a decade previously, when he stood on the 1st at Royal Lytham and St Annes in Sunday's final round. An arrow-like tee-shot at the par-three hole, where Lanny Wadkins once began his Open with a hole-in-one, nearly earned Woosnam an ace, too, and it did earn him a birdie to go into a share of the lead. But calamity was about to befall him.

Memorable Opens often have their own sobriquets: 'The Duel in

215

the Sun', 'The Car Park Open', 'The Ball in the Broken Beer Bottle Open', for instance. Lytham and 2001 will be forever known as 'The 15-club Open'. For the sake of an extra club, Ian Woosnam's one hand was torn off the famous old trophy, and it never went back on again that day.

The Open began quietly for Woosnam, as he shot a one-over-par 72. He used his one-iron for many of his tee-shots, because he had struggled a little in practice with keeping his drivers on the fairway. Keeping the ball below the wind was another conundrum. Worrying about choosing a driver he would be happy with on the breezy links of Lytham was to prove deadly in the finish for Woosnam.

There was only one name in the British newspapers' stories of the opening day, and it wasn't Ian Woosnam's. Colin Montgomerie was the man they all lauded. Could Monty, who was touted as the best European Tour player never to have won a major (interestingly, David Duval suffered from the same label in America), do it this time?

Montgomerie already had seven consecutive European number-one honours to his name, but he rarely performed well at the Open. It was different this time, as his 65 earned him a three-shot lead. Nobody talked about Woosnam. He was not bothered about that. But he did know that his score, spoiled by an indifferent back nine, had not reflected how well he was playing.

When Woosnam shot a 68 in the second round, he at least attracted press interest, even though he was all of five strokes behind Montgomerie, who held on to his lead, if only by a stroke. Woosnam had found the right recipe for scoring better, but he was not totally comfortable with his driving – something that stayed, chillingly, with him throughout the week. As he said at the time:

'I had a few pints [the night before] and it seemed to do the trick. I wouldn't say I played fantastic. I kept the ball in play, made birdies at the right time and really didn't make many mistakes. I just kept mis-hitting my drives a little bit, losing 20 yards here and there. You get a little bit uptight because you've got to get it on the fairway. Even if you're a little behind, you can still get the ball on the green. I just needed to improve the striking a little bit.

'I worked on the range for an hour and a half. It certainly helped. If the wind got up, you got in front of the ball and trapped it because of being in the wrong position.'

Woosnam's tinkering with his driving continued after the third round, but by then his whole outlook had changed. This was a man who, despite being 43, believed he had the game to win now.

It was just like old times. Woosnam and Bernhard Langer played together in the third round and they both shot 67s to zoom to the top of the leaderboard. There was life in the old dogs yet – they were to follow Sam Torrance and become Ryder Cup captains for the next two campaigns – and both veterans harboured hopes of winning.

With pre-tournament favourite Tiger Woods virtually out of the frame and Montgomerie slipping right down the field to only 28th place, Woosnam, Langer, Duval and Germany's Alex Cejka, who at one time threatened to run away with the third round, held a one-stroke lead. It was Woosnam's best performance at Royal Lytham and left him full of optimism.

A few weeks previously, Woosnam had, in an off-guard moment, casually suggested he was getting bored with the game, particularly all the travelling around. After his fine effort in the third round, a mischievous journalist asked him if his 67 had put him back in love with the game. The fiery little Welsh dragon dismissed the question by replying that he was so in love with the game he was going to play '52 weeks of the year, Christmas as well,' snapping, 'Now get rid of the crap.'

He was pleased with his day's work, though, with the exception, still, of one department.

'Conditions were pretty favourable, set up for good scoring. The greens were a little bit faster and drier and, overall, the course was fantastic. It was a matter of trying to get your ball in the right place on the fairways, then try and get it close to the pin and, hopefully, hole a few putts. I played pretty steady. I had to have a few chips and putts on the first four holes, but after that I played pretty solid.

'I don't know whether it was just me, but Lytham seemed more fair. If the ball hit the fairway, you stayed on it. Sometimes, when it gets really bone-hard, you can hit the fairway and your ball jumps into the rough and all sorts.

'Some of the pin placements were a bit tricky. You had to try to stay away from the pins and accept you are going to be 25 or 30 ft away, and hopefully hit a good putt and it goes in, or two-putt and go on to the next hole.

'I must admit, there was one club I was struggling with: my driver in the wind. Downwind, it was all right, but into the wind I just started to squeeze the ball out and hit a weak shot all the time.'

And so the seeds of mischance were sown. Other seeds of misfortune were to follow. Woosnam found out, to his chagrin, that he would not be in the final group out the next day. As he had remembered handing his card in before Langer following the third round, Woosnam automatically thought he would be out with Duval in the final match. This was under the 'first one in, last one out' ruling. Duval, shooting a blistering 65 in the third round, had been first man in on six-under, so was automatically one of the last players out in the final group. Then had come Langer and Woosnam, ahead of Cejka, so one of them would accompany Duval. There is confusion as to why Langer got the nod instead of Woosnam. Was it because Langer had teed off first in the third round? Or did he putt out first on the 18th on the Saturday? Whatever the reason, Woosnam was down to tee-off with Cejka in the penultimate match, followed by Langer and Duval.

In the scheme of things on Sunday afternoon, did this decision also affect the outcome of the 2001 Open Championship? Would an extra ten minutes before teeing off have unearthed and averted the error that would leave Woosnam forever wondering whether he could have lifted the famous trophy instead of Duval? How would the blocks of fate have stacked up? We will never know.

Woosnam went to bed on Saturday night with the best wishes, it seemed, of most of Wales and his home town, Oswestry, ringing in his ears. He didn't sleep that well but was pleased to get to the course ready for practice, with his perennial back problem not surfacing.

Because he had had worries about his driving, he concentrated on that for a time, finally opting for a new driver that had been offered to him on the range by one of the club manufacturers. It had felt sweet when he tested it, and so he decided to play with the new one instead of his normal driver. Woosnam said afterwards that he sent his old driver back to the locker-room with his caddie, Myles Byrne, an Irishman from a caddieing family in Bray, whom he had taken on that year.

Woosnam went to the 1st tee oblivious of what was going to prove a calamitous start to the final day. All could not have begun better. A swish with a stock-in-trade easy swing gave Woosnam a wonderful start to the day. His six-iron carried his ball to inches, nearly holing out. Woosnam tapped in and strode to the 2nd tee on seven-under-par, level with Sweden's Niclas Fasth, who was well into his round, and a shot ahead of playing-partner Cejka and Langer and Duval, who were just teeing off.

Then Woosnam's world caved in. He was crushed by a revelation from his caddie.

'I played a six-iron at the 1st hole to about 6 in., took the ball to the 2nd tee and my caddie said to me, "You're going to go ballistic."

'I said, "Why?"

'He said, "We have two drivers in the bag!"

'It meant we had fifteen clubs – an automatic two-shot penalty.'

A crestfallen Woosnam had to approach the match referee, John Paramor, of the European Tour and relate his awful tale. Paramor confirmed the two-shot penalty. A birdie-two became a bogey-four. Woosnam slammed his cap on the floor and threw the cuckoo out of its nest, hurling the rogue driver behind the tee.

'At that moment, I felt like I'd been kicked in the teeth. It's hard enough playing level with some of the best players in the world, but to give them a two-shot advantage!'

Woosnam had to regroup. But how do you get something like that out of your mind? Well, of course, you don't. Not even if you are 43 and you've been through nearly every scenario in golf. Not this one, you hadn't.

'I still had 17 holes to go in the Open Championship. It was like a battle. I never really got it out of my head all the way round. I kept thinking, "If I hadn't had a two-shot penalty, I would have been leading."

'The next few holes, I felt lousy. I got plugged on the 4th. Everything seemed to be going against me. I felt like picking up and walking in. I was cheesed off.

'I like a good fight, though. I had to get over it. I did. That's the fighting spirit in me. It took me quite a few holes to recover.'

Five holes, to be precise. Then Woosnam made eagle on the 6th.

'The eagle helped a lot. And word seemed to spread around the course about what had happened to me. Even on the 2nd green, the crowd were behind me. They were fantastic. They felt sorry for me. That helped me. It was quite something coming up the 18th.

'I managed to shoot level-par, but I would have finished at least second without that bogey on the 1st. Who knows what might have been if I'd had 14 clubs instead of 15?

'I had been experimenting with two drivers on the practice ground. Myles thought someone else had taken the driver out of the bag and taken it to the locker-room. There were two big head-covers on the two drivers, so he should have spotted that. Maybe he was a little nervous, trying to think of other things, like trying to praise his man, for instance. But it is the ultimate sin for a caddie, not counting the clubs.

'I suppose I should have checked the clubs, but that's what you pay a caddie for. It's the biggest mistake he'll make in his life.'

Added to the quest to find the right driver and the fact that he wasn't in the last group was one more significant point about Woosnam's fateful early moments in the 2001 Open. Lytham's 1st hole is, as amply demonstrated in this passage, a par-three. If it had been a par-four, which would have left Woosnam pondering whether to use his one-iron or a driver, he would surely have noticed the extra weapon. His misery would have been spared, and we may still have had a different champion.

'If I had needed a driver on the 1st, we would have spotted it straight away.'

It wasn't spotted. David Duval was the one holding the Claret Jug with both hands, a winner by three strokes from Niclas Fasth. Woosnam had to settle for a share of third place, a further shot behind.

Not only did the 15th club almost certainly put paid to his Open chances, finishing only third was to eventually cost him a Ryder Cup place. It was a big price to pay for what is, after all, an innocent oversight, punished so severely by golf's pedantic, but mostly necessary, rules.

Woosnam admirably recovered his composure enough that very evening to forgive his caddie such a costly mistake and hold back from firing him. Two weeks later, he did sack Byrne, however, after the bagman overslept and missed their tee-time in Malmö during the Scandinavian Masters. Woosnam had to take on the local caddie-master and break open his locker door to get out his clubs. Byrne had the key – just as, it seems, he had on a fateful last day at Lytham.

2001 TOP SCORES

D. Duval 69–73–65–67 274
N. Fasth 69–69–72–67 277
I. Woosnam 72–68–67–71 278
B. Langer 71–69–67–71 278
E. Els 71–71–67–69 278
D. Clarke 70–69–69–70 278
M.A. Jiménez 69–72–67–70 278
B. Mayfair 69–72–67–70 278

2002, MUIRFIELD: THOMAS LEVET

(Levet lost in a sudden-death shoot-out to winner Ernie Els)

'When I saw his lie in the bunker, I said, "I'm not finished yet," because it was awful. He made one of the best bunker-shots ever seen under pressure . . . Then . . . to get up and down was fantastic. I was happy to push him that far.'

THREE YEARS EARLIER, Jean Van de Velde had tried and failed to become the first Frenchman to win an Open Championship since Arnaud Massey in 1907. It took another three years for Thomas Levet to try to achieve the same feat. While Van de Velde had the better chance of winning, Levet actually went the further of the two, standing on the brink of victory before finally giving best to Ernie Els.

The 2002 Open was set up to be a battle between the two best young golfers in the world at the time: Tiger Woods and Els. Britain's fickle weather and Woods's difficulties in counteracting it badly affected his chances. When push came to shove on the final day, there were four hands on the Claret Jug. And none of those hands were Woods's.

When Levet – with two victories on the European Tour to his credit, one of them notably a four-man play-off – arrived at Muirfield, he says he had no idea what was in store for him:

'When you show up for the Open, you hope the course is not too difficult. When I arrived there, it was an absolute monster! The rough was very, very high. We got lucky that the weather was decent for a few days. It was awful on Saturday, and the scores showed it, but for the other three days we had beautiful sunshine and it wasn't that windy.

'It was playable most of the time, and you could hit a lot of iron-shots off the tee. On the Saturday, though, when the wind really got up, it was impossible to hit irons off the tee. You might not make the fairway, or the hole would become way too long.

'When I arrived there, I knew I was playing well, but in those conditions, when the rough is so high, you need to try to do what you would do with a horse: put the blinkers on. Don't look. Don't worry about what is going on around you. Get on with the job and focus on it only. That's why, I think, I played good that week. I didn't look where the possible "miss" was. I just thought, "Aim at the middle and hammer it down the middle." That was my philosophy for the week, and it worked out pretty good. Perhaps I should do it all the time! If you had the game to do it, fine, but if your game wasn't in such good shape, it was probably difficult to do that. But when the course is set up like it was, if you can do that, it gives you a big advantage over the guy who's hitting it sideways all the time.

'I got lucky that week. I hit it straight.'

Not so straight on the 9th in the first round, though. Lady luck plays her hand at every Open, and this time she was with Levet. With things going reasonably well, he suddenly drove into the right rough on 9, hacked across into the left rough and his ball dived into the thick stuff. After a quick search, he found it, strolled across to check yardages with his caddie – then couldn't find it when he went back! There followed a frantic three- or four-minutes' search before the relieved Frenchman relocated his ball. On such incidents are Opens played out, with the fickle hand of fate pointing one way or another. At the end of the round, though, there was no sign of what was to come for Levet in his modest opening.

'It is imperative you have a good start in a major. I shot 72 on day one. You need something solid, and this was solid enough, even if I was one-over. It was not a difficult day, but conditions were not that easy because the greens were bouncing a lot. I achieved my first goal, which was not to shoot myself out of the tournament straight away. I was in a fairly decent position to make the cut.'

Only thinking about the cut. That was understandable, although Levet was actually only five strokes off the lead held jointly by Americans David Toms, the US PGA champion the previous year, and Duffy Waldorf (making a few heads swim with his rather colourful and flowery shirts that week) and Swede Carl Pettersson. Favourites Woods and Els were well back in the field.

Levet was ready to make a move up, however. He says he was well in the mood to do so:

'Day two, I made no mistakes at all. It was just super golf and could have been lower than that, but that 66 was very pleasant. On a tough course like that, you could settle for par. It put me around eighth place, but what was more important was that the driving and the long-game were absolutely perfect. I don't think I'd hit the ball any better than I did for those first two days.'

The move had been made by Levet, and there were now ominous signs from the two favourites. Els, with a 66, surged into a share of a one-stroke lead on six-under-par with Waldorf, a resurgent Bob Tway, the man who had chipped in to dash Greg Norman's US PGA Championship hopes way back in 1986, Irishman Padraig Harrington, and a Japanese, Shigeki Maruyama. Woods was two strokes behind, sharing the spot with, among others, Colin Montgomerie, who had produced a magnificent 64, and Levet.

Saturday's high winds, armour-piercing rain and clouds that looked as though the Apocalypse was approaching would shatter quite a few dreams. Among those lost forever in the tournament was Woods, who plummeted off the leaderboard, his hopes of the Grand Slam dashed virtually terminally. Montgomerie shot an 84, 20 strokes worse than his previous day's effort. It was a day of the long scythes – scything rain, that is. Levet had it all under control, he maintains:

'My accuracy that week was a great benefit on the Saturday, when the weather was terrible. I was hitting lots of straight tee-shots. I only went into the high rough twice. That was it for the day. I made two bogeys. Everybody was making bogeys.

'The most important thing for me about Saturday was that I avoided all the bunkers around the greens. That is a big key at Muirfield, missing the sand. It certainly helped me shoot a 74, which was better than the average on a horrendous day for a lot of players.'

For the later starters, anything in the early 70s was a good score, so Levet did not lose much ground. Els's 72 kept him on top of the leaderboard, on five-under, two strokes ahead of Dane Soren Hansen. There was a whole gaggle three off the pace. Levet and, notably, Australian Steve Elkington were in the group four strokes behind.

With the number-one favourite seemingly out of the picture, his rivals prepared to make hay as the sun shone again on Sunday, as if mocking Woods's bid to follow up his Masters success.

As the final day unfolded, there was an early surprise in store for the packed leaderboard jostlers. Gary Evans, the injury-prone Englishman who was the European Tour's perennial flatterer-to-deceive, first scrabbled a couple of fingernails on the famous jug. Just as with Steve Bottomley in 1995, though, there was to be no fairy-tale story for Evans, whose histrionics when holing a 40-footer after losing a ball on 17 will long be remembered. Something must have told Evans that six-under, at which he stayed by dint of his unlikely putt, was going to be the mark. However, he promptly bogeyed the last for a 65 and five-under.

That stood as the target for a good while – in fact, for a good deal of Els's round. Evans will forever wonder if his ball had not gone to ground at the penultimate hole, what might have been. If it hadn't been lost, would he still have made par? Or might he have made birdie?

Evans was eventually overtaken by Stuart Appleby, who had lain five off the lead overnight. He also carded a 65 but for six-under. Appleby stayed ahead on his own, as Padraig Harrington also nudged a finger or two on the trophy by going to six-under with a birdie on 17. However, the Irishman then lost his hold altogether by bogeying the last, also finishing five-under.

Levet was the next man in.

'In the final round, I had a really great start. I picked up a couple of shots and then I birdied number 9 to go three-under for the day and four-under for the tournament. From 10 to 17, I was just putting for birdie all the time, but nothing was dropping.

'I could see other guys were having trouble, especially at the par-threes, 13 and 16, so I stayed calm and accepted par after par.

'Then, on 17, I made a monster putt for eagle and suddenly it made the difference between being seventh, which would have been a good result already, to being second. All because of one putt.

'At that stage, I thought, "Oh, my God." Ernie was in the lead, but by only one shot. I've got only the 18th to play, and he has a lot of trouble coming. He has those 13th and 16th holes to come, both playing really tough.

'It was a nice feeling. I said to myself, "Oh, my God; I can do something here." After that long putt on 17, I felt I really could win the tournament. It was such a sweet feeling – very, very nice. It was very different from the feeling you get in an ordinary tournament. This was a major; this was the Open.'

Three years previously, France had flown the tricolour. But while Jean Van de Velde could have made a double-bogey on the last at Carnoustie and won, Levet says he felt he had a more onerous task:

'I decided I had to birdie 18. I knew, somehow, I just had to birdie it. I went after the driver, like I did every day. That day, there was basically no wind. I hit a really good drive and a nine-iron. All I wanted to do was make that putt for a 65. It just went by.'

So now there were two on top: Appleby and Levet. Levet did well to compose himself enough to make the putt going back and sign for a 66. Soon, they were joined by another Australian, Steve Elkington, who also returned a 66. Three hands on the Claret Jug. But would the tall and elegant South African, who had tried and fallen short so many times, end their hopes and wrest their tenuous hold?

Els had already played what was to become the shot of the week when he somehow squeezed his chip from a horrible lie in the bunker at the short 13th to just a foot and made par, rather than taking the double-bogey that looked more likely. That kept him eight-under. Although he bogeyed the 14th, unable to rescue himself from sand this time, Els still looked favourite to win in normal time as he played the 16th. However, proving that Levet knew what he was talking about, Els took double-bogey on the next short hole, the 16th, hitting his tee-shot long and left and then blading his recovery.

It needed a monumental effort of determination from Els, or his Open dreams would be shattered again. A raking drive on 17, a majestic four-iron and a decisive second putt for birdie after a tentative approach put Els on six-under and back in the mix. The final-hole birdie was beyond him, though, and he had to settle for par on the last. As he signed his card, Els knew it could have all gone wrong, and he had to gather his wits and his resources for a play-off. It had been a close call in the end, and now he was going to be pushed to finish the job.

While Levet admired his South African contemporary, he confesses he'd rather not have had Els for company:

'We were waiting and waiting. When Ernie made double-bogey on 16, I thought there could be only us three guys in it. I wished we had only been three!'

But there were four. And for a certain sports psychologist, having two of the quartet as clients left him in two minds. Belgian mental coach Jos Vanstiphout had Els and Levet on his books. To which should he administer his words of wisdom? Levet, typically, saw the humorous side of it all, as the man they call 'Mr Magic' tried to produce two rabbits out of the hat.

'It was funny. He didn't know where to go. I can't remember who he spoke to most – or if at all – I was so focused on what I had to do. I heard he was rushing around not knowing whether to talk to my wife or Ernie's wife while we were out there. He was jumping up and down. Jos was probably the most nervous of the three of us. And he couldn't lose!'

On the course, somebody did have to lose, though. Whose nerve would hold best? Levet had a plan which he hoped would win it for him, as he and Elkington went off first. Rather than play it as a four-ball, the R & A decreed it would be two two-balls, with Els and Appleby following on, much to Levet's surprise.

'The play-off holes were going to be tough. The 17th, the par-five, wasn't so difficult, but holes 1, 16 and 18 were probably three, four and five in difficulty. So it was going to be a stiff test.

'It was very strange in the play-off – one of the strangest things I've known in golf. We were four guys for the play-off and we didn't play together. There are things that would have turned out in a different way, I'm sure, if we had all played together. For a start, I would probably have played 17 a little differently if we had played as a four.

'When we started play-off, I said to my caddie immediately, "Look. What we need is the same plan as we had during the tournament. We need to play these holes the same way as I had in the tournament." I just concentrated on making the best score possible at the four holes, not thinking what might be at the end of them.

'As Steve and I were out first, my first objective was to make par to start off. My goal was to make par, par, birdie, par. I felt one-under was a realistic winning score. It would have been, of course.

'When I made a long putt on 16, a very long one across the green, to go one-under, I was one ahead of my prediction. I thought to myself, "This is looking good."

'Then I hit the fairway on 17, and I felt even better. I said to myself, "Just keep steady. Keep calm. Play the shots one after the other and don't think ahead of yourself. Lots of things can still happen. Don't worry about the other guys; just go forward and play it as it comes."

'I completely blotted out any visions of lifting the trophy. I'd been in positions of winning on the European Tour, on the French tour, and this is something you should never do. Plus, I would say that course was so difficult, you didn't have time to think about that. You had enough things to do around that course than thinking, "I'm going to win the Open." That's one of my strengths: under pressure,

I just think about what I have to do. I take the shot and then another one, then another one. I never think about what might happen if I miss the fairway or the green.

'As I said, I might have played 17 another way if we'd all been together and I knew exactly what was going on. I would have known if they were in trouble, when I was set up OK. I would probably have tried for a much safer birdie. I went for it a little bit too much on the second shot and missed the green, made only par. If I'd hit my second shot on the green, the tournament could have been over.

'Then I bogeyed the 18th, when I wasn't quite so straight off the tee this time. I just had a feeling that dropping a shot at the end, which took me back to level-par, was going to make a lot of difference to the outcome. It wasn't nerves. I just didn't hit the best of drives. It didn't go my way.'

While it hadn't completely gone his way, Levet was still not beaten. His playing-partner, Elkington, bogeyed the 1st, birdied the 17th but then bogeyed the 18th. On one-over, his Open was over. Appleby bogeyed the 16th, birdied the 17th and then bogeyed 18. His bid was over. Els parred all four holes but survived through Levet's final-hole bogey. The Parisian kicked himself for not quite finishing off the job but prepared himself for a tumultuous shoot-out.

'The sudden-death play-off was an incredible sensation. The crowd was really loud. I couldn't hear my caddie and he was only a yard away from me! It sort of made the hairs on the back of your neck stand up. When Ernie missed his putt on 18, we walked back to the tee, and all the way back people were just crazy. The woman driving my buggy was trying to speak to me, but I couldn't hear what she was trying to say. It was impossible.

'When we got to the tee, I said to myself, "OK, stay calm. Just play the hole the way we've played it all week long." I wanted to hit a long drive down the right side, because the rough is very light on the right, then hit a shortish iron to the middle of the green and try to make the putt, like I did all week long.

'It was the only driver I missed left all week. I had been hitting the ball really well that week, and, even hitting it left, a good drive would have passed the bunkers. But I hit it low left and found a bunker. I said to myself, "Steady. Ernie still has plenty to do." When you hit an iron off the tee, like Ernie did, you still have a very long second shot. He was on 210 yards, or something like that. The ball's bouncing and the green's not that big, so I told myself, "Keep the ball in play. You have to make him win the tournament."

'I had to get back to the fairway and then try to hit it close enough to save par. Then, you never know. My plan could work, because he had to go for it and missed the green with his second shot and put the ball in the bunker. When I saw his lie in the bunker, I said, "I'm not finished yet," because it was awful.

'He made one of the best bunker-shots ever seen under pressure. It didn't quite match the one he did on 13 during regulation play, because he hit much closer there – that was also unbelievably difficult – but this one on 18 was under even more pressure and the lie was bad. Then, to hold your nerve after that chip, to hole a putt that was a good 3 ft, was a remarkable thing. To get up and down was fantastic. I was happy to push him that far.

'To get that far and not win is, of course, disappointing, but, as we say, "*Je ne regrette rien.*" It was a great week for me, always exciting right to the very end. A lot of players would settle for being second in the British Open. I gave it all I had, so I have nothing to regret about the week.'

2002 TOP SCORES

E. Els 70–66–72–70 278
T. Levet 72–66–74–66 278
S. Elkington 71–73–68–66 278
S. Appleby 73–70–70–65 278
(Els beat Levet in sudden-death after a four-hole play-off)
G. Evans 72–68–74–65 279
P. Harrington 69–67–76–67 279
S. Maruyama 68–68–75–68 279

2003, ROYAL ST GEORGE'S: THOMAS BJÖRN AND MARK ROE

(Björn led by two shots with three holes to go, but finished tied second with Vijay Singh behind surprise winner Ben Curtis. Roe was disqualified after surging into contention on Saturday afternoon, following the 'wrong cards' fiasco with Jesper Parnevik)

'I hadn't been in that bunker all week. I hadn't even looked at it. When I got to it, I thought, "This is as tough as they come."'

GOLF'S GREAT DANE Thomas Björn had witnessed close up the misery of one of his heroes, Greg Norman, missing out on the Open title in 1989 at Royal Troon, when he watched from in front of the ropes as an 18 year old.

Björn had vowed that he would become a good-enough golf professional to play in the Open. Little did he know that he would suffer the same bitter taste as Norman 14 years later in the Open Championship and have his hand forced off the famous trophy too.

By that time, Björn, already a runner-up in the 2000 Open, had reached a level in the game where not only he expected to win a major, so did all the pundits. His game had been improving year by year, and, as well as finishing second to Tiger Woods in 2000, Björn had beaten the world's best player in Dubai in 2001 in the Dubai Desert Classic after going head-to-head with Woods for all four days of the tournament. This was his eighth stab at the Open title. It seemed that Sandwich 2003 was the perfect time for him to make a major breakthrough.

Björn's hold on the Claret Jug, though, was taken away by one costly shot into a bunker: the formidable trap at the 16th at Royal St George's – a hazard that had dented the hopes of many before him.

But while the sands of time ran out three holes from home on Sunday, in an extraordinary earlier twist to the tale, Björn's chance of winning was dashed through a fleeting act of petulance – as early as the first round. Two needless dropped shots on Thursday were to have a telling effect on Björn's opportunity to break his duck in a major.

The golfing prince of Denmark's assault on the Open trophy began quietly, with a steady enough run over his first nine holes, and, with conditions made difficult by wind and rain, Björn was sitting pretty coming to the penultimate hole. As he played the 17th, he was only a stroke off the lead and had every chance of leading if he could play the final two holes well. Then Björn's fiery temperament took a hold.

Having found the bunker with a rather clumsy wedge shot, Björn was already seething when he climbed into the sand. His temper reached boiling point when he left the ball in the bunker. He whacked his club into the sand. Nick Faldo, watching from a few yards away, shook his head in disbelief. Touching the sand when your ball is still in the bunker is breaking the rules, of course, unless, perhaps, you are in a totally different area of the hazard, when the rule is much more woolly and ambiguous. There was going to be no escape for Björn. A two-shot penalty was on the way.

That penalty hauled him off the leaderboard, as Björn's score was eventually adjusted to a two-over-par 73, giving him a reasonable top-twenty placing. But he knew what could have been. As he said at the time:

'I was playing some of the best golf of my life – two-under standing on the 17th tee. I then hit into the bunker with my third; then, all of a sudden, I'm looking at a double-bogey.

'I don't think I'd left a ball in a bunker for about ten years, and every time I hit a bad bunker-shot – lots of players do this – you just kind of check the sand to find out why you did not hit a good shot. That's all I did. I dropped the club down in the sand to check it. There was a lot more sand than I expected. It was just a reaction to hitting a poor bunker-shot. Unfortunately, I wasn't out of the bunker and I was probably not thinking clearly at the time.

'I didn't realise right away that I had a two-shot penalty. I didn't even think about it until I got out of the bunker. Then there were about six people reminding me what I'd done.

'I was looking at double-bogey and it turned out to be quad [quadruple-bogey]. You have to regroup from there. I then got up and down from short of the green on 18. I hit a wonderful chip to about a foot and saved my par. I got in the clubhouse and looked at how everybody else was shooting over par. That gave me belief that I was still in the tournament and could still do well.'

Björn's 17th-hole aberration sent him five strokes behind the surprise first-round leader, Hennie Otto of South Africa. Otto, with a 68, led by a shot from a revitalised Greg Norman, the 1993 winner at Sandwich, and one of the favourites, Davis Love III. Another dark horse was a stroke in front of Björn: Ben Curtis. Curtis, wide-eyed and playing his first Open after qualifying by dint of a 13th place in the Western Open in America, making his major debut, lay 396th in the world. His opening 72 to command a share of sixth place would be a flash-in-the-pan, of course.

On an opening two days when scoring was workmanlike and rarely spectacular, a 70 by Björn in the second round earned him a share of second place on one-over-par, his quadruple-bogey on the 17th bunker forgotten, as this time it didn't prove so expensive. Only one player was in the 60s in the second round, and Ernie Els's 68 was ten shots better than his opening effort, so The Big Easy wasn't exactly threatening. Davis Love, on one-under, was the man of the moment, leading by two strokes from Björn and Korean S.K. Ho. Curtis, who hadn't even come with a caddie and had hired English bagman Andy Sutton on spec when he arrived, hadn't gone away. Curtis was one of seven players in fourth place, three shots off the lead. Beginner's luck? Possibly.

Round three proved a revelation for Björn. His temperament was as sound as his swing, and a round of 69, when many were still stumbling over Royal St George's many pitfalls, took Björn into a one-stroke lead on one-under-par. He had some formidable opponents directly behind him, though. Love was the man in second place on level-par. Woods, still the bookmakers' favourite, was in the substantial group on one-over, sharing third place. As well as Woods, who was anxious to put right the wrong he felt Muirfield had done him the previous year, top world-ranked players Vijay Singh and Sergio Garcia were only two shots off the lead.

And that dark horse that everyone had expected would have tailed off? Ben Curtis was also in the third-place group.

Curtis was a rank outsider, but Björn was fairly surprised to be contending so strongly, even if he was on the brink of breaking into the world's top echelon, because he had spent much of the early summer honing his swing with his coach, Sam's dad Bob Torrance.

'I'd been trying to build a golf swing for the future, and all of a sudden I'm leading the Open Championship going into Sunday's final round. Building for the future? This was it!'

So Thomas Björn, twice a Ryder Cup hero, one of Europe's big players, prepared himself that night to take on, among others, Woods again and five other major champions, Love, Singh, Nick Faldo, Nick Price and Fred Couples, in what was expected to be an absorbing finale.

While fate waited to deal out its hands the next day, a few hours earlier Englishman Mark Roe's destiny was decided. Roe, while a regular winner on the European Tour, had never really been fancied to win a major – until that Saturday afternoon. A scintillating third round of 67 made him leader in the clubhouse on one-over-par. Could it be the year for the tour's arch-joker? Roe's main claims to fame before that fine performance had been for hitting exploding golf balls off the tee during a pro-am, for once emptying a plate of spaghetti over his great mate Russell Claydon's head in hijinks in a restaurant during a French Open – that kind of thing. This was a seriously good score.

'It was one of the best rounds I ever played, and it was starting to be one of the best tournaments I had ever played. There was something happening out there. I saw my name at the top of the leaderboard and I got calmer, not more uptight, which is kind of strange. You don't expect to be that way, but I was very calm and content with the situation; I was just enjoying it. It was just the way things seemed to be going that week. Everything was good, and I was seeing shots. It was the kind of golf you needed for that course, an old-style course. It wasn't the modern game you needed, where it is 320 yards through the air. It was more of a shaper-and-hands type of course, and I just had good visualisation of all the shots.'

Roe, always the showman, basked in his Open glory. He had just been enjoying talking to the world's media about his first serious threat to win a major − when he was hit by a bombshell.

'I had done all the interviews with ABC and the BBC, and I was just on such a high. I was buzzing with all the interviews. I walked away from one of the interviews and somebody said, "Can you come back to the scorers' cabin?"

'As I'm walking back, I'm thinking, "I've made a mistake on Jesper's card." He'd shot 81, and there were a lot of shots out there. I was thinking, "This is horrendous." There was obviously some mistake been made, to be called back. I was working out how to say sorry to him, but I'm thinking, "He's shot 81, so he's not going to be too devastated." I'll have to say, "Sorry, Jesper. I made a mistake on your card." But I knew I hadn't. I'd checked it, double-checked it and called the lady scorer.

'I remember the recorder's words to me in the box: "34–33, 67. Congratulations. Great round. You're free to go." [The recorder had also been unaware at this stage that Roe had filled in the wrong card.]

'When I walked in, I looked at Jesper. He was ashen faced. I said, "Have I made a mistake?"

'He said, "No. It's worse than that."

'I thought, "What can be worse than that?"

'I looked down and there are the two scorecards side by side. I spotted it straight away. I looked at the rules guy and said right away, "We're disqualified, aren't we?"

He said, "I am so sorry; there is nothing we can do. I have looked at every possibility in the rules and there is no provision for it. So I am sorry but you are both disqualified."

'I was utterly floored. I just looked at everybody, and my first thought was, "No, not today. Not this tournament, please." But you have to get yourself together, because you have to go and talk about it. There was a very brief moment to collect my thoughts. Then I had to come out and do all the interviews again!'

Roe and Jesper Parnevik had committed the cardinal error of forgetting to exchange cards on the tee – something pros do as a matter of course before they start the round, like remembering to put on spikes instead of playing in trainers. Only this time, in the hubbub of an Open Championship, they didn't. They went out and played their rounds together – and accidentally used their own scorecards to record their playing-partner's scores. At the end of the round, they handed them in. At that time, this broke the rule which insisted the scores on a player's card had to be filled in and signed by another player. The rule was unequivocal. They were both disqualified, and Roe went from joy – at what would have been a score only two shots off the lead and would mean playing with Tiger Woods in the final round – to misery. He only blamed himself, however.

'It was 100 per cent my mistake. I have never looked to make an excuse for it. In 20 years, I have never made a mistake like that. In 20 years, I have never made a mistake on my scorecard, and in essence I didn't make a mistake in my scores.

'It was just the time factors. Jesper came to the tee a good deal later than me. I had picked up my card and, in all the excitement in getting ready to tee-off, I stuck it in my bag, and he did the same with his. You change cards with your playing-partner. It is always something you do. It was just a simple mistake to make, but I guess the punishment does not fit the crime.'

Roe had to make the long trek home and then try to get over his anguish. In typical fashion, though, he did bounce back, even if he will never forget his worst moment in golf, the day his chance for Open glory ended in tears.

'I think it probably took me the Sunday of the Open to get over it all. On the Monday morning when I got up, I was absolutely fine. I'm at home with my wife and kids, and you realise then what is important in life. I was very, very upset on the Sunday, though. I cried on the Sunday afternoon when the prize-giving was going on. But only for a lost opportunity, because I would have loved to have played with Tiger Woods on the Sunday of an Open Championship. I have never played with him. It would have been the greatest day in my career, an opportunity to win the Open. It is what everybody dreams about. I am not saying that on Sunday I wouldn't have been nervous – I'm sure I would – but it was *Boy's Own* stuff. I guess they were tears of frustration for a missed opportunity.

'I watched the last round, and, like everybody, I bled for Thomas because of what happened. I watched it, but the emotion came after, perhaps even more so because it was a relative unknown who won it. And the way it was won made me think, "That could have been me."'

There is no bitterness in Roe at his lost opportunity, nor regrets that the performance of his life counted for nothing. His dignity in accepting the circumstances earned him friends worldwide.

'When I switched on my mobile phone, it had run out of text space, which is something like 50 messages, and the voicemail space was full of messages from people from everywhere. I had letters from all over the world. Later, I had a letter from a steelworker in Virginia saying the whole gentlemanly way I went about things was the reason his father had taken up the game of golf and why he, too, had taken it up. It was a lovely letter, and I have kept them all. The funniest came from an old friend and fellow touring pro, Mark Davis. He left a voicemail message which said, "Roey, you twat; you've spoiled my weekend!"

'I would never be bitter. There are so many good things in my life and so many things which matter more to me than the game of golf.

I love the game of golf, but as I said at the time, it is not that my children were ill or anything or my wife had had an accident. It is all about perspective. It was a huge day, and Sunday would have been a huge day for me, but that is life. You pick yourself up, dust yourself down and get on with it. There is nothing else you can do. I will very often think about it, and it will always be ever present in my golfing thoughts. It is not something I have a problem with, but it is something that I am constantly reminded of. Every pro-am I play, they say, "Don't give Roey the scorecard!"'

Ironically, in 2005, the R & A relaxed the rule that disqualified players not exchanging cards. Two years too late for Roe.

'It is brilliant that no one will have to go through what I did, just because they forgot to swap cards over on the 1st tee. It can happen on the 1st tee of big tournaments with all that is going on. It may happen again, but obviously now no one will be punished. I think it is a great move. I am really pleased that something good has come from my mistake. I would like to think that the way I handled it at the time, and what I went through, was possibly a small influencing factor. It will be good for any professional not to have to go through the emotional roller coaster I went through on that Saturday, when I had an opportunity to change my life.'

On Sunday, Björn had his opportunity to change his life.

He had slept well, not worried about his position on top of such an acclaimed leaderboard. In fact, it was because it was such an impressive array of talent on top that Björn went to the 1st tee unafraid. His theory was that everyone was expecting one of the major champions in the pack, especially Woods, to win, so he had nothing to lose and the pressure was off him. He tried to stop thinking about the task ahead by playing with his children and sharing cups of tea with his wife, Pernilla. The whole family was there with him in a rented house.

Even though he had tried to push thoughts of winning out of his mind, it was a rather nervy start for Björn, and it cost him a bogey on the 1st, which meant he was no longer the sole leader. However, he soon worked off his nervousness and, by the turn, he had more than cancelled out that opening blemish with three birdies. He had needed to. A name not familiar to golf fans at the Open had stormed to the top of the leaderboard. Ben Curtis was not only refusing to go away but showing he was there to stay.

Björn refused to be fazed by Curtis's charge. Playing coolly and calmly, cutting out errors with good course management and taking advantage of advice handed out by his experienced English caddie, Billy Foster, the Dane soon threatened to bring home the major bacon, as Curtis at last showed signs of folding up ahead.

As he headed for home, caddie Foster was optimistic he would at last walk alongside an Open champion. Seve had not been able to pull one off when he worked for him and nor had Northern Ireland's greatest latter-day golfer, Darren Clarke, another of his illustrious bosses. A terrific par-save on the 12th kept Björn ticking over.

Soon after, he put daylight between himself and the rest of the field with a birdie on the famous and infamous 'Suez Canal' 14th. At the formidable par-five – with invading out of bounds on the right, a deadly stream, which gives the hole its name, and cross-bunkers to navigate on the way in – Björn first split the fairway, eased a comfortable six-iron up and then produced a brilliant wedge to just over a metre. He briefly went three strokes clear of the field. But the two defining holes of the 2003 Open were now coming up.

'On 15, you have to hit driver. At all Opens, the key is to stay out of bunkers, so that might mean hitting irons at some holes to do so. You couldn't do that on 15 if you were going to have any chance of parring the hole. It wasn't a bad tee-shot, but my ball took a bounce to the left and finished up in the bunker. I was pretty well certain to make bogey then.'

Dropping a shot on the 15th seemed like just a small stumble in Björn's triumphant march home. He still led by two when he strode onto the 16th tee.

The deadly short hole at Royal St George's had killed off many an Open hope, with its right-hand bunker acting like a magnet to seize on balls hit by players brave, or misguided, enough to go for the flag and not quite get their shot right. With the flag cut into a slope that ran down to the bunker, any shot missed on the right would provide serious trouble for its owner.

Because of Björn's bogey at the previous hole, his playing-partner Love, whose Open hopes had faded, went first and hit a peach of a shot at the flag.

Björn had his own plan for the hole:

'I was very determined. I stood up and aimed at the same spot in the grandstand, a little round mark which was the Open Championship logo, that I had aimed at every day. I got ahead of it a bit and it started off just left of the flag. That caused it to get caught in the wind, which was blowing left to right.

'I hadn't been in that bunker all week. I hadn't even looked at it. When I got to it, I thought, "This is as tough as they come." My ball was sitting on an upslope, with a big rise in front of me. The danger then is you are always likely to hit it short – the one thing I knew I couldn't afford to do.'

What Björn also found out was that his ball was in the heaviest and deepest sand in the trap. The 16th bunker had more sand in it than most on the course, anyway. It was going to need perfection in bunker-play from Björn, right at a time when pressure was on the Dane most. Would he be able to ease his ball out of the cloying sand – or would he catch it too cutely and knife it way past the flag and through the green?

'I had two options: either try and hit a really perfect shot or hit the ball 40 yards or so past the hole, then be faced with an impossible shot coming back. I tried to hit a decent bunker-shot. It came out fat and I left the ball in. I tried to hit another decent bunker-shot. But it again came out fat.

'The third bunker-shot was the best I ever hit in my life, because the ball was 2 ft under the sand in a footprint. It went 5 ft past, and somehow I gathered my thoughts, took a deep breath and holed the putt.'

Björn now needed a birdie to win. Or he needed two pars to get into a play-off with Curtis, who had set the target of one-under-par by holing a testing, double-breaking putt of 10 ft to save par on the last.

The 17th, of course, was not exactly Björn's favourite hole. He tried to shake the thought out of his head, but the ugly memory of his quadruple-bogey there on the first day would not go away. The 17th was to confound him again.

'My drive on 17 wasn't that bad, but I caught a real horrible lie in the rough. I knocked it up and then hit a wonderful chip. My ball touched the hole but ran on a bit. I missed the putt coming back.

'All of a sudden, your head drops, because you know you need to make a birdie-three at the last, which is not an easy hole. You're normally happy to make par at the 18th, but I couldn't afford that. I didn't make birdie. I hit another great chip but it stopped just short of the hole. Par. That was it.'

Thus, with Singh also finishing one stroke light, the Open Championship had, arguably, its most unlikely winner of recent years. His collapse at the death haunted Björn for over a year. The nightmares came in thick and fast.

'I kept dreaming about my ball rolling back into that bunker like a giant snowball.'

And he wasn't allowed to forget his mishap the week after the Open, when he bravely turned out for the Irish Open at Portmarnock.

'This little kid shouted out, "There's the guy who lost the British Open." If he was 25 years old, you'd want to bash him one. But he was ten . . . and he was right.

'It was a double-bogey at the wrong time. When it happens to the guy that leads the tournament, then it becomes a big issue. It becomes a big disaster. It happened to me and I accepted it.

'When you're in that situation, I don't think people understand how focused we are. You almost don't have time to be nervous. You're so determined about what you have to do. And all of a sudden these things happen. But you're so focused. You almost feel like your head is in the ground. You don't see anything. That's exactly the way it felt. I never thought about things that could happen to me over the closing holes that could be disastrous, or anything. I just thought, "Keep hitting one shot at a time." I was surprised when it happened, because it came out of the blue. I didn't feel nervous in the sense that I couldn't handle it. That's just the way it is. You've got to live with it.

'I have no other reason than to be proud of what I did, and I have every confidence for the future. But if you're not disappointed at throwing away a three-shot lead in the British Open, there's something wrong with you.'

2003 TOP SCORES

B. Curtis 72–72–70–69 283

T. Björn 73–70–69–72 284

V. Singh 75–70–69–70 284

T. Woods 73–72–69–71 285

D. Love III 69–72–72–72 285

2004, ROYAL TROON: ERNIE ELS

(Els lost in a play-off to Todd Hamilton)

'That putt . . . I'm going to be thinking of that putt for a good while, I can tell you.'

THE YEAR 2004 should have been the most memorable of Ernie Els's career. It turned out to be the most frustrating. And the 2004 Open Championship proved to be the most frustrating time of all for the man they call The Big Easy.

By the time Els fetched up at Royal Troon, he had been squeezed out of a maiden Masters title by Phil Mickelson's electrifying finish at Augusta. Els had to settle for his second runner-up honours there, when it looked as though he would keep Mickelson out of the winner's enclosure yet again.

Then, at Shinnecock Hills, Els was just two strokes off fellow South African Retief Goosen's lead going into the final round of the US Open. A double-bogey at the 1st ended Els's hopes almost there and then. A closing round of 80 sent Els into obscurity – well, to ninth place – when he had looked ready to win that major again.

Never one to be daunted by such setbacks, Els was the bookmakers' favourite to take the 2004 Open title. Tiger Woods was in a slump. Mickelson had never played the Open well and nor had Goosen. Of course, there were many others who could stand in his way, but Els was the man most fancied to be lifting the Auld Claret Jug again.

In the end, all these mighty forces were bettered by a journeyman

– a journeyman in the truest sense of the word. Todd Hamilton beat the odds in 2004. Never again would Oquawka, Illinois, just be famous for an elephant. Ernie Els, for one, will never forget 2004 and Royal Troon.

Els had played Troon when the Open stopped off for its two previous visits, missing the cut in 1989 when he was an amateur and finishing a distant tenth behind the winner, Justin Leonard, in 1997. Coming into the Open on the back of a third place at the previous week's Scottish Open at Loch Lomond, Els was optimistic.

Woods was patently off-colour. Els, who had implied that his greatest golfing foe had as good as put the hex on him for several years, when he was unbeatable to some extent, was now proving he was a mere mortal after all. He felt Woods had 'come back to the field a little bit'.

With Woods not so much of a threat, would the in-form Mickelson finally work out how to win an Open? Mickelson, though, seemed to be falling between two stools. The left-hander, who had finally broken his major duck with victory at Augusta, appeared rather too obsessive about Troon, too anxious to win. Mickelson missed the cut at Loch Lomond after spending more time practising at Troon than concentrating fully on the Scottish Open, and many a pundit was saying that that kind of compulsion would only end in tears.

What increased Els's will to win was a throwback to the previous month. He was stung by certain comments made about him over his last-day performance at Shinnecock Hills in the US Open, which were pointed out to him at Troon. It had been reported that some USGA officials, perhaps going on the defensive about criticism over the Shinnecock greens, especially in the final round, had suggested Els had thrown in the towel with his 80 on the Sunday in the US Open. If Els had needed a spur to go all out for his second Open title, this was it.

'They shouldn't have said that. How do you give up? That was the most ridiculous thing I've heard in my life. I've never given up on any round of golf in my life. If I'd given up, I would have shot 100. They had no idea. They lost the plot. To take one of the best golf courses in this entire world and to make it a farce like that . . . They had egg on their faces. I was striking the ball so pure and my putting was good [at the US Open]. Everything was falling into place nicely. But I could see Saturday afternoon; I could see the golf course going. We had that wind blowing that evening and then, the next morning, it [the course] was just gone. I made that six on the first and Retief made birdie – a three-shot swing. Your whole mindset changes after one hole. I felt really good about that tournament.'

So now with an extra reason for winning, Els practised with vigour and liked what he saw in this major course. Ironically, as it was to turn out, he enjoyed the Troon greens in practice.

'It was a very fair course, a good test of golf on a very tough course. The rough, not terrible. You could get the ball out of the rough, so it makes it more exciting. Sometimes you have such deep rough you can only get the ball out to the fairway and it takes the activity out of the player's hands. Depending on the wind, you had to have a pretty sharp short-game to make birdies on the front nine, and coming back to the clubhouse there are a lot of difficult par-fours, so you had to drive well and hit a lot of long irons. The greens were great. They were running beautifully.'

It sounded like the perfect course for a man determined to make it third-time lucky that year after two disappointments. One punter that week had faith in Els. A £62,000 bet was laid on the strapping South African, reputed to be the biggest golf bet of all time. When he copied Gene Sarazen's feat and holed-in-one – with a wedge rather than a five-iron – at the Postage Stamp, the mere 123-yard 8th, everyone was wondering if the punter had had divine help when laying his money down.

By the time Els got to the penultimate hole of the day, another par-three, it was looking an even better bet. Then came the first mishap of the week. A double-bogey on 17 left Els nursing a two-under-par 69 and only thirteenth place, when it looked as though he might lead. As with every Open Championship, this act was to have a telling effect when the tournament unravelled on Sunday night. It cancelled out his ace on the 8th. It was just one of several cases to come, where misfortune or misjudgement landed a left-hook on the chin of Ernie Els.

'It was unfortunate what I did on 17. I just pulled a five-iron left and I had a bit of a downhill lie in the bunker. But it wasn't the most difficult shot I've ever had in my life. I just messed it up. I thinned it into the bank in front of me and I made five from nowhere.

'It was disappointing. From such a highlight on the 8th to such a low-light on the 17th.'

Els's second ace in a major – his first came in 1997 at Winged Foot in the US PGA Championship – at least helped to put him in the running after the first round. Soon-to-be Ryder Cup players Paul Casey and Thomas Levet held the one-shot lead after 66s. Levet had won the Scottish Open the previous week and was having a second stab at winning the Open after losing out at the death two years earlier to Els. Michael Campbell of New Zealand took third place, and there were nine more players between him and Els.

Todd Hamilton, having shot a modest level-par round, had not got round to talking about Norma Jean yet. Another American dark horse did get the chance to let the world know who he was, after the second round completed. Els stayed well in touch by shooting a second 69, but he trailed Skip Kendall by three strokes.

Following Ben Curtis's shock win the previous year, the pundits were wary of writing off what they considered were no-hopers. Kendall's 66, including a mammoth 60-ft eagle putt on the long 16th, earned him a one-shot lead over Levet, the Frenchman clinging on to hopes of completing the job this time. Els was in a group of five in fifth place, once again grateful to the Postage Stamp, often his most unfavourite hole, for mailing his fifth successive score of 69 at Troon (following on from three 69s in 1997). Whereas he had aced the formidable little hole the day before, this time Els found one of the infamous sentinel bunkers at the par-three, somehow squeezed out a shot to 30 ft from a perilous lie, and saved his par, when he was staring another double-bogey in the face.

That 30-footer, though, was the only silver lining to black clouds starting to form over Els's putting ability that week.

'You know, 69 is never a bad score at any major championship, but I was pushing a little too hard, trying to score really low. We had good weather again, so I felt I could have shot better than that. I got really frustrated with the putter.

'At the 8th, I could have made anything, and I walked off with three. I guess all the mess-ups I've made around the course I've made at the Postage Stamp. So that was a great three after the hole-in-one.

'Apart from just not being comfortable with the putter, I felt I hit the ball the way I hit it at Shinnecock. If you're on the leaderboard, you've played well.'

Sharing fifth place with Els? Having shot a 67, now was the time for Todd Hamilton to relate the story of Norma Jean, the name of the elephant buried in the town square of Oquawka, population: 1,500.

Unlike Ben Curtis or Skip Kendall, Hamilton did have a string of victories to his credit. Like 1998 runner-up Brian Watts, his journeying had taken him to the Far East for most of his career and had provided him with thirteen titles, ten of them on the tough Japanese circuit. He had also won the Honda Classic on the US PGA Tour that year. Hamilton was no rabbit blinking in the headlights.

He was quite a story-teller, too, talking about the time in 1974 when the circus came to Oquawka and a lightning bolt killed Norma Jean. The elephant was too heavy to take away, so they laid her to rest where she fell.

Perhaps the most significant fact about Hamilton, though, was his penchant for links golf. Having moved from Illinois to Texas, his home course in Dallas was set out in links style, and he was familiar with all the sorts of shots you needed in the management of Troon. When the tournament reached its denouement, that experience proved vital.

Ernie Els knew all about Todd Hamilton. They had come up against each other a few times, and Els knew he was up against a dangerous opponent when they played together in the third round. Hamilton proved just how dangerous. His 67 on the Saturday put him a stroke ahead of Els on eight-under-par.

'I knew Todd from Japan when I played there quite a bit in the early '90s. Todd was quite a star over there. He was really pretty big in the East, especially in Japan. It took him a while to get his card on the US Tour, but he's always been a quality player. And he had a really good game for Troon.'

While Els observed that Hamilton would 'take some beating tomorrow', the tall South African was also wary of the three players one stroke behind him in third place. His arch-adversary in 2002, Thomas Levet, was there. So was the man who had made winning an obsession at Troon: the Masters champion Phil Mickelson. Having shot a 73 in the first round, Mickelson's salvage operation was complete and he was looking for a major double, when he had not won even one until his triumph at Augusta. To enhance the mouth-watering prospects of Sunday's finale, Els's compatriot Retief Goosen, the man who had seen him off at Shinnecock Hills in the US Open, was also there in third place. And just to add even more spice to the recipe, Tiger Woods had found a modicum of form and had half a glimmer of a chance from four strokes back.

Even though he was patently unhappy with his putting, Els was in the mix for a third successive time in that year's majors. Surely he would not fail this time?

Early salvoes were fired before it came down to an Els–Mickelson–Hamilton tussle. Levet chipped in from behind the 4th green for eagle to join the lead. His friend and playing-partner Barry Lane holed an eagle putt there to lie one shot off the lead. Then Mickelson also chipped in at the 4th for eagle to nose into the top of the leaderboard too. The Troon crowd could hardly keep pace with the drama.

Hamilton bogeyed the 1st and fell back to second place. Els birdied the 3rd and shared the lead with Mickelson. Levet lost ground up ahead. Goosen stayed quiet all afternoon. Els and Hamilton birdied the 4th. It looked like a straight fight then between Els, Hamilton and Mickelson. Hamilton picked up another shot on the 5th to go back into the lead on his own on nine-under. Els had said he would be dangerous, and Hamilton, after his nervous start, was proving him right.

It was nip and tuck. Els bogeyed the 5th. Mickelson, in the match in front, nearly drove the 7th and then almost chipped in for eagle before tapping in for birdie. Mickelson and Hamilton shared the lead on nine-under-par.

Then came two of the three defining holes for Els that shaped his 2004 Open. Having moved into a share of top place with a birdie on the 7th, he crashed down the leaderboard by double-bogeying the 10th. Here, he drove into the heavy rough and gorse and had no hope of reaching the promised land in two shots. In fact, he needed five more. With the toughest hole to come – indeed, one of the most difficult in the world: the four-hundred-and-ninety-yard par-four 11th by the railway line – Els was wobbling badly. When he again drove into gorse, his Open bid looked over.

There followed, though, one of the most extraordinary shots seen in an Open final round. His ball did not dive right into the bush but teetered in the folds of a branch about 2 ft above ground. Els, a great cricket fan, played what could loosely be described as an agricultural slog and dislodged his ball far enough to go for the green. A determined iron to 12 ft needing just one putt and Els somehow saved par. Another double-bogey and the curtains coming down had seemed a much more likely outcome. Relief flooded over Els and kept his hopes alive.

'It was unbelievable. I don't think I've ever seen that happen. I don't know if it's ever happened in a game of golf. It was just hanging there on the gorse branch. Obviously, it was a huge break, because if the ball goes right into the bush, I've got to take penalty drop and it's then pretty well all over. Somehow, I got it out of there. I was quite nervous. I know the guys who do the clinics hit the ball that way and hit it 200 yards, but I was just trying to make a contact. I made a great four.'

Els's remarkable rescue act was crucial, because Hamilton, who had lost ground by bogeying the 10th, birdied the 11th hole to go back on top, with Mickelson on the popular mark of nine-under-par again.

Els was now two shots off the lead, and Mickelson was clear

favourite to add the Open to his Masters title. He had not dropped a stroke since the 17th hole of the first round and had rarely looked likely to do so. The 13th, though, proved the unlucky number for Mickelson, and the hole, in the end, scuppered his chances of the double, as he missed the green from virtually nowhere to make a bogey-five. Mickelson's hand was torn from the Claret Jug, never that week to return.

It looked as though Els's hand would never regain its hold, either. However, his salvage operation on the 11th seemed to reignite his hopes. A solid putt for once that week saw him birdie 13. Only a stroke behind now.

Hamilton refused to be caught. He increased the lead to two shots again by chipping in at the 14th. The cut and thrust continued. Mickelson birdied the 16th. So did the final pair out on the course. Hamilton was ahead still by two. With Els's putting touch now firmly with him, he birdied the 17th, the testing two-hundred-and-twenty-two-yard par-three that in 1989 helped consign Wayne Grady and Greg Norman to the runners-up platform. Hamilton was ahead by only one shot now from Els, with Mickelson beaten.

Finally, the enormity of what he was on the brink of achieving, plus the sheer presence of one of the biggest men in golf – in more ways than one – took its toll on Hamilton. He lashed his drive right and into the grass, with little chance of the sort of recovery Mark Calcavecchia had made so tellingly from near there 15 years before. Hamilton's second shot was a heave across the fairway and into further rough, close to the spectator fencing. Although he warranted a free drop, Hamilton could not persuade his ball to skip any closer than two-putt territory. Two putts for bogey left him staring into the abyss of defeat. Els, with a magnificent raking second shot, had hit the green in two and had a ten-footer for birdie to better him.

For three days, Els's putting had let him down. But over the final seven holes, it had improved vastly. All he had to do was coax this one in and a second Open Championship title in three years was his.

Suddenly, though, Els's refound putting prowess deserted him again. He didn't give the ball enough forward spin and, inevitably running out of steam, it veered on the low side of the cup and ran past. Only par – and into a play-off with the man alongside him, who had hardly dared watch the final action of 72 holes. Els again faced a four-hole play-off, also his second in three years, with the vision of that putt already filling his mind.

'I played really well coming in, and to make those putts, just trying to get back into the race, was a hell of an effort. I had a chance on 18, but I just couldn't get the ball high enough. I just never got the ball running at the hole.

'I had such a good second shot. It was such a weird pin placement, where, if you were short of the hole, you had such a difficult putt. If I had known that, I would probably have hit it past. That putt . . . I'm going to be thinking of that putt for a good while, I can tell you.'

If that putt will haunt Els, soon he was to have another one very similar, to add to his nightmares. But with Hamilton waiting, he had to try to shrug off his disappointment at the way he had allowed a golden chance to go begging.

'If you start thinking about what happened on the 72nd hole too much, you're going to be in trouble. I felt good going into the play-off.'

Both men parred at the 1st and 2nd holes, the opening two of the play-off. Then the 17th stepped in to add the scalp of Els to those of Norman and Grady. A tee-shot left at the par-three and Els did well to scuttle his pitch onto the green falling away from him. Hamilton, with the honour from the start of the play-off, had overcome his nerves to hit the green. He missed from 15 ft. Els was inside him by 3 ft – but also missed the putt.

One shot ahead now, Hamilton was on the brink of Open glory and in sight of being the second dark horse in succession to carry off the oldest major honour in golf. Just like in real time, though, Hamilton stumbled. His drive again skewed right. This time, his ball found a spectator walkway which was classed as ground under repair. He got another free drop, finding a favourable lie. If they were not guiding it, the gods seemed to be taking more than a passing interest in his ball.

Els winged another fine iron into the heart of the green again, once more about 10 ft from the flag. Hamilton chipped up 25 yards short of the green. There seemed three possible results now: a win for Els with a successful birdie putt and Hamilton failing to get up and down; sudden-death if Els holed out and Hamilton did get up and down; or sudden-death if Els missed the putt and Hamilton couldn't chip and putt.

It was none of the three.

Pulling out what he called his 'hybrid' – a 'Texas Wedge' in the shape of a 14° one-iron-type club he uses to either bump-and-run around the green or fashion his shots off the tee – Hamilton ran his ball to no more than 2 ft. Par was certain. Now Els had to rely on what was normally his strength. He had to birdie . . . or else. If he didn't, it really was curtains this time.

His ball refused to obey. Els's fragile putting that week had cost him dearly. A third major in a row had gone by the board.

'At the 17th, I pulled my four-iron. I was trying to hit a similar shot to the one I did in regulation play. I hit it further left. I was trying to stay aggressive and make another birdie. Then I had a pretty difficult chip-shot. I then just hit a poor putt. It was a makeable putt, only 12 ft.

'On the 18th, I had a perfect look at it from about 10 or 11 ft. I didn't read it properly. Well, I read it properly but it wasn't the right line. I hit on the wrong line and it broke right.

'I didn't quite play the play-off good enough. I just couldn't get the right read on the putts. I had my chances, but I've got to give a lot of credit to Todd. He hung in there. He obviously had a game plan, and he stuck to his guns. I felt that I could get more aggressive, go after the par-fives and get close to the par-fours and have shorter shots. He played conservatively, and his short-game was just unbelievable. That little shot he played on the last hole he played quite a few times in the tournament. It really worked out well.'

Thus, Els was left disappointed for a third successive time in 2004 majors. It didn't get any better. He finished fourth in the final major: the US PGA Championship.

'Getting so close in a major and not winning is very tough to take. Losing any of them was hard. I just came up a little short each time. I gave them all my best shot.'

2004 TOP SCORES
T. Hamilton 71–67–67–69 274
E. Els 69–69–68–68 274
(Hamilton won four-hole play-off)
P. Mickelson 73–66–68–68 275
L. Westwood 72–71–68–67 278

2005, ST ANDREWS: COLIN MONTGOMERIE

(Runner-up Montgomerie lay just a stroke behind eventual winner Tiger Woods at the turn on Sunday)

'The bogey threw me. The wind switched and I hit the wrong club. I didn't quite get the same momentum coming home after that.'

TO LOSE AN Open by five strokes does not sound as if anybody had a hand on the Claret Jug but Tiger Woods. However, in 2005, Colin Montgomerie came as close as he had ever done to winning the Open Championship. And when Montgomerie turned for home in Sunday's final round, the man who was to go on and win an eighth European order of merit did fleetingly wrap his fingers around the famous old vessel.

Montgomerie had rarely performed in the Open Championship. He had been runner-up twice in the US Open, once after a play-off, and finished third on his debut in that major. In the US PGA Championship, he had also lost in a play-off. His best result in the Open, though, was the same as his top finish in the Masters: tied eighth.

In 2001, Montgomerie briefly laid a finger on the Jug when he led after two rounds of the Open at Royal Lytham and St Annes. That year, however, he faded to only 13th. The previous year, he had half a chance when going into the final round at Royal Troon just about in touch with the lead. Sunday was not his day, though, and he slid to only 25th. It looked as though this home title was never going to be really, truly within his grasp.

Then, at 42 years of age, Montgomerie performed at his best in the major, fittingly in front of his adoring public at the Home of Golf: the Old Course at St Andrews. It was a highly creditable showing, too. Montgomerie, once a regular of the world-top-five club, had slumped to 83rd in the global order by the time 2005 got under way. With the painful break-up with his wife, Eimear, it was hardly a wonder that the career of Europe's top golfer between 1993 and 2000 took a nosedive.

St Andrews 2005, though, saw Montgomerie return as a force. Not quite a force that was good enough to defeat the world's number-one golfer, but a good-enough force to give Tiger Woods a great run for his money.

Not many people know, though, that Montgomerie might never have had his best Open – that he might never have got past the first round – and that he might never have gone on to become European number one for an eighth time. If it had not been for meticulous club technicians in the travelling Mizuno workshop, Montgomerie might have been disqualified for playing with an illegal club.

Because the St Andrews fairways are quite unyielding, playing normal, shorter irons can produce too much 'bounce'. So Montgomerie, always striving for perfection, took with him a couple of specialist wedges, designed especially for links play. If they worked out, he fully intended using one or the other of them, perhaps both, in the tournament. He was not happy with the feel of them, however, so he decided he wanted them reshafting. His coach, Denis Pugh, took them to the Mizuno workshop next to the practice range for new shafts to be put in. There, alarm bells went off when the technicians, Tommy Yamaguchi and Terry Terazono, inspected the clubs. Workshop boss Andy Kikidas warned Pugh that the grooves on the wedges were too big and they might be illegal. Pugh took them to the R & A and, when they checked them out, sure enough, the officials told him they were dubious that the grooves conformed. If Montgomerie had played with them, he could well have been disqualified. The clubs never went back in the bag again, and Monty's week wasn't ruined.

When he began his bid on the Thursday, there was scant sign that Montgomerie would be hard on Woods's heels that week. While Woods shot a 66, six-under-par, to earn himself a one-shot lead over Mark Hensby, Australia's new-found major force, Montgomerie compiled a modest 71 in the first round. That wasn't even good enough for a top-20 spot. The Saltires, kilts and wigs were not yet in evidence, and Monty's fan club was hardly vocal.

As Montgomerie came to the end of a second-round 66, however, his supporters were in full throng. There was a huge crowd at the final two holes. They were there to salute Jack Nicklaus. The Golden Bear was making his final appearance at the Open and, in unprecedented scenes at the Old Course, took his bows and his accolades and posed for pictures on the Swilcan Bridge. Then Nicklaus rounded off his final appearance by holing a curling eight-footer – on a similar line and length to the one which finally defeated Doug Sanders when Nicklaus won the St Andrews Open in 1970.

A little while after the legend had taken his leave of the course, Montgomerie holed an even-longer putt on the 18th. This one was 12 ft. It earned him an appearance alongside Tiger Woods the next day. Montgomerie's successful closing putt meant he had leapt all the way up the leaderboard to second place.

Could it be his turn at last? Could the best player in the world never to have won a major end his drought at the Home of Golf? There was a long way to go, but the portents were better this time than they had been in 2001, when, at Royal Lytham and St Annes, he had led after two rounds.

Montgomerie may have been trailing Woods by four strokes, but his followers were in no doubt that their man could prevail this time. Montgomerie was convinced their support was paramount in his big finish and his position, and that his gallery might carry him all the way. And he was delighted his putting was showing great signs of improvement.

'That birdie on the last, that 12-footer, was a very important putt.

I had been leaving my putts short, but this was a much more decisive putt. I felt if I could keep putting like that, I had a chance.

'The crowd were great to me. They had been building up to see Jack's farewell. I was very glad they stayed on to help me home. I was three-under-par for the last five holes, and there was a lot of credit to them for helping me do that.'

With Woods in such seemingly indomitable form, though, Montgomerie recognised the enormous task in front of him. If Woods carried on playing like he had − a 67 to follow his 66 − then everyone might be playing for second place. Those fickle bounces on often brick-hard fairways might be the only way for Woods to slip up and drop the odd stroke or two.

And drop the odd stroke or two he did. Not enough, though. On a windy afternoon, Montgomerie out-shot Woods by one, with his fans urging him on at every grandstand and from every vantage point in front of the ropes. Woods three-putted early on and also twice drove into gorse. He ran up two penalty-shots during the round.

Somehow, though, the world's number-one player scrambled through it all, even making par after taking one of his penalty-shots. His finish was impressive, too, ensuring he held a two-shot lead over José Maria Olazabal, and he kept three ahead of Montgomerie and Retief Goosen. He first rolled in a 12-ft putt to save par on the Road Hole 17th, and then hit the final green and took two putts for birdie.

Montgomerie bettered Woods by two strokes going out, and when he birdied the 10th with an incisive six-iron approach to only 4 ft, he was only a shot adrift of the man he knew he had to beat if he were to at last break his major duck. His fans were ecstatic by that time. However, they were quietened somewhat on the 11th, as he bogeyed to drop back. That hole was to prove his nemesis the next day.

The Road Hole was not as kind to Montgomerie as it was to Woods. His second bogey of the day went on the card at the 17th. Showing great determination, though, Montgomerie fought back and holed a 40-ft putt on the last for birdie and a round of 70.

'It [his putt on 18] was vital to me. It was just one less shot I had to find. It was a difficult day and Tiger had a couple of drives he wouldn't have been happy with. The wind picked up. It came right across the course, and all of a sudden there was no hole that was straight in or straight down. The course dried out, and it was difficult to get the ball close to any pin. Our scores proved that. I played quite well for two-under. Nothing much went wrong. But it was difficult to get the ball close to make birdie putts.'

Chilling words. That was to be true the next day. But, while it fazed Montgomerie, it was not such a problem for powerhouse Woods.

Montgomerie's old problem of leaving putts short returned to him, too. That was something he vowed to get right in the final round. He was determined not to disappoint a crowd that were giving him their all.

'The crowds were fantastic. It was quite unbelievable. There were about 15 grandstands out there and it was a standing ovation on every one of them. There are no words to describe how you feel. It's so exciting and so lovely to feel the warmth of support from a whole nation. It was quite unbelievable to come up the last and finish the way I did. I felt them willing the ball in on the last.'

That funnelling putt on the 18th left Montgomerie three shots behind Woods. Olazabal thus had the honour of appearing with the world number one for the final round. The Spaniard had already played the opening two rounds with Woods and acquitted himself well. Now he lay just two strokes adrift of the lead. Olazabal, even more than Montgomerie at that stage, had a tentative hold on the Claret Jug.

Retief Goosen was Montgomerie's partner. The question of whether Montgomerie might have performed better alongside the world's best player was a moot one. But Montgomerie had certainly enjoyed his third round and showed not a shred of nerves nor lack of concentration the previous day. He had noticeably revelled in playing with Woods. Olazabal's renewed vigour and Monty's bogey on the 17th on Saturday, though, had ended his hopes of a final-day showdown with the favourite.

With the final round beginning quietly for Woods with four pars,

Olazabal and Montgomerie kept their hopes alive and so did Bernhard Langer. Twenty-one years after Langer had made a strong bid for the Open title at the same course, the 2004 European Ryder Cup captain contended strongly again in the final round. Langer stayed in contention right until the 15th, where he perished in the sand, running up a double-bogey.

Olazabal, with a stunning 35-footer on the 4th, cut his deficit behind Woods to a solitary stroke. One hand wrapped around the Claret Jug handle for Olazabal.

Montgomerie's second birdie of the afternoon, two putts for a four on the par-five 5th, left him only a shot off the pace, too. His supporters went wild. Several blond wigs fell off and Saltires were raised higher. At last, Woods was in a fight.

The world number one, though, as if recognising he might be caught, then distanced himself again, birdieing the 5th, too.

His two-shot lead over Montgomerie lasted only three more holes, however. And had Monty's eagle attempt from 25 ft on the 9th, after hitting the green with his drive, come off, instead of his ball diving away late, there would have been a tie on top. The birdie tap-in, though, left Montgomerie heading for home only one shot behind. At this juncture, Montgomerie's hand was at its firmest on the Auld Claret Jug in his career.

What followed next highlighted the 2005 Open. In the space of two minutes, the title was decided.

On the 10th, Montgomerie had not got close enough to make the birdie that would lock him and Woods together. Then, on the 11th, with the wind causing confusion with club selection, Montgomerie fatally decided on a six-iron instead of a seven. His ball plunged through the green. He chipped up to 7 ft and missed the putt to bogey. At very nearly the same time, Woods also made bogey on the 10th. Oh, what might have been?

That error of club selection on the 11th – well, maybe not an error but treachery by the unpredictable gusts that day on the Old Course – was the end of Montgomerie's challenge. His tenuous grip on the Jug handle was released.

'The bogey threw me. The wind switched and I hit the wrong club. I didn't quite get the same momentum coming home after that. When Tiger birdied the 12th, that was that.'

His push for a maiden major honour disappeared altogether with a three-putt bogey on 13, and Woods soon went up another gear. Birdies on the 12th and 14th extended his lead to unassailable proportions. A bogey on the 17th, where discretion became the better part of valour to avoid any serious late mishap, when Woods decided not to tangle with the Road Hole Bunker, was a mere hiccough.

Just before Woods played up to the 17th, Montgomerie's par-saving putt on the last to keep him a stroke better than the waiting Fred Couples, and subsequently also Olazabal, was greeted with the sort of roar accorded Open champions.

'The crowd were phenomenal. Even when they realised I wasn't going to win, they knew my job in hand was to finish second. They helped me in that cause.

'The pins were set in very difficult positions. It was nigh on impossible for me to get the ball close. And the wind made things difficult, too. But I gave a great effort and it gave me great confidence that I'm capable of doing well in the Open.

'In hindsight, it would have possibly been better for me if I'd been playing with him [Woods]. He had a great advantage of knowing exactly what was happening, because we were about a hole ahead or a hole and a half ahead, so he knew exactly what was going on.'

While he was defeated, Montgomerie was back as a force and with hopes still for the future, despite his age, of capturing the Open title that had eluded him for so long. His brave attempt at winning in 2005 at St Andrews encouraged him in the belief that he could still add a major victory to his otherwise impressive golfing CV. Regardless of whether he does or does not do that, his victory bid at St Andrews will still be one of the highlights of his career.

'It doesn't affect me that I haven't won a major. It hasn't changed me, and I don't think it will if I win one. Maybe it will be a relief more than anything else, but I am happy with what I've achieved in my career.

'It was eight years since I'd contended that well in a major. After three years in the wilderness, it was fantastic for me to have a resurgence.

'And there's no disgrace in finishing second to the best player in the world.'

2005 TOP SCORES

T. Woods 66–67–71–70 274

C. Montgomerie 71–66–70–72 279

J.M. Olazabal 68–70–68–74 280

F. Couples 68–71–73–68 280

EPILOGUE

WHILE I HAVE witnessed a good many of this book's Open near-misses, two of my illustrious colleagues have been there for all of them and here give their views on what might have been.

PETER ALLISS has tasted the disappointment of seeing an Open chance disappear while he was a player, and he has looked on as a television commentator as hands have been torn from the Claret Jug:

'I thought when Doug Sanders got down in two from the Road Hole Bunker in 1970 it was all over. That's because if you had to pick a hole with the least amount of Open fear, you'd think the 18th would be in the top two. You can't really believe you could miss the fairway or you'd not get the ball on the green in two. It's simple enough, I suppose, to take five. But I thought he'd won. And everyone thinks Nicklaus cruised through in the play-off, but he had to get up and down for birdie on the last to win, so it was no walkover, and Sanders twice came within a whisker of winning.

'I was commentating for Birkdale in 1983 when Hale Irwin walked up to his ball and had an air-shot. We'll never know how expensive that was.

'Just missing out on the Open? Well, Jack Nicklaus, can you believe, has been second half a dozen times. In fact, his record in majors would be amazing even without any victories at all, if you think how many times he was second and third. With a bit more luck, he could have won another 15 or so majors. And I think if you analyse it, Nicklaus has probably screwed up less than anybody in the game!

'There's always something in Opens to decide what's going to happen. Take Nick Price's putt on the 17th at Turnberry in 1994, such a blow to poor old Jesper Parnevik. I'm not sure about not looking at scoreboards. If Nicklaus thought it would be two five-irons and an eight-iron, that's what he would do. It would come immediately into his brain. There have been so many over the years . . . if they had only done this, or only done that.

'Whatever's said about Tony Jacklin missing out in 1972, he made a total mess of the 17th and didn't even finish second. That was Jacklin's mistake. He let . . . whatever it was . . . get to him. From being twenty yards short of the 17th in two, and Trevino through the back of the green in four, it should have been game over. Trevino had a tremendous amount of good fortune all week, holing bunker-shots on the fly, but Jacklin threw that one away.

'In 1975, Peter Thomson thought Jack Newton was full of courage and that he had the balls to win, but that's when we really saw the coming of Tom Watson. Jack did have courage, though, and he only lost at Carnoustie because of being bunkered on the 18th in the play-off.

'We saw a lot of raw talent in 1976, when Seve first came on the scene. We didn't know he'd go on to hone it to a high level of sophistication. Only 19, and he might have won the Open. It was the start of a wonderful period for European golf, which Seve headed for many years.

'The 1977 Open was quite remarkable – shame there had to be a loser. Nicklaus and Watson were like a couple of heavyweights punching away at each other. The drama of the final hole was extraordinary. The rest of the field were mere mortals. I remember Hubert Green, when he went up for third prize, saying, "Well, I won the tournament I was playing in!"

'In 1982, Nick Price should have won. Over the last five or six holes, he missed fairways and caught bunkers. They were shots that you didn't expect from somebody who'd had a fair deal of experience by that time and who was a renowned striker of the ball. It came as a big surprise to me when he let that one slip. That same year, Bobby Clampett ran away with it over the first two rounds. I was commentating with Mark McCormack, and he said, "I'm just going to the bookies to have a bet on how many strokes he'll win by." But he didn't; he fell back and had a miserable time over the last two rounds.

'Tom Watson made a dreadful mistake in 1984, a cardinal error of club-selection on the 17th. He was possibly two clubs too many.

'In 1988 . . . if I were leading the Championship by two, with a round to go, and I was offered a 68 before the final round, I'd say, "No. I'll stay in the clubhouse." It wouldn't have been enough. For Seve to have shot a 65 was remarkable. I remember the little chip Seve made on the 18th that almost went in the hole. Nick Price was beaten then and shot a 69 to lose by two. I felt very sorry for Nick. He played quite beautifully all week.

'The 1989 Championship was one that Greg Norman threw away in the end after a magnificent final round to get there, and we mustn't forget Wayne Grady. He also had a great chance. Greg must have thought it was all over when he started the play-off birdie–birdie.

'For the 1999 Open, it was, I think, the saddest piece of commentary I've done in my career. I put it on a par with Neil Fox missing the kick in the rugby league final when all he had to do was put it over from ten yards under the posts to win the cup, or Devon Loch in the Grand National, who somehow contrived not to win. My father, Percy, played with Arnaud Massey, who won in 1907, and I was thinking, "Well, a Frenchman's going to win this year." I was sitting working with Alex Hay, and Jean took his driver out of the bag on the last hole and we almost covered our eyes, thinking, "Oh, my God!" He hits it and he's then going to do this, going to do that . . . He may still think he played the right shot; I don't think he played the right shot at all. Then I think he should have hit an eight-iron, then a pitching wedge on the green and three-putted and won the thing. You could say he was unlucky clattering into the stand

and coming back where he did, but his golfing brain disappeared. The ball was in a foot of water. But to hole the putt he did, to get into the play-off, was truly remarkable. At the time, I thought, "What the hell are you doing? For God's sake, mop him down; give him a large brandy." It went on and on and on. It took half an hour to play the last hole, then there was another half-hour while he changed his clothes, then there was the play-off . . . They all played pretty terribly in the gathering gloom and rain, and then Lawrie finished three–three and, at the end of the day, totally deserved the Claret Jug. For Van de Velde, though, it was an awful, awful thing to happen to anybody. Without doubt, he was the most visible loser of the Open.

'Thomas Björn in 2003? For all the talk about modern equipment, gurus and fitness and all the rest of it, players do not play golf with rifles. Your brain can tell you to aim for the middle of the green and you still end up in the bunker on the right. Or you take the wrong club and go ten yards too far, ten yards short . . . I don't think Thomas would be aiming for the flag. Anyone who aims at the flag when it's six or eight paces from the edge of a huge bunker, in such a commanding position, when you've got a green the size of a tennis court on your left, knows he has made a mistake. He then tried to play a canny bunker-shot that didn't come off, and that was the end of his story. I just think he misdirected his tee-shot.

'And there we have it. What could have been. The only chance I ever had was in 1954, the first one Peter Thomson won. I fiddled about silly, silly, silly things. I could have been a couple of shots better than Thomson. All these players I've talked about will say the same thing. I was 23 at the time. People said to me, "Don't worry; you'll have plenty of opportunities again." I played plenty more times but never had that opportunity again.'

RENTON LAIDLAW, that doyen of golf-watchers, a writer and broadcaster for over 40 years, has also seen close-up how Opens have been won and lost:

'The fellow I feel sorriest for would be Bernhard Langer. I think because of what he's achieved in golf over the years, the way he's played it and the manner in which he's played it, he's been a terrific ambassador for the game. It would be nice if the name Bernhard Langer was on the Claret Jug.

'Peter Oosterhuis is another we'd like to have seen win but never quite made it. He was close in 1974 when he finished second to Gary Player, and he was in the running in 1982.

'As far as the others who have come close, it's noticeable that a lot have gone on to win after nearly doing it. I think you've got to lose it to win in it. Nick Price, for instance, in 1988 at Lytham. He'd already come close before that at Troon in '82. I remember sitting with him at Lytham, though, and funnily enough we had the trophy with us. He said to me, "I just want to put one hand on the trophy and I'm going to have two hands on this trophy some time."

'I said, "I certainly hope you do."

'Of course, he didn't that week, but then he came to Turnberry and did it. And he did it, you can argue, because Jesper Parnevik made a wrong decision playing his second shot at the last . . . or he didn't quite know what the situation was at the time. As far as Nick went, it balanced out.

'Talking of balancing out, Greg Norman was looking to win again in 1990 but got annihilated by Nick Faldo, and then got his own back in 1993. In fact, the 1990 Open was one of the best. Nick was in majestic form that week, and Greg didn't have one hand on the Claret Jug for long.

'It would be difficult to look back over the last 30 years and say, "That was a duff Open." It's changed a bit now because of modern technology. The skill of the older players that gave them the edge over the rest has been rather lost. That's not to denigrate a Ben Curtis or a Todd Hamilton, but it's allowed these fellows to come in and have a chance of winning – before they've had a chance of losing.

'In the old days, it was the big names that won it, because they were able to play the shots that you needed under pressure to win an Open Championship. It's much more open now. Far more people can come to an Open with a chance of winning – assuming, of course, Tiger Woods isn't on his best form!

'A lot of players will never win an Open because they just don't believe they will, even though they are pretty good golfers. Belief has a lot to do with winning and not quite making it. Seve has always had incredible belief.

'Doug Sanders might have had belief but did miss a short putt. You really did feel for him. You only have to stand on the 18th green at St Andrews to see how difficult putting can be, though, even when the pressure's not on. The 18th at St Andrews is built over an old burial ground. There was a big hole there and they had to build it up. The green does slope more heavily than you think. But there are some players destined to come close and never win. Was Doug Sanders a good-enough player to get his name on the Auld Claret Jug? He really did battle so hard the next day but still lost out to Jack Nicklaus. With players like Curtis and Hamilton winning, that question doesn't count nowadays. In those days, it did. Doug was a good player, a great entertainer, but was he good enough to win an Open? Maybe not.

'Move forward 35 years, and Monty played really well at St Andrews, but had he enough experience from the past to win? He had a pretty awful record. He was buoyed up by the crowd this time; he's a fellow who responds to people saying "Well done, Monty", "We love you, Monty". And I think it was Tiger Woods who also inspired him to have his best chance. But there was no way, over the last six holes, that Tiger was going to let his lead slip. I don't know whether Colin would be able to beat a Tiger playing his best, which he was at the 2005 Open.

'Ian Woosnam I felt sorry for at Lytham, with a two-stroke penalty. Would he have come that close without the penalty? Tony Jacklin was going really well until a thunderstorm in 1970, and he never recovered from Lee Trevino chipping him out of the 1972 Open.

'Thomas Björn was one of the highest-quality players to miss out on an Open Championship title. It wasn't an easy bunker-shot, but he could go into the bunker at Royal St George's and walk off with a four any time. I think there's a lot of destiny involved. If it's your week . . .

'I would have loved Jean Van de Velde to have won, because he's such a colourful guy, and he was so unlucky for the ball to hit the corner of the stanchion on the stand and bounce back over the Barry Burn. In 999 times out of 1,000, the ball would have just dropped down the other side of the Barry Burn. Then he got hit by the tide coming into the burn. It wasn't to be.

'I also felt a bit sorry for Wayne Grady in 1989. It would have meant so much to Wayne, who's not the most extrovert of golfers but reliable, sensible, likeable. It wasn't meant for him, either. He never got another chance. Parnevik, or his caddie, should have checked the scoreboard in 1994, but it wasn't to be.

'In 1976, here was Seve, a laddie from Spain who didn't speak any English, playing some of the greatest shots we'd ever seen. He missed out. If he could have kept the ball on the fairway, he might have won. But he wasn't ready. In 1979, he might not have been ready, but he believed in himself so much no one could stop him.

'If they are in that upper echelon, they will get another chance. Simon Owen, leading the Open with two to play. You say, "This is my chance." Did he win? No, he didn't. Simon never did it again. Steven Bottomley finished third in 1995, and now he's out of the game. There are a lot of players who nearly won and then did. But there are a lot of players who nearly won and disappeared.'